Enda McDonagh

The Making of Disciples

TASKS OF MORAL THEOLOGY

Michael Glazier, Inc.
Wilmington, Delaware

First published in 1982 by:
MICHAEL GLAZIER, INC.
1723 Delaware Avenue
Wilmington, Delaware 19806
Distributed in the United States, Canada and the Philippines
by Michael Glazier, Inc.

0-89453-285-5 (Michael Glazier, Inc.)
Volume 5 of *Good News Studies*

© Enda McDonagh 1982

Origination by Photobooks (Bristol) Ltd.
Printed and bound in Great Britain by Biddles Ltd.
Guildford and King's Lynn

THE MAKING OF DISCIPLES

Contents

Acknowledgments

This book was prepared and written during my tenure of the Huisking Chair of Theology at the University of Notre Dame. For the opportunities which that post provided, I wish to thank the Huisking family and the administrators at Notre Dame, particularly the President, Father Theodore M. Hesburgh, and successive chairmen of the Theology Department, Fathers David Burrell and Richard P. McBrien. Many other members of the Administration and Faculty provided support and stimulus during these years but I would like to pay special tribute to my colleagues in Ethics or Moral Theology, Stanley Hauerwas, John Howard Yoder and Edward Malloy. My most important single resource person was my graduate assistant, Sister Patricia Scholles, ably assisted by my secretaries Julie Thorson-Smith and Millie Peters. Their work was completed by my Irish secretary, Mary O'Malley.

As usual I am greatly indebted to Gill & Macmillan in the persons both of the Managing Director, Michael Gill, and his very dedicated editor Bridget Lunn.

Sources

Jesus Christ and Friends (The Furrow, December 1981)
Orthopraxis (Proceedings of Catholic Theological Society of
  America, 1980)
Liturgy (Conference on Moral Theology, Notre Dame, April
  1980)
Moral Education (Towards Moral and Religious Maturity,
  Conference at Senanque, May 1979)
The Holy Spirit and Human Identity (British-Irish Theological
  Society, Maynooth, 1980)
Prayer and Politics (*The Furrow*, September 1979)
Love, Power and Justice (Conference on Prophetic Theology, St
  John's University, New York, July 1980)
The Dignity of the Undignified (*Concilium*, ed. Jacques Pohier
  and Dietmar Mieth, 1979)
The Business Corporation (Conference on Judaeo-Christian
  Vision and the Business Corporation, March 1980)
Redemptor Hominis and Ireland (*The Furrow*, October 1979)
Church and State in Ireland (*The Crane Bag*, 5/1, 1981)
Agenda for Irish and British Moral Theologians (*The Church
  Now*, Gill and Macmillan, 1980)
Peace and War: A Task for American Moral Theologians
  (Conference of European Churches, Bucharest, March
  1982)

Introduction:
The End of Moral Theology

It is not entirely frivolous to suggest an end to moral theology and moral theologising, even in the renewed forms in which it has been practised from the 1950s through the 1970s. There are of course too few moral theologians, too few perhaps to keep it alive. And the interests of that few are still too limited to formal questions of Christian autonomy and heteronomy, of specificity, of consequentialism and its alternatives, or to substantive questions which range little beyond sexuality, bio-ethics and a touch of war. With such limited obsessions the verdict might well be suicide; moral theology dying at the hands of its own practitioners, to the accompaniment, perhaps of sighs of relief both from pastors and penitents who suffered and suffer from the stringent confines of its earlier manual presentations (still influential) and from 'liberated' Christians who find succeeding presentations vague in vision and loose in directive.

Before pronouncing a final verdict it might be well to recall the famous physicist Lord Kelvin's judgment on the end of physics in 1904, just before the physics of the micro- and macro-cosmos exploded with quantum physics, relativity and their further developments. More relevant and crucial are the implications such a verdict would have for the theological enterprise in general. Scripture studies might be reduced to a simple historical study of interesting historical documents—a temptation many scripture scholars might not want to resist. More significantly still, dogmatic theology could be exposed as a self-enclosed study of historical formulae and philosophical speculation without any of the impact of saving truth (*Heilswissen*) traditionally taken to be characteristic of Christian preaching and teaching. In many ways dogmatic theology has suffered more from its separation from life than moral theology has

1

suffered in its separation from the central truths of Christianity, their narrative account and primary formulation in Scripture and their historical development in the doctrines of the Church. The attempts to develop a separate moral theology, which really began in the sixteenth century as a way of providing guidance for confessors, dealt a serious, perhaps lethal blow to dogmatic theology emerging as separate study of doctrine with its historical and speculative methodology. The theology of Christ or of the sacraments in that tradition was no less distorted than a fundamental moral theology constructed from a weakened tradition of natural law or a moral theology of the sacraments that busied itself exclusively with questions of validity and liceity. The limitations of manual moral theology had their exact parallels in dogmatic theology. Moral theologians recognised some of their own limitations more quickly. Without a parallel awakening among dogmatic theologians their attempts at renewal were bound to be truncated. For various practical reasons the separation of dogmatic and moral theology and of both from scripture studies remains the dominant mode. There are however sufficient indications that the mode is coming under increasing question. The end of moral theology, provided it is accompanied by the end of the self-enclosed dogmatic theology, could prepare the way for re-birth of an integrated theology that will still permit and demand various emphases, even specialisations. In the other sense of end as purpose, the end of moral theology and of the moral theologian must be to provoke and promote such conscientisation among theologians in general and provide some guidance to how a new integrated theology of Christian truth and life might emerge.

This book reflects the writer's attempts over a couple of years (1979–81) to use moral problems, issues and traditions to develop such an integrated theology. At its deepest level this demands interaction and integration of theory and praxis which all theologians must seek. In specifically Christian terms the best expression of the end of all theologising is the making of disciples. It is certainly the end or purpose which should characterise theologians who take as their starting-point Christian and moral experience and living. In one way or another the chapters of this book attempt to promote this end or goal of (moral) theology by examining some of the tasks necessary to its achievement. The making of disciples translates

2

for this theologian into basic or moral general tasks together with the more particular tasks whose particularity derives from more defined aspects such as the social and economic or more defined communities such as Ireland.

Moral and Christian experience and living as expressed in the life and practices of the Church community are receiving increasing attention from theologians, Protestant and Catholic, fundamental, doctrinal and moral. The self-conscious correlativism between faith and culture which Paul Tillich proposed and explored reflects ancient Jewish and Christian traditions of attempting to mediate between divine presence and activity and human presence and activity both within and without the communities of Israel and of the Church. Theology has always, at least implicitly, sought to explore critically this interaction. The current interest among biblical scholars of setting the Christian (and the Hebrew) Scriptures in the social, political and cultural backgrounds maintains a tradition as old as the apologists, Clement of Alexandria and Augustine. The new school of liberation theologians is more specifically interested in politics and power structures and the responses demanded by their distortion within the Third World, between the First and Third Worlds and as affecting specific deprived social groups such as women within the First. (The theologies of the Second World have to be to a large extent guessed at, but no doubt their experience of Communism and its power distortions heavily influence theological reflection). In the modern world major Catholic thinkers (to be more parochial for the moment) regard as significant partners in dialogue their social, political and cultural peers. This is evident in near-classical theologians dealing with classical problems such as Edward Schillebeeckx in his magisterial works on *Jesus* and *Christ* or Karl Rahner in the whole course of his *Theological Investigations*, or Bernard Lonergan in his *Method in Theology*. More self-consciously innovative fundamental theologians John Baptist Metz in *Faith in History and Society* and *The Emergent Church*, or David Tracy in *Blessed Rage of Order* and *The Analogical Imagination* carry on similar dialogues. The near total outsider Rosemary Haughton, particularly in her excellent recent book *The Passionate God*, draws on human experience of loving and its expression in romantic literature to perform that most theological of tasks, discovering and uncovering the God of Jesus Christ in the most precisely human realities.

3

Moral theologians have always had to keep close to certain aspects of human experience. Contemporary exponents do not attain to the depth and range of dialogue to be found in these liberation, doctrinal, fundamental and ultimately unclassifiable theologians and their colleagues. Yet they must have something important to contribute to the developing dialogue between faith and experience, Christian theory and Christian praxis, because of their preoccupation with Christian living and Christian praxis.

In promoting the integrated, dialogical and communicative theology which the time and its tasks demand, moral theology can recover for theology that most concrete of living and believing realities, the disciple of Jesus Christ in the community of disciples, as starting point, subject and goal of theological reflection. The *disciplina* of the *discipuli* forms the original starting point for reflecting disciples and should issue in a richer, more self-conscious grasp of Christian meaning as well as a greater commitment to Christian living. In this fashion disciple-ship could constitute one crucial way to developing dialogue between faith and culture, including politics and economics, between Church and world, between Christian eschatology and human history, between reflection, contemplation and engagement, between Christian praxis and its theoretical understanding and exposition. In the context of such an integrated theological enterprise theologians with a moral bias could recover for themselves a role and a confidence that are to a large extent absent at present. Such role and confidence (the confidence of Christian hope with all its implications) could attract more good students of the *disciplina* than are available at present.

By adopting discipleship as one dominant theme of their reflections and explorations, theologians, with a doctrinal or a moral bias, are compelled to address the Scriptures in text and context more directly and seriously than some doctrinal and moral traditions of the immediate past. The address must however have an active and not just an intellectual or theoretical bias. The Scriptures must be read as accounts of activity by people active in response to the call to be disciples. The hermeneutical problem is not simply one of translation of meaning from a first-century to a twentieth-century world, but a dialogue between the meaning-ful or faith-ful activity of first century disciples and the meaning-ful and faith-ful activity of

4

twentieth-century disciples. Responding to the call of Jesus Christ as it is mediated through word and Sacrament and cosmos, ecclesial community and human community, is the first meaning-ful and faith-ful act of the disciple. It constitutes what some of the medievals called a *theologia prima*. The further exploration and development of that call occurs in deliberate reflection and the committed activities of prayer and 'politics' (taken in a wide sense frequently used today of organised service of the neighbour). Such developed activity of the whole Christian provides a *theologia secunda* which may not be confined to simply intellectual exploration but includes the richer understanding which comes from doing the truth. Attempts to express this *theologia's* activities in a connected verbal account, conceptual or narrative, or more correctly both, always limp behind the reality. Written theology is always inadequate to theology as lived and understood in Christian discipleship and must continually refer back to that activity to be supplemented and corrected. The theologian who ignores his discipleship commitment will rapidly become a word-spinner. The disciple who ignores his theological responsibility very easily becomes a mindless activist. Theory and praxis, reflection, contemplation and action demand the attention of all disciples in varying degrees. And those disciples with a theoretical bias, who provide written theology, must be somehow active themselves and in communication with disciples with an activist bias. Written theology and its more complete correlate in the reflection and activities of disciples are community works in which theological writers and speakers act as articulators of the current community's faith/praxis, of its continuity and discontinuity with previous historical phases of the community of disciples and as stimulus, challenge and partial guide to the future of that community.

The community of disciples depends on its continuity with past Christian communities and its fidelity to the originating communities of Jesus and Israel. But the achievements of the past are also, in the divine economy, promises for and challenges to the future. The impact of that future is being realised here and now in the in-breaking of the Kingdom, already inaugurated but not yet finally come. Disciples are called to recognition, service and promotion of that Kingdom. Disciples with theological responsibility for articulating and exploring that recognition and service are also directed towards the future and the God of the future who is coming in the Kingdom begun in Jesus. That future orientation belongs to all disciples and not just to the class of professional writers and teachers of theology. Sensitive Christians of various kinds, including especially more prophetic disciples like Mother Teresa or Helder Camara or Martin Luther King, open us up to the further realities of the oncoming Kingdom. The writers and teachers of theology will, on the basis of their studies and engagement, ensure systematic attention to the future and unpredictable God of Israel and of Jesus Christ. This attention to, sensitive and alert waiting upon, the further coming of the Lord exposes the essential tension in theology between past and future, the essentially unfinished and provisional character of theology, and the dependency of theologians and other disciples on the gift of the Spirit to lead them into further—and finally all—truth that Jesus embodied.

The Theological Tasks of Disciples

This book records some of the theological tasks of disciples from the more basic to the more specific. These tasks are determined by the general announcement and call of Jesus Christ himself, that 'The time is fulfilled, and the kingdom of God is at hand, repent, and believe in the gospel' (Mk 1: 14–15). The call is specific more precisely from the first direction to the fishermen, Simon and Andrew, 'Follow me and I will make you fishers of men', through his various rebukes of the disciples for their failure to understand, to the more demanding and precise 'If any man could come after me, let him deny himself and take up his cross and follow me' (Mk 8:34).

Discipleship involves first of all a personal relationship with Jesus the Christ. What did that mean for the first disciples? What can it mean for disciples to-day? How far are disciples in our time following the person of Jesus as those first historical disciples, however haltingly, did? Do today's disciples respond to the spirit of Jesus as one might respond to the spirit of Socrates or Gandhi? Is there a living and personal Spirit of Jesus through which one enjoys a personal relationship with the risen and living Christ who is truly the man of Nazareth and the Son of God? In the first chapter these basic questions of discipleship are put.

Two obvious constituent features of discipleship are life and prayer. The chapter on praxis pursues the theme of orthopraxis

6

as not only constitutive of discipleship but also normative for the traditional range of theological disciplines, scripture studies, doctrinal and moral theology with their various subcategories. How praxis and theory interact to form the disciples forms the *leitmotif* of chapter two. In chapter three the question is asked whether worship and prayer in the liturgy are expression or source for christian morality and the life of discipleship. In attempting to relate the mystical and the moral and in exploring the relationship between liturgy and moral understanding the theologian has to confront the most profound mysteries of discipleship and its role of service to the Kingdom.

In chapter four recent work on moral education is examined in the light of the demands of discipleship. Exploring the pervasive yet unique role of the Holy Spirit in establishing the human identity of disciples completes the section on basic tasks.

The social, political and economic demands of discipleship could, up to a few years ago, be described with confidence as the most neglected area of moral theology and of discipleship. That is changing but not systematically or quickly enough. Some of the tasks which theologians face are at least begun in the chapters comprising Part II of this book. Although again they began as papers for different audiences at different times in the years 1979 to 1980, they reflect the author's increasing preoccupation with the social dimensions of discipleship and its key-role in theology.

Part III attempts to ground this theology more precisely in local Churches. By discussing the tasks of Irish disciples and theologians, which have surfaced in various ways in earlier chapters, the author seeks to speak out of and to the society and the Church which formed him and to which his debts therefore are greatest. The debts extent beyond Ireland. In the final two chapters I attempt to repay something of what I owe to the Churches in Britain and the United States of America by examining tasks which affect them particularly, if not exclusively.

The provisional and fragmentary character of this book may at least be partially atoned for by a strong sense of the central reality: the gift and call of Christians and their theologians to be disciples of Jesus Christ in life, in reflection on it and in the interaction between life and reflection. I have no doubt that more profound and systematic expositions of this central reality will come from an increasing number of theologians in the years immediately ahead. Discipleship as a theological theme is about to become fashionable if it has not already done so. The fashionableness will pass, yet the call to the disciples who are theologians, and the significance of that in the present attempts to transcend some old artificial theological divisions, will remain. The end of moral theology will be both the making of disciples and the remaking of theology.

PART I

Basic Tasks

I

Jesus Christ and Friends

Despite its reputedly 'high' Christology St John's Gospel contains one of Jesus' most intimate descriptions of his disciples, as 'friends'. The loving dimension of such a relationship might be taken for granted in the context of the Gospel, but the mutuality, even equality, which it suggests is surprising in an account of Jesus Christ who is above all one with the Father. This and similar problems within the Gospels themselves illustrate difficulties we have as contemporary disciples of Jesus. How do we understand and describe our relationships with him both as Jesus of a particular geography and history and as risen Christ? Is this a personal relationship for each of us? What can such a personal relationship mean? How far is it like or unlike our personal relationships with our human family and friends? How far is it like or unlike the personal relationships which the first disciples had before or after Easter?

Two Theological Eras

   In pursuing these questions it is important to recognise that there are (at least) two theologies or religious understandings, drawn from two different religious cultures, at work in most of us today. I have in mind the two very different phases of Christian understanding separated by the work of Vatican II. That work was itself incomplete. It did not achieve or even attempt a contemporary Christology. The work is still in the process of being implemented, in a Church that has proved both marvellously resilient in face of great change and marvellously resistant. Yet the implications of Vatican II for relationships with Jesus Christ as centre of our faith have gradually emerged, not least in the controversial explications of current Christologies of a Schillebeeckx or a Küng or a Boff. Together with a range of

11

other Catholic theologians they represent a response to movement generated by what Rosemary Haughton has called 'that superbly destructive Council'. That movement has not yet been completed; the destruction or demolition of old forms and structures is still continuing or is at an uneasy and uncertain halt. We live in the overlap of two theological eras and share in that confusion.

Before the Council
Christology before Vatican II as presented, for example, in seminary manuals and catechisms displayed the certainty, the clarity and the limitations of Chalcedon. (Karl Rahner in a commemorative volume for the fifteenth centenary of Chalcedon may have been the first contemporary Catholic to recognise that Chalcedon had the inevitable limitations of historical achievement.) The *certainty* of 'truly human and truly divine' set the parameters of further development. The *clarity* seemed no less impressive. In hindsight this certainty and clarity were reinforced by emphasis on and sensitivity to the divinity in most official and academic discussion. Uncertainty and obscurity on this issue could not be tolerated. The humanity, despite its clear formal protection, did not seem to interest pastors or theologians to the same extent.

In such a theological setting personal relationships with Jesus Christ rested firmly on his divine nature and so on his divine presence to believers. Relationship with Jesus Christ was above all a relationship with the Son of God, with God. His humanity and ours were, of course, essential to the relationship but this was for the believer in his beliefs, his prayer and his day-to-day living, primarily a relationship with God, whom he worshipped, loved and feared. A review of theological understanding and attitude in the three areas of faith, prayer and *praxis* may help to illuminate and confirm this position.

In terms of beliefs about Jesus Christ or the material content of faith, the knowledge attributed to him offers a convenient illustration of the dominance of divinity. This knowledge included the acquired knowledge which a human being derives from experience. Without it Jesus could not be described as human. It also included infused knowledge. Above and beyond these, Jesus enjoyed the beatific vision which seemed to make all his other knowledge superfluous and call in question his genuine

12

humanness. This difficulty was considered but solutions tended to recognise the prior call of his divinity and its demand for beatific vision at whatever cost to the humanity. Similar tendencies were discernible in discussing the related topics of the human consciousness and human personality of Jesus. He was certainly one person in two natures but the person was simply divine and this made the divine nature appear as dominant. In so far as Catholics of this era were exposed to a monophysite temptation (and which Christians are not?) the one *phusis* was divine.

The centre of Catholic prayer then as now was the Eucharist, the Mass. The centre of the Mass was the act of consecration. The most immediately impressing effect of that was the Real Presence. This presence with the awe and worship which it inspired was a divine presence, the presence of God. The transformation of bread and wine into the Body and Blood of Jesus Christ as renewal of his sacrifice to the Father and in response to his Last Supper injunction would be unacceptable, even unintelligible theologically unless Jesus' humanity was fully recognised. Yet in the spirit of the times the divine presence predominated in attitude of priest and people alike. And this was symbolised in the very separation of priest and people, the use of Latin, of sacred vessels and vestments. The priest was a man apart as God was apart. This apartness of God strongly reflected the Old Testament tradition of his total otherness in spite his being with us in authentically human form in the tradition of the New.

Outside the Mass, and within it for some of the faithful, the humanity of Jesus was honoured through prayer in the Stations of the Cross and devotions to the Sacred Heart, in the mysteries of the Rosary and in Marian piety generally. Ejaculatory prayer to which people were commended and which they practised also reflected a personal intimacy with Jesus in his humanity. Yet the centrality and obligation of the Mass with its sense of the divine presence remained the peak and the norm of all Catholic prayer. In the relationship of prayer Jesus Christ as truly divine was fully if awesomely available.

In what might be termed a 'high' ecclesiology the primary image of the Church was the Body or the Mystical Body of Christ. Catholics lived 'in Christ', a favourite phrase of St Paul. They were, in that other Pauline phrase, members of the Body of

13

Christ. This was a mystical union, hence the description, Mystical Body. While the image of the body underlined Jesus' humanity the force of the word mystical and the obvious relation with the Eucharist tended once again to stress the divine presence. Responding to one another in Christ could produce a tendency to reduce not only the humanity of Christ but also the humanity of respondent and respondee. Loving people for Christ's sake seemed sometimes like ignoring them as people in their own right. The urgency and depth of the call of Jesus Christ in the neighbour gained much from the powerful image of the Body of Christ. In terms of one's personal relationship to Jesus it gained immediate practical expression. It would not, however, be unfair to see here once again the personal relationship as with the risen Christ rather than the ministering Jesus of Galilee and so with the divine rather than the human. Generally it could be said that this theological era in the Catholic Church did not develop a theology (as opposed to an apologetic) of Jesus' historical ministry. Without such a theology, attention to and understanding of the human being Jesus suffered.

The Christology of the first era was formally complete. The human and divine dimensions of Jesus Christ were upheld. Yet in faith content and in prayer, community and living, the divine Christ took precedence over the human and in a parallel development the glorious and risen Christ tended to eclipse the ministering historical Jesus. Indirectly at least, Vatican II, in its treatment of liturgy and the word of God, the Church, its relation to other Churches and to the world, suggested a rather different emphasis in understanding and relating to Jesus.

Vatican II and after

Although Vatican II had no explicit treatment of Jesus Christ or Christology, certain aspects of faith, prayer and action offer ways of understanding the Council's thrust in matters Christ-ological.

The most directly relevant of these was the Council's document on revelation, its treatment of the word of God and the further document on the historical study of the gospels.

Thus inevitably the life and ministry of Jesus was brought back into the forefront of discussion. This discussion is still being intensely pursued by Catholic scholars adapting from, criticising and developing the work of their hitherto more advanced Protestant and Anglican colleagues. Whatever difficulties have emerged in interpreting what are essentially faith-documents so as to yield authentic words and deeds of Jesus, a great deal more is known with varying degrees of certainty and probability about the times and life of Jesus than was apparent immediately before the Council. Knowledge and interest have fed on each other so that whereas in the late fifties Catholic interest focused on the glorified and divine Christ, in the late sixties and seventies the focus has been on the ministering, suffering and human Jesus. The conviction that whatever else Jesus was, he was a man, characteristic of some popular views of these developments, offers a neat counterpoint to the earlier popular and no less simplifying slogan, that whatever else Jesus Christ was, he was God. It is to some extent the presumed conflict of these two slogans which most starkly reveals the two religious cultures and two theological eras within which most Catholics still live.

The first official document of the Council was that on the liturgy. In its theological emphasis on the Mass as the action of Jesus Christ and the communal action of the Church, more dynamic dimensions were opened than simple emphasis on the Real Presence previously allowed. Subsequent practical development in language and structure made explicit the involvement of all believers in the recalling and representing of Jesus' offering to the Father. This association of all with the priest is now symbolised by the priest facing the people, lay people joining in the readings, assisting in the administration of Holy Communion and receiving Communion in the hand. The mutuality and equality of all as friends of Jesus with clearer attention to Jesus drawing his disciples about him to hear his word and join in his table-fellowship, emerge in the renewed liturgies. The relationship with Jesus begins to assume more of the characteristics of human person to human person relationship after the fashion of Jesus and those first disciples.

The primary document of Vatican II was the Constitution on the Church. The primary image of the Church in that document was that of the people of God. This people is a pilgrim people answering the call first issued by Jesus to the disciples to come, follow him. As a pilgrim people the Church is still *in via*, on the way. It follows the Jesus who has passed this way, the Jesus who *was*. It is consoled on the journey by the food and drink which embodies the encouraging and empowering presence of Jesus, the Jesus who *is* with them always. They look forward to the Jesus who *is yet to come* in glory. This threefold relationship to the Jesus who *was*, who *is* and who *is to come* combines interest in and insight into the historical Jesus and the glorified Christ, the divine Son of the Father and the human son of Mary. The intimacy with and distance from Jesus Christ, past, present and future will help illuminate our earlier questions about the kind of relationship we have with him.

The relationships of the pilgrim people with one another require love of neighbours as friends of Jesus and so of one another. This may seem to lack the depth and urgency of fellow members of Christ's Body or being Christ to one another, which still of course applies. Yet friendship speaks of intimacy, distinctiveness and distance in a way which could easily be overlooked in Body of Christ talk. And the image of God's people coheres more easily with Vatican II's recognition of other groups of Christians as Churches, peoples also following Jesus Christ on his way to the Father, peoples who belong to the *qahal*, *ecclesia*, the called people of God. In other documents the Council extends its understanding of God's saving call to other major religious traditions, particularly the Jewish tradition and people which had suffered most from a narrow and tragically persecution-prone vision of the Church as a very exclusivist club. In the full vision of the Council and its consequences, the divine call and human response embraced all people of good will. The service of the Church, of the explicit disciples of Jesus Christ, extended in love to all, particularly the suffering and oppressed. The work of justice, of liberating the oppressed and caring for the victims, was recognised as an integral part of preaching the good news of Jesus Christ (Synod of Bishops 1971). Relationship with Jesus Christ clearly extended to all, but reached its high point in love and service of the excluded and marginalised. This derived from the example of Jesus' own ministry and of Jesus' own victimhood. In a fresh view of Jesus' influence on our practice, ministering in the name of Jesus has sought out the victims as a primary location of Jesus in our world. Intimacy with and distance from Jesus turns on our intimacy with and distance from the least ones (Mt. 25).

Breakthrough

In trying to understand the nature of our relationship with Jesus Christ the new emphasis on the humanity of Jesus creates, for all its initial attractiveness, problems of intimacy and distance which are not readily resolved. The historical question-marks which biblical scholarship has posed to questors for the Jesus of history are part of the problem. Given that they have been in some measure resolved, and they will never be completely resolved, we have the assurance of discerning in defensible historical terms the outlines of Jesus' life, ministry and death together with some of his genuine words and deeds. Such achievement and assurance enable us to relate to Jesus as we might to any great figure of the past, like Socrates or Alexander the Great, Gandhi or Martin Luther King. Their lives and thought and achievements could be an inspiration to us in our own living so that we could fairly describe ourselves as their disciples. Some current writing and thinking about Jesus may fall into this category. But it is clearly not adequate to how we think of ourselves as disciples of Jesus. We believe that his call to his first disciples operates also for us, that it is somehow our historical call also and that the path of the first disciples indicates our path today. Intimacy and distance in the case of Jesus Christ and Christians, is not described simply in terms of historical distance and intimate sharing of an ideal.

In pursuing the meaning of discipleship, then or now, there is no escaping the death and resurrection of Jesus Christ. In the aftermath of the death and the cowardly desertion by the disciples, expectations that he might be 'the one to redeem Israel' (Lk. 24:21) had vanished for the moment. The Easter events and experiences had a transforming effect on the downcast disciples so that their hearts were burning within them even before they recognised him in the breaking of bread (Lk. 24:30–32).

The resurrection and glorification of Jesus have many rich and powerful dimensions. Here it may be useful to concentrate on one, the breakthrough of humankind to God and of God to humankind. This double breakthrough in Jesus which the early disciples experienced as Jesus living beyond death, risen, raised from the dead, was the basis of their new faith. Such faith transcended the hesitations and pettiness of their earlier state and eventually led them to share Jesus' destiny, to drink of the

17

cup of which he drank and as he had foreseen. And this breakthrough must be the basis of our faith, our personal acceptance of Jesus as saviour, the person in whom our salvation was achieved through the definitive human access to the saving life of God and the definitive divine access to the broken, sinful life of humankind. Union with the historical human Jesus on his saving journey through Galilee and so to his death at Jerusalem, is a condition of discipleship and of sharing in the breakthrough. There is no access to the risen Christ, to the divine saviour except in his footsteps along the stony, painful way of history. Our ability to join him on that journey depends on our conscious decision and on growing understanding of what discipleship means as we discover it through setting the New Testament in dialogue with our lives. There is no escaping the Jesus of history for the genuine, explicit twentieth-century follower. Our personal relationship with him is constantly nourished and modelled on the discipleship accounts of the New Testament.

Yet we have to push still further into the New Testament and the Christian tradition if we are to do full justice to the relationship. In his crucial breakthrough to the Father and the Father's breakthrough to humankind Jesus became the New Adam, the new head of the human race. What was achieved in him was radical enough to merit description as New Creation, the call and formation of the New Israel, enjoying a New Covenant. With such rich imagery we begin to understand how, for example, Jesus as new head of the race can in the fullness of his presence to the Father be intimately accessible to all human beings. Jesus of Nazareth is available to all who seek him not just as a Socrates or a Gandhi, as model and inspiration, but by God's breakthrough to humanity in him, as new head and as living and loving friend.

In such a capacity he accompanies us in our search for God. The God of the breakthrough, of the kingdom which has been inaugurated in Jesus Christ, is still the God ahead of us, whom we await in hope. In that expectation we are instructed by the Jesus who *was*, as recorded in the Gospels and lived in the community of disciples. Jesus is also among friends now sharing the new life which his breakthrough achieved and which goes so far as to identify his friends and disciples as members of his Body and living in him. They are not simply friends but brothers and sisters and co-heirs, sharing in his Sonship of the Father.

18

And yet they remain in hopeful anticipation of his coming in glory, when God will be all in all and distance will give way finally to utter intimacy.

The Distance and the Intimacy

The two eras may be gradually converging into a richer understanding of Jesus as human and divine and a fuller understanding of our relationship with him in its diverse distances and intimacies. The recovery for theology of the human life and ministry of Jesus promises an intimacy that could not be achieved by the heavy emphasis on the divine element in the Chalcedonian formula. To be truly human Jesus had to be human as this particular Jew of this time and place. Access to him as human depends on understanding the time, the place and the Jew. The obstacles to any such complete historical understanding are enormous, totally forbidding for some scholars and critics. The promise of intimacy with Jesus the Jew is threatened by the limitations of historical research, not to the point of abandoning the search but certainly as a warning to the easy assumption that return to studying the life and ministry of Jesus will offer and ready unparalleled intimacy. For all the awesome distance which separates us in our history from Jesus in his glorified presence to the Father, it is still that glorious presence and its intimate realisation for us which ensures and explains our vital access to the Jesus of Nazareth. Intimacy and distance operate in divergent yet complementary ways in relating us to the historical and risen Jesus.

The developments of Vatican II itself, for all the promise of intimacy which a people's Church and a people's liturgy offer, face this paradox of a new intimacy creating a new distance. The use of the vernacular in the liturgy was defended and attacked as overcoming the old distance and attempting to introduce a new intimacy. Coupled with more active participation by the laity and the priest's joining the circle of the celebrating community, a more intimate setting was certainly achieved. The fresh attention to the liturgy of the word and to memorial and celebratory aspects of the Eucharist suggested, further, a new sensitivity to the historical Jesus and his saving actions. This was undoubtedly the result, at least in churches and celebrations where such intimacy and attention were seriously sought. Yet in the best of celebrations one would have to admit that the vernacular for instance introduced its own new distance. The very accessibility of the language rendered the reality in some ways more strange, more distant. The inadequacy of human language and gesture in mediating divine realities became more evident as the language and gesture became more familiar. This is not a question of poor translations and poor choice of word and gesture, although we suffer frequently from those also. It becomes a deeper problem as the pitiful inadequacy of even the best words and gestures strikes us more deeply. Return to Latin and separation of the priest and people would now simply displace the true sense of distance and replace mystery by mystification. The present danger is that the failure of the new liturgy to fulfil the promise of intimacy and intelligibility will lead many (young) people to give up on the possibility of access to Jesus and to God.

The shift in the intimacy and the distance also affects new images of the Church and of its mission in the world, including the mission of justice. The 'people' image and its close allies, disciple and friend, suggest a mutuality and equality with one another and with Jesus that overcome the distances of more hierarchical models. Yet the differentiation and distinctiveness proper to people and friends also establish a distance, a respectful distance. The differentiation and the distance are important to a mature community of believers.

As people of God and disciples of Jesus Christ the Catholic Church relates more naturally and easily to other groups of disciples and to all those in sincere search of the good and the true. In ecumenical terms the different Christian Churches all draw on the inspiration of the Jesus who *was*, are empowered by the Jesus who *is* with them and look forward in hope to the Jesus who *is to come*. Disciples all, they might be expected to find their deeper differentiation as Christian communities and traditions in fuller unity under the leadership of Christ. In service of the world the call of disciples to preach, promote, and discern the kingdom provides a rallying point for Christians' common action. Increasing collaboration in their basic mission could and should bring closer integration in intimacy with the Jesus who calls and who commissions. Without greater coming together of disciples in the diverse Christian traditions it is difficult to discern fidelity to Jesus in their pursuit of his kingdom.

20

Questions remain

Is our relationship with Jesus a personal relationship? The initiative in this relationship lies with Jesus. He is the one who calls us. The Jesus who calls is the Jesus of Nazareth, the Jesus who *was*. We understand that Jesus primarily by attention to those witnesses and accounts which have been recognised and preserved for us in the continuing community of disciples. We have critical access to the Jesus who *was* by our historical study and prayerful meditation on the New Testament. That access is rendered living here and now by the presence of Jesus who *is*, who is present to us now in virtue of his breakthrough, in his death and resurrection, to the omnipresent Creator and Father of us all. This presence, realised by the gift of the Spirit whereby we too say Abba, Father, is in that sense tripersonal. Yet we make bold to say 'Our Brother', 'Our Friend', 'Our Lord and Master Jesus Christ'. We may presume to speak of Jesus and with Jesus in personal relationship terms.

The power of the presence of the Jesus who *is* overcomes the distance we inevitably experience from the Jesus who *was* and here we differ in important ways from the first disciples. That new intimacy which they also experienced in the aftermath of resurrection involves its own distance for although he is with us he is yet to come in all his fullness and glory. We wait upon him. We look forward in hope. We shall yet see him as he is. The interruption of death in our family and circle of friends reminds us that we have also yet to see them in all their fullness and glory. The relationships we enjoy with one another are models for our relationship with Jesus. Yet they are subordinate to it. Despite their apparent concrete intimacy they are also haunted by that elusive combination of intimacy and distance which characterises our relationships with Jesus Christ.

21

2

Orthopraxis

At a certain level it might seem superfluous, even tautologous, to speak of moral theology and orthopraxis. What is moral theology about if not the conduct, the right conduct, the orthopraxis of Christians? The relatively late distinction between dogmatic or doctrinal theology and moral theology as it began to prevail from the seventeenth century was based on a distinction between the study of revelation as truth or truths to be believed by Christians and a study of the practical or moral demands which they had to fulfil. In that sense dogmatic theology took care of orthodoxy while moral theology might be said to take care of orthopraxis, if the expression had been around. Despite the apparently radical developments in moral theology, particularly in the last thirty years during which the manuals that had dominated the scene since 1600 suddenly disappeared, that general picture of the scope and relationship of dogmatic and moral theology still prevails. In an effort to do justice to the complexities of that persisting view of the relationship and to the challenge facing it from the current theological interest in *praxis* and *orthopraxis*, it will be necessary to rehearse, from the moral theologian's viewpoint, some fairly obvious features of the conventional distinction between doctrinal and moral theology in theoretical conception and actual realisation.

The actual development of moral theology as a distinct discipline with its own teachers and text-books was largely due to the post-Tridentine emphasis on the training of confessors. Of course, theological treatment of morality was as old as theology itself. Since the thirteenth century at least it had coexisted with summaries for confessors which derived from the Penitential books first introduced by the Irish monks. However, from the

22

seventeenth century moral theology, in its predominant mode, began to offer a comprehensive outline of Christian conduct and especially misconduct on the basis of moral law organised under the headings of the ten commandments. This outline was later elaborated in terms of natural law argument and increasingly supplemented, if not overshadowed, by the provisions of canon law. The earlier relationship with an integral theology never entirely disappeared. In the Dominican and other traditions the virtues rather than the commandments provided the architectural structure of the discipline as well as a more obvious connection with the basic doctrinal truths of creation, redemption and grace. Such speculative moral theology, however, made much less impact than the practical moral kind which these traditions had also to provide. Important individual attempts were made to broaden the scope of moral theology beyond the needs of confessors and to introduce a full-scale theology of Christian living directly related to the themes of doctrinal theology, as for example, in Tübingen in the early nineteenth century. But it was not until these last decades and particularly in the aftermath of Vatican II that the manuals, their scope and their approach were finally seen as inadequate. At the fundamental or introductory level, moral theologians have been trying to integrate moral theology more fully into the total theological enterprise by relating it more closely and more directly to the work of biblical scholars and dogmatic or doctrinal theologians. (I continue for the moment to use these terms, despite their obvious limitations, because they have been the traditional correlatives to moral theology. Newer terms within the Catholic ambience such as systematic or critical theology do not convey this distinction and contrast.)

The current renewal marks an important break with and advance beyond the manual tradition. It is now possible to speak with much more conviction of moral theology as a theology of Christian living deriving from an analysis of the event of Jesus Christ as 'the way and the life' correlative to the dogmatic analysis of that event as the truth. Doing the truth that is Jesus Christ becomes the starting point of moral theological analysis and the core of its conclusions. Orthodoxy and orthopraxis seem to fit together neatly as the concerns of dogmatic and moral theology respectively; and in such a theological world the problems confronting us here could be reduced to some further elaboration of moral theology as analysis of Christian living and charter of orthopraxis, both deriving from the truths of orthodoxy. Unfortunately or perhaps fortunately, that is not the theological world theologians really inhabit.

It is certainly not the world moral theologians inhabit. The return to Christian sources in Scripture and doctrine has had a significant impact, particularly on fundamental or general moral theology. Yet even here one sometimes gets the impression that the overall vision and approach, the broad theological framework centred on the events and truths of salvation, do not affect so intimately the analysis of such general moral themes as human freedom and responsibility, moral norms, conscience and development. They seem more affected by some traditional and contemporary philosophical, psychological and even sociological insights. It is difficult, for example, to find in fundamental moral theology a thorough discussion of the Cross as central to Christian living or a corresponding analysis of the meaning of the Cross in moral theology.

Moving from the more general discussions of fundamental moral theology into the more specialised areas of Christian life and practice, connections with specifically Christian events and truths tend to become more tenuous and vague. This is, of course, a generalisation to which there may be many exceptions for particular authors discussing particular problems. And it is a generalisation applicable primarily to the Western world. The special cases of Latin American and other third world theologians are not considered here because these do not operate primarily as moral theologians, although their work has moral implications as we shall see. Some moral theologians with a narrative interest might also be excepted at times. Biblical sources may be invoked simply to provide directly moral teaching in the conventional mode rather than any broader and deeper access to the structure and mystery of Christian living. For all their polite deference to the great salvific events and truths, moral theologians feel bound to get on with more exacting analysis of particular moral questions from homosexuality to political violence in ways basically akin to the ways of their manualist predecessors. Appeals to biblical theological insights appear as an exhortatory overlay or the result of soft-headedness or muddle-headedness. Sometimes they are. What is at issue here, however, is not the adequacy of the strictly (i.e. non-theological) moral analysis or the soft-headedness of the theological, but the recognition that most moral analyses and moral theologians operate with categories and modes of argument that seem to owe nothing to Christian faith or theology. To see such analyses as comprising a theology of Christian living and so a charter of orthopraxis for Christians is not at first sight convincing and may presuppose certain relationships between faith and ethics, indeed grace and nature, which may be questionable but are seldom questioned by Roman Catholic moral theologians.

Moral theologians tend not to question certain theological presuppositions, and this is in part due to their acceptance of dependent relationships on biblical scholars and dogmatic theologians. The accepted roles of biblical scholars as determining what exactly the Bible or founding tradition was saying and of dogmatic theologians as translating that into meaningful categories and language for contemporaries defined the role of the moral theologians as applying their findings to contemporary living. Their work was dependent on and derivative from the dogmatic theologian and biblical scholar. In so far as they were concerned with (Christian) praxis, their work was dependent on and derived from the (Christian) theory elaborated by the dogmatic and biblical scholars. The inevitable remoteness (as the moral theologian saw it) of doctrinal truths and debates from more pressing moral issues may have led moralists to ignore or detach themselves from scriptural and dogmatic studies, but it did not alter the priority given to these studies or the structural dependence of moral theology on them.

This relationship led to some curious consequences in Roman Catholic theology. The theology and the theologians enjoying the greatest academic prestige were dogmatic. (This has altered in the last couple of decades to include scripture scholars.) As long as the student body was made up exclusively of ordinands to the priesthood, moral theology and moral theologians enjoyed a certain practical primacy. For the mixed student body of today, moral theology is much less significant as theology. It is frequently treated as a supplementary or subsidiary study and described simply as ethics. Its derivative and dependent position has become, if anything, more marked.

The dependent and frequently detached position of moral theology has undoubtedly impoverished it and this impoverishment is not confined to moral theology. The primacy which dogmatic theology enjoyed as theory tended to isolate it in an enclosed academic or at any rate theoretical world. Some of the great dogmatic theologians of our own day, such as Rahner and Schillebeeckx, have echoed Aquinas and Augustine in tackling the practical and ethical dimensions of Christian truth. Yet the predominant treatment of the great traditional dogmatic themes, unity and trinity of God, creation, incarnation, redemption and resurrection, has involved study and development in an ecclesial and intellectual atmosphere that effectively removed them from the living and doing and questioning of the body of Christians. The intellectual and theological attempts of moral theologians to analyse that living and doing did not for the most part enter into the questioning and analysis of dogmatic theologians. The faith they were clarifying was primarily an intellectual or cognitive stance, a theoretical one. Practice would come later, as application. This led, for example, to a Christology noted for its fidelity to traditional formulations and its almost complete unawareness of how acceptance of Jesus involved a total way of life. This could only be subsequently reflected on and analysed as comprising intellectual (cognitive) and practical components in such a way that the former were continuously influenced by the latter. The primacy of theory evident in the historical primacy of dogmatic theology succeeded to a large extent in sealing off theological understanding of Jesus Christ from the questions and the insights which following Jesus Christ as a way of life must inevitably produce. The current interest in a practical or political Christology, in understanding Jesus through living discipleship, reflects a broader preoccupation with praxis and the theory-praxis relationship. It also reflects a dissatisfaction with a kind of theologising that gave the impression of being entirely removed from the realities of church and world within which theologians and Christians must also live and act. The twenty-fifth chapter of Matthew's Gospel (how we know Jesus Christ) may well combine with Marx's second thesis on Feuerbach (on truth as a practical question) in undermining some cherished theological structures. At least the primacy of a theoretical dogmatic theology uninfluenced by the practical needs of the time and from which a practical or moral theology derives, is no longer unquestionable or unquestioned.

The Praxis of Discipleship

Praxis and orthopraxis are not traditional Christian terms but are legitimately and usefully employed today. The orthopraxis or right conduct of Christians is the conduct, way of life or praxis appropriate to disciples. Moral theologians of Christian background must seek to clarify the praxis of discipleship. Other modes of expression for the task of moral theologians have been and are used. I choose disciple and discipleship as suggesting a more dynamic reality then simply Christian or Christian believer while at the same time attending to the distinctively Christian character and biblical origin. Discipleship is also a traditional theme in Christian theology although it has in modern times been discussed more in spiritual and ascetical theology. Fritz Tillmann made a heroic effort to give it a central role in the renewal of moral theology with his massive pioneering moral work *Die Nachfolge Christi* in the 1930s. It has continued to exercise an influence in the work of Häring and others in contemporary moral theology. J. B. Metz has introduced it into considerations of fundamental theology although his interesting and explicit application of it to Christology occurs in his brief work on the religious life which would hitherto have been classified as spiritual theology. Karl Rahner and Edward Schillebeeckx attend to it in their fashion in a variety of ways and works, while Bernard Lonergan's key use of the notion of conversion in his *Method in Theology* bears effectively on the role of praxis in theology and so relates to discipleship. A consideration of discipleship does not provide the only way into Christian theology or necessarily the best way even for moral theologians. It does seem to me, however, a valid way and one which may throw helpful critical light on what Schillebeeckx, Metz and others have described as the critical problem in contemporary theological hermeneutics, the relationship of theory and praxis.

Discipleship is not a single and complete principle from which further principles and finally the detail of Christian behaviour and living may be deduced. To treat it as such would be to revert to the old order of according primacy to the theory or meaning of discipleship as elaborated in biblical studies and systematic theology, which must then be translated into practice or applied in moral theology and moral living. Human and Christian moral living cannot, without enormous impoverishment, be interpreted as the translation or application of some *a priori* blueprint. The richness and creativity of moral living as recorded in human history and experienced in our own lives go far beyond the accounts—formulated or that could be formulated —of morality known at the time. Indeed the formulations themselves, in affairs sexual or economic, must be continuously reformed and transcended in the light of human experience and the fresh insights it provides. The moral life has characteristics of the adventure or the journey, demanding improvisation and innovation as challenges occur; and responses are demanded and become possible which were not and could not have been predicted. Of course in discerning and responding to the challenges, the moral agent invokes and employs the resources acquired in the past, either by him personally or by the community to which he belongs. But they will not always be appropriate or adequate, except in so far as they stimulate him and give him sufficient hope to risk discovering and creating the new responses of the future. The future as the zone of human freedom may not be reduced to the officially prescribed and technologically planned. The integrity of the *humanum*, to borrow Schillebeeckx' phrase, requires the kind of openness and freedom which the bureaucrat and technocrat in government and corporation find so inconvenient but which the Christian feels obliged to protect and promote. Freedom in and of the future is essential to the free and creative discipleship s/he has undertaken.

The normative account of discipleship as praxis and of the freedom, creative discovery and innovation involved in it is found in the Gospels and within the New Testament generally. It is a standing reproach to moral theologians that they have for so long neglected the New Testament or that when they turn to it, as they do more frequently nowadays, they tend to mine it for particular moral teachings and concepts without first surrendering, for example, to the narrative character of the gospel stories themselves in their accounts of discipleship and the narrative character of much of Jesus' own moral teaching. The recovery of narrative as theological source which we are witnessing today has much to contribute to moral theology, provided we have the commitment and the skills necessary to enter into it in an appreciative, creative and yet critical way. Gutting *The Brothers Karamazov* to find some illustrations for students, or confusing on the other hand the roles of genuine

28

narrative, its analysis in literary criticism and conceptual moral analysis, will not provide an illuminating narrative theology.

But to return to the praxis of discipleship in the New Testament! The original call to which the disciples responded in freedom did not reveal very much of what was involved. Indeed after several years they were still subject to crucial misunderstandings about Jesus and their own discipleship. The slow painful process of learning through living with Jesus which they experienced went through a critical stage at Easter and Pentecost. They did not, however, thereby escape the further conflicts and innovations which the break with Judaism and the mission to the Gentiles involved. The Spirit who was to lead them into all truth did not demolish the human ways of difference, discussion and discovery as the disciples undertook their task of preaching Jesus as Lord in whom salvation is available to all.

The praxis of discipleship to which Jesus called and in which we are engaged and were engaged long before we discovered many of its implications, is continuously nourished and illuminated by reflection and reappropriation of the New Testament documents. Nicholas Lash speaks helpfully here of performing the Scriptures. Subsequent narrative accounts of how discipleship has been lived and understood in the history of the Church offer similar nourishment and instruction. In this connection the Dutch theologian Frans Haarsma has recently drawn attention to changes in hagiography as indicative of 'changes in the structure of religious experience of our time and culture'. For our purposes the changes underline differences in paradigms of discipleship. Mother Teresa, for example, is for so many today a more readily recognisable type of disciple than Padre Pio was, John XXIII than Pius XII. And Dag Hammarskjöld, Martin Luther King, and Dorothy Day reveal aspects of discipleship that were largely obscured in the past. It would be a mistake to push the change in religious consciousness and/or paradigms of discipleship simply in one direction. Haarsma, like other Europeans, has to take account of the impact of secularism on all religous thinking to an extent and in a manner only patchily known in other parts of the world, including North America. (One is reminded of some of the work of Andrew Greely here.) And in Europe there are many 'modern' Catholics who would cherish Padre Pio above Mother

Teresa. Although it is not possible or necessary to enter into all the complexities of religious consciousness with their implications for models of discipleship, it is necessary both to recognise certain trends or fresh discoveries and to advert to the continuing complexity and confusion. Biography as source of moral theology on the model of theology offered by James McClendon, for example, cannot offer any single clear and definitive theory or model of the praxis of contemporary discipleship. To presume to do so would once again be attempting to subordinate praxis improperly and to close off freedom and openness to the future. That is not the way in which narrative is intended to work as theological inspiration and illumination.

Returning to the primordial narratives of discipleship in the New Testament it is important to recognise that Jesus came within a particular community and tradition, that of Judaism, that his first disciples belonged within the same community and that the ultimate break was gradual, painful and confused, if definitive and irrevocable. In discerning and following his own mission and in inaugurating his disciples into it, tradition and community in retrospect at least can be seen to include acceptance and affirmation, criticism and negation, transcendence and transformation. Luke's account of the opening of his mission in Nazareth takes Jesus to the synagogue and to the reading of the Isaian text (Lk.4:18-19, Is.61:1). This acceptance and affirmation of the tradition and laws of the Old Testament characterised the accounts of his early life also and provided throughout his life the immediate context and basis for his way of life and that of his disciples. He had not come to destroy. Not one jot or tittle of the law should pass until all should be completed (Mt. 5:17-19). As for the official teachers of the law and their deficiencies, as he saw them, the disciples were to attend to what they said but not to what they did (Mt.23:2). The obedience even unto death which Jesus exemplified involved careful regard for the tradition into which he had been born, which come from the Father through Abraham and Moses and the prophets. Only on the basis of this affirmation and acceptance could he discover and preserve his own identity as the one in whom all these things were fulfilled. Only his own self-interpretation within this tradition enabled the disciples on the way to Emmaus to understand him finally as the Messiah, the climax of the law and the prophets, not the misunderstood and misguided victim (Lk.24: 25-27, cf.24:44-47).

The acceptance and affirmation led, in the very appropriation and living of the tradition, to conflict, criticism and negation. The refusal to accept the subordination of human beings to the sabbath was a symbol of Jesus' growing distance from the official interpretation of the tradition and his growing distance from the official interpreters (Mk.2: 23-8). His praxis and self-understanding, developed out of the tradition, ended in mortal conflict with the praxis and self-understanding of contemporary religious leaders and their Roman political masters. His negation of the tradition, as understood by them, was supported in his life and teaching by the memories of David or Elijah or Abraham, the subversive memories, to use Metz's phrase, of the tradition which he cherished too much to submit to non-historical and non-living orthodoxy, an orthodoxy imposing insupportable burdens on the people. The people whose burdens primarily concerned him were the disreputable and excluded, the conventional sinners from harlots to tax-collectors (Lk. 15: 1-2). His friendship and fellowship with them, presented as symbol of the kingdom promised by the prophets and inaugurated, as he saw it, by himself, created irreconcilable divisions and cost him, as he thought it should cost a friend, his life.

The criticism and negation of the tradition as received and of the community leaders as receiving it, were clearly not intended either as a simple rejection of the tradition itself or as an archaeological restoration of some previous historical expression and living of it. The aim was at once more conservative and more revolutionary, no less than transcendence through transformation, preserving the thrust of the tradition, indeed following it through to the point where it had to be transcended and therefore radically and totally transformed. Perhaps the *Aufhebung* of Hegel and later of Marx may be the most appropriate word in our time for the intention and impact of Jesus. In that kind of framework we may hope to do justice for contemporary Christians to the continuity and discontinuity of Old and New Testaments or Covenants.

Every generation of disciples is born or reborn into a tradition and a community through which it encounters the reality of discipleship both in living authentic modes and in dead

31

inauthentic modes. The disciple's praxis derives from and so affirms the tradition of discipleship inherited and encountered. That mixed inheritance already contains much that is inauthentic and distorting and, therefore, in need of criticism and reform. And of course even at its most authentic, it will be in itself inadequate to the new challenges of living history and new generations. The affirmation, criticism and transcendent transformation will still be called for from the disciples of Jesus, even if the eschatological fulfilment of his transcendent transformation lies beyond their history. The transformation and liberation in history achieved in Jesus Christ must be re-presented, realised anew in the historical conditions of each Christian, of each society and of each age. That is the thrust and the task of Christian discipleship. The cost of it is scarcely likely to be less than he paid: in Eliot's phrase, not less than everything. But to that we shall return.

The demands of discipleship to affirm and to appropriate the tradition, to criticise and to negate it and so to transcend and transform it in creative fidelity to the life, death and teaching of Jesus Christ may be structured and analysed in various ways. For the purposes of this paper and with the focus more precisely on the tradition of moral theology, I will suggest the need and possibly the way to affirm, criticise and transform that tradition, first by considering two crucial aspects of moral theology, and then by invoking two evangelical themes, to a large extent neglected by that tradition but, in my view, of particular relevance to today's task.

The 'Reasonableness' of Moral Theology

Catholic moral theology continues to pride itself on its reasonableness. Its conclusions, it maintains, are arrived at or at any rate are defensible by reasonable analysis of human experience as moral—that is, as right or good and so to be done—or wrong and evil and so to be avoided. By a careful and consistent application of reason over the ages and in diverse historical circumstances, a continuous but not unchanging set of principles and guidelines has been developed. A number of comments and qualifications are in order here. While Catholic moralists in the main adopt a teleological or consequential starting point for their moral reasoning, following in this, they believe, Aristotle and Aquinas, they are not in the main

32

exclusively teleological in their overall understanding or in the analysis of particular areas of human behaviour. And I do not myself think that their reasonableness is tied eventually to a teleological as opposed to a deontological analysis or to some combination of the two. I do think, however, that their reasonableness is more closely conditioned by some other general features of the system. The first of these is a sense of the reality and recognisability of the human, independently of sin and grace. The theological constructs of pure nature and pure reason have played and continue to play, however disguisedly, a powerful role in much of Catholic moral analysis. It is to a large extent from this base that one derives the universal principles of natural law morality, still so strong in the Catholic tradition. Even so acute a thinker as Karl Rahner, and one who has apparently distanced himself from the older distinction of nature and grace, had to invoke a formal existential ethic to account for the concrete particularity of Christian morality as against its universal and essentialist principles. In theological terms there is, of course, no pure nature to be observed and analysed and no pure reason to do so. This translates psychologically, sociologically and historically into people conditioned and limited by all their circumstances, good and evil, seeking or not seeking the good and the right.

In such a search, reason will play a decisive role, and the *humanum*—the realities and possibilities of the human—will provide the basic material. But if either reason or human reality and possibility are abstracted from their ambiguous history with all the psychological and social conditions and limitations, the abstracted reason and humanity are bound to prove misleading.

In a manner akin to the hardening of Jewish tradition among some of Jesus' contemporaries, any moral tradition, including the Christian, can become enslaved—and this is part of human sinfulness—to the psychological, social, economic, political and broader cultural conditions of an epoch. No moral tradition can exist in isolation or abstraction from these, but Christian morality, with its origins in the protest unto death of Jesus Christ, is obliged to retain its distinction and tension by a critical stance towards the cultural ambience in which it lives. It has not always done so, remaining either the uncritical captive of a past cultural and political achievement or equally uncritically

33

surrendering to a new one. The affirmation to which Christians must certainly attend, and which the Catholic tradition of morality with its view of reason and the *humanum* at least in theory upholds, must be kept in tension with the critical and the negative which have been more a feature of the Protestant theological tradition and some of its predecessors right back to Augustine, if a new and transformed praxis and understanding of discipleship is to be attained. This will occur in action and at some cost before it is recognised and promulgated in theory. It might be worth re-examining some of the shifts in Catholic moral teaching on peace and war or religious liberty or usury or slavery or contraception with a view to seeing how far the previous affirmation had become simply an accommodation to current social circumstances or whether the subsequent affirmation (in transformation) is no less an accommodation to new social circumstances, without in either case any of the critical distance or pain of negation which is to be expected of a Christian in the world. I may remark in passing that much of the polarisation we experience in the Church is in my opinion due to uncritical surrender on either side to past and present social visions or ideologies.

This reflection on the 'reasonableness' of Catholic moral theology may be summarised as follows. Reason must be used critically not only in relation to the arguments proposed for and against a particular moral position or conclusion but also in relation to the overall social circumstances and vision within which the moral position is alleged to make sense or nonsense. The critical stance will usually be costly and painful, not least because it will arise out of an engagement or commitment and concomitant praxis by which a new position will be established, understood and witnessed to.

Elizabeth Anscombe's frequently quoted remark that 'in modern philosophy we have an incorrigibly contemplative conception of knowledge' (judged as knowledge by being in accordance with prior facts) is very applicable to too much of Catholic moral theology, which needs to turn more self-consciously to knowledge through doing and to be willing to pay the price for that. In this context the Cross as an epistemological tool may not be so far-fetched as appeared at first sight. Moral theology, for all its need of reasonableness, has to transcend the mere reasonableness of *nous* to reach the more comprehensive

34

understanding of faith and the Cross which will continue to appear as foolishness to the non-transcending *nous*.

Personal and Social

The second feature of traditional and renewed moral theology which merits comment here is its personal character. Like its reasonableness, this feature of moral theology is valuable, indeed indispensable. Like reasonableness it also bears marks of particular historical epochs so that for the most part it has operated as an individualism rather than simply as a personalism. The combination of cultural, philosophical, political and economic factors which created an individualistic ideology to which moral theology also submitted is too complex to discuss here. Criticism of individualism within moral theology derives today from general moral sources and, more specifically, theological sources. There is increasing awareness of the more significant moral demands as deriving from large social groups in questions of peace and war, hunger and population, technology and ecology, economic and political oppression and liberation. These demands can be met in turn only by organised group action with its suggestion of the group as moral subject recognising and responding to group needs. This requires a closer look at how groups are already interacting; it also requires a growing awareness of how far all of us are, even if unconsciously, engaged in a group praxis that is often destructive of other groups. Such moral activity, the awareness and critique of it and the call to transcend it, have been stimulated and illuminated also by the work of European theologians attentive to the role of praxis—in particular, political praxis—in theological understanding and critique as well as by liberation theologians, of the third world and by the first-world feminist and black theologians. The effects of all this on Christian praxis and so on its theology as moral theology will undoubtedly be very profound, not only in rearranging the priorities between large-scale social problems but also in changing the very way we recognise and conceptualise moral problems *tout court*.

The praxis of disciples must always be personal but personal within a community context and commitment that is not expressed in the coexistence of the individual worlds of modern liberal society, with its protected rights, privileges and powers, but by a community consciously seeking the emancipatory solidarity of the inbreaking kingdom, if I may adapt some ideas of J. B. Metz and Frances Fiorenza. How the morality of property, of communications, of punishment and prisons, to take a few random examples, will appear in that transformed praxis and moral theology cannot be simply predicted *a prioi*. The current technology of moral analysis, overwhelmingly derived from individualist considerations, will certainly be put to the test, and one hopes, eventually and fruitfully transcended.

Friendship and Kingdom

It may be opportune here to invoke my evangelical themes as throwing further light on the praxis of discipleship and its theology. The two themes of friendship and kingdom are intimately related to discipleship in the Gospels. The designation by Jesus of his disciples as friends in the final discourse in the Fourth Gospel and the self-conscious witness to the meaning of that friendship in the commitment to laying down his life (Jn. 15: 9-16) connects with and transforms much that is evident in the Master-disciple relationship as recounted in the Synoptics. His proclamation and inauguration of the kingdom provide the focal point of service for the disciples in their first mission and final commission. The personal and communitarian features of discipleship are evident in the combination of friendship and membership in the kingdom which Jesus offers.

More intimate links and further specification of friendship and kingdom as distinctive of discipleship may be derived from Jesus' befriending of the outcast and marginalised and his indicating that fellowship with them was both a symbol of and reality of the kingdom, the reality for which he gave his life. Indifference to the excluded, accommodation to the including and excluding power of historical society, is clearly at variance with the example of Jesus and the role of disciple. The myriad exclusions, by power and money, race, sex, even geography and history, with which historical society is riddled, are clear counter-signs of the kingdom. To endorse them, even silently or unconsciously to accommodate to them, is to signal one's rejection of the kingdom, one's breach of the friendship to which Jesus has invited his disciples. In a particularly moving way Metz extends the inclusivity of Christian discipleship and friendship to embrace the excluded of history, the victims of past oppression, and employs this as criterion and critique of our current pretensions to discipleship. Given such a praxis and criterion, theologians of discipleship will have to examine very closely their own way of life. There is a heavy price to be paid for a theology which presumes to discuss discipleship and recognises the way to do so as giving at least equi-primacy to praxis.

Before every active moral theologian decides to abandon the discipline in face of such terrifying demands, I may add a few words of consolation. Apart from the fact that the first disciples were a pretty mixed lot, and if one is to judge by Peter's prevarication and Paul's temper, continued to be so, the friendship and the kingdom are always, of course, *in via*, and moral theologians cannot expect to escape the limitations of human sinfulness. But they may not use this as an excuse for self-indulgent accommodation, much less for self-righteous denunciation of others. And all Christian theologians and all Christians are committed to discipleship; so where shall the moralist go?

Yet Christian discipleship cannot involve or appear to involve fresh insupportable burdens. And it is not primarily a matter of human achievement. It is a response to the inbreaking kingdom realised in Jesus Christ, which itself is gift, empowering and transforming gift, the gift we call the Spirit. The new law, Aquinas reminds us, is internal to us by the presence of the Holy Spirit, uniting us with Christ. Under the influence of this gift, illuminating and transforming us, we become and behave as disciples. The surrender to the Spirit is no less demanding for us than it was for Jesus but is not something we achieve on our own or of ourselves. The praxis of discipleship requires our creative and total response, but the gift is primary.

Finally as a theology of the praxis of discipleship, moral theology will be once again properly theology. In seeking to understand discipleship in and through praxis and reflection on it, the moral theologian is engaged in discerning and promoting the inbreaking kingdom, the coming of the God of Jesus Christ in power and glory. The goal of his endeavours is then the discernment and presentation of some grasp of God himself, the only properly and fully theological task.

3

Liturgy

The liturgical renewal, theological and pastoral, which in recent decades has so enriched the Church, particularly the Catholic Church, has had important if still limited effects on developments in moral theology or Christian ethics. One of the pioneers of current development in moral theology, Bernard Häring, has turned his interest increasingly to prayer-life and its theological understanding, although that interest has been more in charismatic prayer than in formal liturgy. Other more classical moralists, such as Paul Ramsey, have written substantial papers on this topic. There is an emerging sense of the necessity of integration between the liturgical life of the community, personal prayer life, what used to be described as spiritual and ascetical life, and Christian living in the world (formally treated in moral theology). This is evident in much liturgical, theological and spiritual writing and in the many institutes and courses to be found in North America and throughout the Christian world. It would be foolish to repeat and unnecessary to review the results of this work here. Yet the duty of moral theologians to explore the relationship between liturgy and morality, from their perspective and with their skills, is for the most part incomplete. It will be my task in this chapter to carry that exploration a little further.

Liturgy as Celebration: Relating the Mystical and the Moral
The frequent use of the phrase 'celebrating the liturgy' clearly does not find its primary justification in the faces, voices, attitudes and actions of the participants. To the observer they may often be very uncelebrating indeed, with their solemn faces, faces verging on sullen, even, their reluctant responses, their distractions and irritations, their bodily awkwardness. Not that

38

secular celebrations, civic or domestic, may be any less lacking in mental or bodily ease and joy. The experience of celebration cannot be simply summoned or commanded. It can be prepared for, stimulated, encouraged. Whether the experience actually occurs for all of the would-be celebrants depends on factors that cannot be precisely planned or fully computerised. In their unpredictability, in their tantalising stretch beyond one's grasp, and in one's need to receive them, they resemble the theological concept of grace. In liturgical and many other human situations they are grace, freely given by the Lord of the celebration to be humbly and freely received by its participants.

Liturgical and wider human celebration focuses on critical historic events in the lives of people or of a people. In Christian liturgy, the primary events are the life, death and resurrection of the primary person, Jesus Christ, but not as an isolated person or remote past figure but as the fount and head of a people brought into being and continuously shaped by him and by these events.

Remembering is central to Christian liturgy and indeed to all celebration, even such clearly future-orientated celebrations as that of marriage. Remembering includes recall of person and events in story and symbolic form. Such significant recall of the past releases the past into the present, allowing formative forces to emerge and be appropriated as part of one's identity. It releases the past into the present and simultaneously releases the remembering person and community from the imprisonment and impoverishment of the merely present. Identity is deepened, renewed, appropriated more strongly and fully in the present as the forces and resources that entered into past shaping are harnessed to meet the future.

The particular identity in question here, that of Christian community and Christian believer, involves identification with Jesus in sonship of the Father. Recalling in celebration involves entering the life, death and resurrection of Jesus Christ in a way that enables us to say Abba, Father. The celebration attends to and awakens this dimension of our existence by attending to and awakening us to the once for all grace and achievement of Jesus Christ. Remembering in Christian liturgical terms is sharing. Person and events are not merely recalled but participated in. The grace and gift of the Spirit is given anew so that recognition of God as Father in Jesus' sense of recognition becomes available to us. The impact of the past on the present is to

39

give access to the Father of all ages. At the heart of all liturgical remembering lies the present experience of God. The grateful celebration of God's care for his people in historic narrative, symbolic action and ritual prayer provides the setting and medium for experiencing, after the fashion and by the power of Jesus Christ, his God as our Father, for experiencing God as God. In Christian liturgy history is the way to mystery, the human activity of celebration the way to mystical experience.

The liturgical link between celebration, remembering, identity and mystical experience has profound significance for Christian understanding of morality. These four elements themselves occur in varying forms and degrees in the responsible and responsive life called moral. Celebration of people, of human events and achievements, forms an important part of human living, whose moral significance has been much neglected. In such celebration we honour, render our due, give thanks and express our love for people past or present. In that realisation of moral value and virtue we are ourselves enriched and extended. We achieve a fuller self-understanding, self-appropriation and self-identification. Such moral response and development transcends the categories of duty and goal, or any simple classification of a deontological or teleological kind. For me it constitutes the paradigmatic case of moral behaviour, moral relationship and moral living.

The parallel between Christian liturgy and morality so understood need not be laboured. For the moral theological task the parallel is less interesting than the intrinsic connection between Christians celebrating one another and their celebrating Jesus Christ. The meaning and shape and thrust of their celebration of one another must be patterned on and informed by their celebration of Jesus Christ as new Adam, first-born of all creation, head of the new creation, unique son of the Father and unique brother to all. In celebration-liturgy and in celebration-morality remembering, sharing, identifying and responding may be characterised by an awareness or experience of mystery and presence which evokes awe, self-transcendence, ecstasy. It is this mystical awareness, which we have already noted as part of Christian liturgy, if not always a recognised part, which offers the deepest insight into the relationship of liturgy with moral behaviour, moral virtue, moral formation and moral character. (I have deliberately listed together these four characteristics of

40

the moral agent or subject, because they are so frequently treated separately even by moral theologians who from their tradition ought to know better.)

Moral behaviour in its typically interpersonal form has at its core some recognition of the other, in his irreducible otherness, in his mystery, and, according to Christian understanding, in his embodiment and revelation of the ultimate and divine other. By the light and power of Jesus Christ, unique Son and brother, every human being shares and is called to embody and reveal the divine and ultimate other. Moral response to a human other has the potential of encounter with the divine other. Moral behaviour or activity is open to that awareness of the divine which at its more intense, spontaneous and gratuitous is called mystical and at its attentive, concentrated and reflective may be called contemplative.

The mystical and contemplative awareness which liturgy should foster and moral activity render possible may, at least in its more mystical realisation, appear to escape time and history. Yet it is never simply instantaneous in its realisation, preparation or aftermath. Moral activity is part of a historical process or of the growth of a person, who acquires insight, skill, orientation and commitment over a range of possible situations, interactions and responses. The insight, skill, orientation and commitment which a person develops in a particular area of moral response corresponds to the traditional concept of virtue. The growth in such insight and skill over the various areas provides moral formation and the total impact of all this on the moral development of the human person adds up for me to what Stanley Hauerwas has so excellently described in terms of moral character. Such a crude summary does scant justice to the subtleties and dialectic of the interchanges between moral activity, virtue, formation and character. Those particular interchanges are not my primary concern here but rather the interchange between liturgy and morality, focusing for the moment on what I have chosen to call the mystical element in both.

The more particular feature of the 'mystical' element which emerges here is the relationship between the time-laden, temporal, historical and developmental dimension of both liturgy and morality and the ecstatic, out-of-this world and out-of-all-time feature which is also characteristic of both in certain

41

intense expressions and experiences. This link masks a nest of theological and philosophical problems on the relations between action and contemplation, between movement and rest, between process and completion, between dynamic and (ec)static, history and transcendence, time and eternity or, most fundamental of all, becoming and being. In liturgy the historical events and their narrative provide the setting for the symbolic but still temporal and dynamic actions and equally temporal prayer responses through which the mystical is encountered and ec-stasis occurs. In the historical process of moral living and becoming, being is encountered and achieved, and the worshipping, contemplative, ecstatic dimension of morality experienced. It may be in wrestling with this link between active and contemplative as realised in both liturgy and life that new light can be thrown on the classical problems of relating the just person and justice or virtue and action, or on the more contemporary problems of relating fundamental option and particular decision or an ethics of character and an ethics of story, to attend to Stanley Hauerwas once again. At any rate it does seem to me that in both liturgy and morality serious attention must be given to their mystical elements and to the basic identity between these mystical elements as far as Christians are concerned.

The 'mystical' experience which the liturgy may stimulate is properly called grace or gift, ultimately the gift of God himself in his communicating presence. In a celebration ethics the stimulus to celebration is clearly gift and finally the personal, human gift of the others (and the self) to be celebrated. In Christian terms they are properly described as grace, God-given enrichment for us. According to the analysis provided here they are not only God-given but God-communicating, rivalling the grace of the liturgy. In the experience of the moral subject moral activity, unlike or at least more than liturgical activity, seems a matter of achieving rather than receiving. To use theological terms a matter of merit rather than grace. The liturgical connection and a more perceptive analysis of human and moral activity suggest that the receiving is at least as important as the achieving and in certain aspects prior to it. This is evident in the conception, birth and early development of the child, who is passive recipient of life, food and love and only gradually as it learns to walk and talk and so take possession of itself becomes an achiever. The balance shifts between receiving and achieving but within the web of cosmic, familial and broader human relationships the need to receive persists. It might be fair to describe this human capacity to act and to respond morally as a creative receptivity or a receptive creativity. The gift which summons and empowers belongs no less to the structure of moral living than it does to the structure of liturgy. Through the liturgy Christians are enabled to recognise, give thanks for and cooperate with this basic structure of human existence as it derives from and tends towards God. To acknowledge and live out this aspect of receptivity is essential to authentic human and moral identification and fulfilment.

An immediate difficulty appears to arise for morality with this stress on grace and receptivity. What about the striving and the struggle, the race to be run, the reward to be won in this life or the next? Does not the receptivity we have been discussing encourage personal quietism in a way often condemned by the Church or social passivity and resignation to the exploiting *status quo* in a way sharply exposed and excoriated by Marx and his followers as the real role of religion? While the priority of the given and, its reception may be appropriate to the liturgy, morality in an attractive and effective sense would seem to give priority to the challenge, the struggle and the achievement.

It is not simply a matter of opposing moral experience and understanding to liturgical or theological understanding. In the Christian scriptures and tradition there is considerable emphasis on human effort, the possibility of its failure or success, as well as on divine grace and its necessity. The difficulties of reconciling these two aspects have been partly reflected in the age-old debates about grace and freedom and about the relation of evil to a good and all-powerful God. Such debates can never be finally resolved as a resolution presumes an adequate conceptual structure for the God-man relationship.

There is, however, an important if subordinate aspect which affects our discussion and may be more tractable. The effort and struggle which moral living clearly involves may not be ignored or played down. It is not only part of immediate experience but also illuminating, stimulating and at least encouraging if not empowering for others who face similar difficulties. Moral heroes and their struggles constitute a constant source of moral understanding, inspiration and perseverance for many people who might otherwise feel unable to cope. The reality of responsible failure with or without struggle requires acknowledgment of the reality of achievement also. Without some experience of achievement or some prospect of it moral living would collapse in despair or absurdity. All this turns on the crucial moral realities of freedom and responsibility. Without the possibility of personal achievement these crucial realities would be meaningless. Personal freedom, responsibility, effort and success or failure, however qualified by cosmic, social, historical or theological conditions, from illness to sinfulness, go to the heart of moral living and moral analysis.

Yet the receptivity and gifts enter no less into moral living than do activity and achievement. Aside from the stage of child-development alluded to earlier, the adult depends for moral insight on some moral community or communities. This insight should be personally appropriated and may be deepened and transformed so that it in turn contributes to the fuller moral understanding of the community. Yet the basic material elements, the moral concepts and categories and the skills to employ them derive from the community as gifts. Their most creative transformation and realisation can never erase that fact.

It is not just a question of acquiring moral understanding in a community. Our personal lives and activities, with all their moral implications, become possible in a set of given cosmic, social and historical structures which are not of our own making but given to us. Ultimately it is, as already indicated, the human others who are given and give to us, directly and indirectly, who attract us, summon us and enable us to reach out beyond ourselves in moral response and return re-created and enriched. The initiative each one has to take and the struggle he or she has to make may not obscure this givenness or graciousness and the receptivity it evokes and completes. The more evident, intense and profound grace and receptivity at work in the liturgy should not, of course, obscure the responsibility and active response which should also be present. Liturgical grace and receptivity can illuminate and deepen our understanding of the moral life, while moral responsibility and activity can strengthen in turn effort and response in liturgy.

As this section has been mainly concerned with analysing the 'mystical' connection between liturgy and morality, it may be worth recalling that the receiving and achieving structure turns on presence, the presence of the other, human and ultimate, and on awareness of that presence. Letting that presence get through, surrendering to it in its reality, its potentially enriching reality, letting it be itself for one: these are some aspects of the mystical core of liturgy and morality. These reveal the receptivity of the subject and at the same time focus and centre him in contemplative fashion. It is a focusing and centring that provide stability, enabling the person to come together in a unity that becomes source of further development and flourishing. Perhaps the best image of personal development in faith and morality which derives from 'mystical' encounters and awareness, liturgical and moral, is that of a flower opening in the presence of the sun and under the influence of its light and warmth. This 'flowering' reveals a further aspect of the gift/achievement and receptivity/activity dimensions of liturgy and morality. At its most profound it may be translated into the 'flowering' of the Father in the presence of the Son and 'the flowering of God' in human presence. But to these I shall return.

Liturgy and Moral Understanding

The traditional opposition between the mystical and the active may be paralleled by opposition between the gnosis of elect individual or small elite and knowledge by the community, available for public examination and debate. The connection between the mystical element in liturgy and morality could suggest some kind of moral as well as religious gnosis and remove personal moral understanding and judgment from the public domain. Such moral understanding has characterised certain theories and practices of moral knowing and discernment. More recently they derived from existentialist attitudes and movements among European philosophers and theologians. These attitudes combined with a more crude individualism and pragmatism in Britain and the United States to issue in a situation ethics popularised by, for example, John Robinson and particularly Joseph Fletcher.

It scarcely needs to be said that the Catholic tradition of liturgy is far removed from gnostic exclusivism and elitism or any crude individualism. This remained true, I believe, even in its most clericalised forms which, through the separation fostered by caste, language and role, undoubtedly led to some privileges

45

for the clerical caste and some mystification for the Christian people. Recent reforms have sought to correct this by making liturgical celebration a celebration with the whole believing community actively participating. The experience of the mystical, of the divine presence, discussed earlier, is available to all participants as far as the rite itself is concerned. And the moral living which may lead to experiencing such a sense of presence is not restricted to any special group but presumed to be characteristic of all Christians and to be discernible and describable by them.

The historical background of Christian liturgy and the public or social character of its celebration provide the context for the learning experience always associated with the liturgy. For our purposes we may restrict that learning to a fuller understanding of Christian living, of the meaning, direction and particular ways of Christian moral response. The role of liturgy in such moral learning and guidance gives historical and social form, human flesh and blood to the experience of divine presence and to the associated summons, empowerment and response uniting liturgy and life.

Every liturgical celebration recalls and re-presents the story of God's self-communication to humankind and humankind's response as culminating in the life, death and resurrection of Jesus Christ. The culmination in Jesus Christ is critical and indeed normative but not exhaustive of the interaction between God and humanity. The liturgy in its remembering attends to the historical Hebrew background from which Jesus himself came and to the new stage of history which he inaugurated. Remembering and retelling of the story and events of Jesus Christ and their wider historical context, the liturgy provides illustration and instruction in abundance about Christian living, the way of response to God and to neighbour. In this fashion it enters into the essential moral education of Christians, an education which is extended and applied in homily, sermon, instruction and catechesis which normally accompany the retelling. The biblical narratives and their liturgical commentary are intended to reveal the basic meaning and direction of Christian living and frequently to offer concrete illustration and direction on the particular ways of responding and behaving. At least a Christian cannot claim to be serious about his way of life as Christian if he does not listen to and carefully seek to understand, appropriate and live out the moral message embodied in the biblical narratives, their persons and events. How a Christian should do this involves questions beyond my scope here. The interpretative interactions between historical biblical narratives and contemporary narratives of churches and Christians or the interpretative interaction between Christian moral understanding and Christian moral praxis will be considered here only in some limited ways suggested by the relationship between liturgy and morality.

In liturgy narrative, symbolic action and prayer come together to enact or re-enact the crucial events of the historical relationship between God and humankind. Christians are called and enabled to participate in that re-enactment, to share in particular in the events and experience of Jesus Christ. Such participation demands and provides an understanding of the meaning and structure of Christian life as a life of sonship/daughterhood of the Father and brotherhood/sisterhood of one another. Two critical aspects of moral understanding for Christians are immediately revealed. The meaning and structure of sonship/daughterhood and brotherhood/sisterhood exceed any merely formal expressions in so far as they are rooted in the narratives about Jesus' life and death, and about the anticipatory events of the Old Testament and subsequent events of the New. What it means to be son/brother after the fashion of Jesus is illustrated in a variety of ways in his own personal life as well as in the teaching he offered of himself or confirmed in the Jewish tradition. This grounding of the liturgy in the biblical writings and events enables the participants to learn how sonship has been exercised by the unique and normative Son and how that has been anticipated and subsequently interpreted in a range of different situations by a range of different people. Sonship as discipleship or following of Jesus gains concrete guidance from the words, actions and person of Jesus Christ as they become accessible in the liturgy. Imitating Jesus, accepting him as one's model finds symbolic yet living expression in liturgy. The combination of reading, symbolic action and prayer enables the participant in the liturgy to share the attitudes and activities of Jesus in ways that shape his own pattern of living.

This is not just a matter of internal inspiration, still less of mere external imitation as one might imitate a hero or a movie star. It is through liturgical recall and re-enaction, a confrontation with Jesus Christ in his way of life and a summons to follow it or imitate it. Yet it goes deeper as Jesus indicated discipleship and following would. It must be a sharing and not just an imitation or following, a sharing of his mind and attitudes, particularly his attitudes to the Father and the neighbour. And it is a sharing of his death as well as his life. If anyone will come after him . . .

The model of Jesus Christ with which one is continuously confronted in the liturgy is illuminating and challenging. The symbolic rehearsal of his life and death in liturgical celebration enables Christians to role-play their way into deeper understanding of what a follower of Christ should be and do. The powerful literary and dramatic impact of particular liturgical celebrations and of the liturgical year provide the Christian with a constant opportunity for remembering and reforming who he is and is to be. Such a remembering and reforming should enter into his moral awareness and sensitivity and into the historical embodiment of that awareness in decision, action, virtue and character. A liturgically shaped way of life and a liturgically shaped morality have in the liturgy itself enormous resources of moral understanding, from the more general meaning and orientation to the more precise demands of different situations.

The impact on awareness is not confined to the powerfully evocative narrative and symbolism. Through narrative and symbolism the Father reaches out in the risen Son to touch and transform understanding and action. The 'mystical' encounter plays its part in illuminating the Christian vision of life and morality as well as focusing on the transforming power whereby the Christian lives out that vision. The sense then of the other, of the holy, which liturgy and prayer define and refine, sheds a glow of light on all our relationships and their demands. This prayer-sense provides a sensitivity to people and their needs which can and should forcefully influence our moral judgments and responses. And in a way hinted at earlier it provides perspective on the relative significance of moral demands and the conflicts they may generate.

In the discussion so far, the liturgy has been for the most part treated as source of moral understanding. Yet Judaeo-Christian tradition, to which it belongs, has always insisted on a certain priority of moral living over liturgy to the point that an immoral way of life renders liturgy meaningless or at least unacceptable. The warnings of Amos or Isaiah, of Jesus or Paul, about the emptiness of liturgy and prayer which is not an expression of moral living attend to the other note of the relationship between liturgy and living, how living must fulfil certain conditions to enjoy authentic liturgy. My interest here is in the understanding, moral and religious, which this relationship promotes or hinders.

In the course of one's life and in the broader communities to which one inevitably belongs, certain moral values and insights are fostered or obscured. Indeed in the very moral doing and living one acquires a new grasp of the morality of what one is doing, a more real as opposed to a more theoretical grasp although this in turn affects the reflection and theoretical or conceptual grasp. Moral understanding turns critically on this interaction between praxis and theory. This also applies to the understanding and Christian existence and living of Christian discipleship, available through the liturgy. Discipleship in its moral dimension is illuminated, more deeply and securely grasped by the experience of the liturgy. And the same liturgy involvement and understanding is related to the quality of life of the disciple. The life which the disciple brings to liturgical performance obviously qualifies his ability to participate, to respond creatively to what is divine initiative. In so far as his involvement and creative response in liturgy are limited so is the understanding of Christian living which liturgical performance offers. The interaction between liturgy and living applies at the level of moral understanding and awareness so that the more developed a disciple is morally, the more fully he is capable of entering into the experience of the liturgy and so increasing his understanding (and performance) of the demands of discipleship.

Liturgy operates then as source of moral understanding but the understanding it provides is influenced in turn by the prior moral commitment and sensitivity of the participants. The dialectic of theory and praxis which operates in both liturgical and moral awareness and performance is compounded by a dialectic of liturgy and moral living in the life of the disciple.

Some further insight into liturgy as source of moral understanding and some protection against a possibly vicious circle between liturgy and life may be derived from more detailed considerations of the tradition on which the liturgy as moral teacher draws. The narratives and symbolic events reveal the meaning and direction of discipleship living but in a situation in which the enactment of the liturgy summons participants to particular expressions of that meaning and direction and judges/condemns certain existing expressions of meaning and direction. The liturgy in this sense has a prophetic role, announcing the way of discipleship and denouncing the waywardness of disciples. In its central use, recalling and representing the life and death of Jesus Christ and in the particular texts and symbolic actions involved, liturgical celebration offers goals, values, standards and critique. From the judgment of Adam and Eve through the decalogue and sermon on the mount to the story of the good Samaritan, the readings of the liturgy inform, evaluate and inspire its participants. The symbolic acts in Eucharist, baptism or penance offer similar insight, criteria of judgment and motivation or inspiration. Celebration of the liturgy provides prophetic witness of how they are to live for the community of disciples and, through them, for the world at large. The new life dimensions of baptism or the community meal character of the Eucharist, the summons and empowerment to repentance, conversion and reconciliation in penance, have much to say about the concrete life of discipleship. And so with the other symbolic actions of the Christian community.

It is worth reflecting that the prophetic witness, call and judgment which the liturgy embodies, and sometimes in harsh detail, is not necessarily general or vague in its content, or soft-centred, flabby and permissive in its demanding. The urgency and stringency of the prophetic tradition which the liturgy is to continue should prevent such weakness. There has been a continuing temptation to translate all moral demand into legal form in order to emphasise, as it is supposed, its strength and clarity. Some moral demands may be appropriately expressed in such legal form, although not all. The legislation of love or even of the broader reaches of truth and justice becomes rapidly meaningless. And the arguments from strength and clarity are not nearly as compelling, even in certain restricted areas like respect for life and sexual relating, as is sometimes supposed. The historical and even strictly liturgical contexts in which, for example, we find the decalogue suggest that this apparently classical legal formulation of morality has to be understood more broadly. The prophetic and wisdom teaching of the Old Testament and Jesus' general manner of moral teaching reinforce what he termed the primacy of moral truth over moral law, of morality proposed, in a variety of idioms, as truth to be done over morality imposed, in one particular idiom, as law to be obeyed. Indeed the very doing of the liturgy is doing or enactment of the basic truth by which our lives and moral activities are to be structured. There is also a certain primacy to be accorded to the doing of the truth over the understanding and so the proposing of it. At any rate the dialectic already noted here applies within liturgy as within morality. The significance of the liturgy derives from its recall and re-enactment of the person, life, death and resurrection of Jesus, from its providing confrontation with, access to and participation in the primordial and normative doing of Jesus. This 'doing' of Jesus, only properly grasped in our own 'doing' of discipleship, provides the fundamental and normative moral truth for Christians but it cannot be reduced to simply legal formulation or even fully grasped conceptually so that it can be proposed as a comprehensive way of life, as a charter of truth to be done. Yet the attempts at conceptual grasping and truth proposals are necessary and possible for the continuing free and critical fidelity of community and person to Jesus. The legal expressions can also be helpful in confronting disciples with the starkness of Jesus' way. What is important to remember is that the best grasp of moral truth available and still more the best legal formulation of moral truth have an approximate and provisional character. This approximate and provisional character does not vacate them of truth or render them useless as moral guides. It simply underlines their limitations while urging and preparing for better grasp and more appropriate formulation.

The symbolic character of the liturgy offers a basis for moral understanding and doing which is at once a solid, continuous and even normative reference-point and at the same time allows for openness, change or discontinuity and creativity. Analogies with works of art from music to literature are helpful here in the very structure of the liturgy and its capacity to mediate to participants new self-understanding and commitment. From this liturgical basis it may be more easy to move to the role of the

51

imagination in moral understanding and doing. A limited use of imagination is required in all moral response and living in so far as one has to reach out to another world in another person or community. The sympathy and empathy integral to such human responses are functions of a person's imaginative powers. More creativity and, radically, imagination is at work in moral breakthrough where a particular person's or community's moral world is restructured or recreated. Jesus is the major figure in this kind of moral restructuring. It is in remembering him that Christians are inspired to restructure their own worlds. Remembering breeds reforming and of the most radical kind. The great Christian heroes or saints attained this reforming through a remembering which fired their moral imaginations. The moral heroes of our time, a Gandhi, Hammarskjöld, King or Mother Teresa have shown that moral imagination, sparked in some degree by the remembering of Jesus. And the touchstone of the breakthrough remains its cornerstone or base, the liturgical recall and re-enactment of the work of Jesus.

To take the role of liturgy in moral understanding for Christians beyond the sketchy outline presented here, it would be necessary to interact with so much of what we have heard about scripture, tradition, the church and the value of moral argument. Scripture and tradition have figured, however inadequately, and I confine myself at this point to a couple of brief comments on church and moral argument.

Liturgy is church activity. Remembering, understanding and reforming through the doing of the liturgy are community exercises in which the individual disciple participates but which he cannot achieve on his own. The moral understanding thus attainable through liturgy is in the context of community understanding. However personal it may be to the call and destiny of the particular individual, it derives from and must be tested against broader community understanding. Paul's advice to the Corinthians on sharing meals in the context of Eucharistic celebration combines this attention to personal capacity with other needs of the community. In more critical situations the community understanding and need must be recognised and responded to but it may also have to be confronted and transcended as Paul himself did in conflict with the Judaisers. The fulfilment of this law which Jesus in Matthew's account sought meant also its own transcendence and conflict with its guardians. Yet the transcendence and the conflict must be out of love for the community and are finally authenticated or rejected, Gamaliel fashion, by their eventual value to and acceptance by the Christian community. In promotion and protection of the community's understanding, as in the promotion and protection of its liturgical celebrations, certain structures and persons have a critical responsibility and role. The appeal to liturgy as source of moral understanding and activity does not undermine those structures or people but it does not, of course, uncritically endorse their every word and act.

For all the vision and the power of the appeal to liturgy, many Christians and Christian moralists may feel that it leaves untouched the difficult problems of moral analysis and moral decision-making in concrete situations. To suggest that the perspective and commitment arising out of the 'mystical' encounter promoted by the liturgy and, in this analysis, also discernible in moral activity, have no bearing on the analysis and resolution of concrete problems is to misunderstand seriously how far such encounter and commitment enter into our perception and response to others in every situation. The more particular recall of God's relationship with humankind and, above all, of its realisation in Jesus of Nazareth illuminates in endless ways the moral dilemmas one faces from fidelity to a marriage partner to sharing the goods of the earth. The liturgical participation in the response of Jesus through his life and death offers understanding through doing that is critical to all moral analysis and has been overlooked by the attenuated rationalism of so much of that analysis. The couching of that analysis or its results in legal terms has compounded the difficulties. Recognition of the provisional character of all moral understanding and of the possibility and indeed necessity of its imaginative and creative transcendence for person and community offers a more fruitful context for developing Christian insight than the casuistry, however closely reasoned and carefully nuanced, of the way out. The obscurities which will undoubtedly remain and the temptations to self-interest which bedevil all analysis will demand a continued attention to critical intellectual analysis and to the community's voice officially articulated, even though they cannot fully and finally remove the obscurities and protect against the self-interest.

Liturgy, Morality and Kingdom

In the previous sections liturgy and morality emerged as ways of access to the mystery of God and of humankind and as a means of discovering and understanding the more particular praxis of that access. The interaction and mutual influence revealed liturgy as both source and expression of moral life and moral understanding. In this section I wish to reflect on liturgy as source of structure and direction in the complex and overlapping contexts and communities in which we lead our moral lives and see how in turn liturgical celebration is called to express and evaluate our moral performance.

The sacramentality of Christian life, as it is focused in the liturgy in particular, confronts the opacity of creation in its very material density. Through cosmic elements such as bread and wine, water and oil, access is sought to the creator of the cosmos. The traditional doctrine of creation emphasises the grand distance between creator and cosmos and the limited condition of that cosmos as expression or reflexion of the creator. (Only with humankind did creatures become images of God.) This opacity to divine communication and human recognition was reinforced by human sin and human estrangement from the cosmos and its management. In sacrament and liturgy Christianity has learned how this estrangement has been overcome as the creation becomes new creation and the cosmic elements, hitherto opaque and resistant, become a new medium of divine-human dialogue.

The symbolic use of such elements in liturgy fully accepts their cosmic and created character. There is no question of eliminating the grand distance between a living, loving God and his cosmos. Yet awareness and respect for the value and beauty of cosmic realities are restored and transformed by their integration into the redeeming and transforming exchange between God and humankind realised in liturgy. This awareness and respect provide one immediate basis for an ecological ethics (and aesthetics). Without any romanticisation of nature or any subordination of true human needs to elitist conservationism, regard for the cosmos in its created origins and redeemed dignity finds its due place in Christian morality. The liturgical indicators of this ethic find their fulfilment in the Pauline vision of a cosmos straining towards its final redemption and transformation in virtue of the achievement of its Lord and head, its first-born, Jesus Christ.

54

With this liturgical awareness of the dignity of the created and material world, it would be possible and valuable to reflect on the divinely given, divinely restored and divinely transformed reality of the human body. The dualism between matter and spirit, or body and soul, which dominated certain Christian movements with its elevation of the soul and denigration of the body, still affects much Christian moral thought and practice. Attention to the health, beauty and pleasure of the human body has been greeted with suspicion by many theological and spiritual writers. Pleasure has been particularly suspect in a way that hindered, for example, the development of an intelligible and persuasive sexual ethic and sometimes provoked a reaction of libertinism as escape from the guilt, fears and restraints of a repressive ethic. Liturgical celebration of the material world including the human body fosters an integral attitude to human being as body-spirit being, and summons Christian believers and moralists to fresh moral evaluation of body, beauty and pleasure.

The integral attitude to human being fostered by Christian liturgy offers particular help in facing up to another dichotomy, disastrous for so much moral analysis and moral living, the dichotomy between individual and group or—more correctly and humanly—between person and community. The difficulties associated with the misperception of the relationship between person and community for the most part derive from an exaggerated (and ultimately vulnerable) individualism, and I consider this misperception to be still one of the most deep-seated, pervasive and distorting in moral analysis within the western Christian tradition and, for that matter, within the western moral tradition *tout court*. It will not be corrected, however, simply by more sophisticated and sensitive analysis separated from a praxis and consciousness that precede and finally escape any complete theoretical grasp. It is precisely here that the praxis and consciousness offered by liturgy could help to release western Christians and their moralists from the prison of individualism and protect them at the same time from a new imprisonment by collectivism. An individual celebration of the liturgy (the work of the people) is a self-contradiction. Liturgical activities are community activities in which the individual Christian participates. The source of that community reality is Jesus Christ as head of the body of which Christians are

55

members. In a reinforcement of that imagery they are described not only as members of Christ but as members of one another. The further intensification and complexification (to borrow Teilhard's word) of that imagery as the members form one body by eating the one bread, which is the body of Christ, at least clearly excludes being or behaving as a Christian on one's own, doing one's own Christian thing in liturgy or life.

The parallel description of Christians as sharing the sonship and brotherhood of Christ respects the personal differentiation but insists on the close familial unity of those who may address God as Father. Sharing the sonship and brotherhood of Jesus Christ means sharing together his life, death and resurrection, symbolically achieved in the liturgy. Recognition of the Father by thus sharing Jesus' recognition of him is simultaneously recognition of one another as brother and sister. This recognition is no mere theoretical conclusion, no polite doff of the cap or shake of the hand but a performative recognition grounded in the performative recognition of his Father by Jesus himself. The interplay of consciousness and performance, characteristic of Christian liturgy (and moral living), combines here with the interplay between performative recognition of the Father and performative recognition of neighbour, and the interplay between the discovery and identification of the community of brothers and sisters and the discovery and the identification of the personal self of the Christian. The praxis and consciousness, developed in liturgy, of the community as a community of persons and of the person as person in community, offers a basis and source as well as a realisation and expression for moral living and analysis which transcend any individualism or collectivism. Such understanding of personal and community response, with harmony on moral analysis, would have profound repercussions, I believe, on a whole range of issues covering truth and communications, respect for life, development, distribution and conservation of natural resources, and human sexuality, marriage and the family. To go beyond simply formalistic attempts to move from liturgical performance and consciousness to such issues, dialogue must include historical background as well as an analysis of current possibilities and needs. In issues of communication for example, the information explosion, the role of advertising, the public's sense of the right to be informed and the person's sense of a certain right to privacy pose new and complicated moral issues. Yet the creative self-communication of the Father in the liturgy through the Son to person and community, calling for and enabling self-communication of humans with God and with one another and so establishing deeper community and fuller personal identity, illuminates issues of communication in terms of respecting and developing the person and promoting community.

The person and community interaction in liturgy has its own historical setting and is subject to a range of historical influences, as we have seen. Liturgy too can become the prisoner of structures and ideas which may derive from and in turn confirm the cultural, political or economic *status quo*. The continual return to the Jesus of the Gospel and the continuing subversive presence of his Spirit provide the stimulus, light and power to break out of such entrapment. The break-out for liturgy and liturgical community is of course break-in by God and his Spirit. This in-breaking we otherwise describe as the coming of the kingdom or reign of God. Liturgy constitutes a symbol, realisation and celebration of the in-breaking kingdom in which person, community and cosmos are to be transformed and glorified. Again the liturgical reality provides the vision and the power whereby human moral achievement is seen in its final dignity and ultimate dependence, in the receiving and achieving of the kingdom.

The kingdom motif in liturgy emphasises again the social and cosmic range of Christian living. It calls attention further to the historical realising of that kingdom, as something always in process but never finally achieved in history. This historical coming and becoming which repeated liturgical celebration reveals and promotes finds its parallels in moral living. Here it would be important to maintain the distinction between liturgical or ecclesial community and kingdom and follow this through by distinguishing the general historical social context within which a person lives and such particular historical contexts and communities as the political, the economic, the familial and so on. How liturgical and ecclesial community and activity announce and promote the coming of the kingdom within society in general and so maintain their distinction from but witness to the economic, political or familial is critical to understanding fully the mission of the church and function of the liturgy in history and their impact on morality. It would however take us too far afield at this stage and I have discussed it extensively elsewhere.

My final observation on the relation between liturgy and morality will centre on the future orientation of liturgy in so far as it is awaiting and expecting the coming again of Jesus as Lord, the final fulfilment of the kingdom. The expectancy which the liturgy in its performance generates mentally relativises and calls in question what has already been achieved in history in development and transformation of cosmos, person and community. It opens history to continuing and indeed radical transformation. If in its remembering it endorses the necessity of continuity, its expectancy offers the challenge of change. The relation of continuity and change embodied in the liturgy in its historical and eschatological dimensions applies with equal force and perhaps greater obscurity to moral living. In personal terms the moral development, the formation of character and the possibility, even necessity, of conversion indicate some of this force and obscurity. In community terms continuity as safeguard of personal identity and development has to confront radical change or discontinuity. As continuity and change interact in moral praxis so they do in moral understanding or theory. Liturgy offers certain help in coping with this continuity/ change problem in morality by exposing its necessity, offering certain models for its understanding and realisation and providing the hope that is necessary to survive.

The liturgy with its expectancy and realisation of the in-breaking kingdom also offers a way of understanding the provisional and relative character of moral achievement in face of eschatological fulfilment. What can be achieved is not all. Yet however limited it may be it is a necessary way of contact with the kingdom in history. Without that contact as indicated in liturgy and expressed in moral life, there will be no prospect of further and final transformation of humanity and cosmos. Response to and contact with kingdom in history provides the critical base for fulfilment beyond. In that sense historical moral achievement retains for adults an essential role and an absolute value, a value that mediates the finally absolute value of the kingdom and forms the base for the ultimate transformation. In this context of kingdom and history with its correlative components of person and community one may begin to make some further sense of the relative and absolute in Christian morality.

The illumination, reassurance and hope which liturgy offers morality as its source, and which it realises for morality as its expression, centres precisely on remembering the liturgy as the way of continuity with the definitive achievement of Jesus Christ on the Cross and also as the way of anticipating the discontinuity which the Cross already symbolises and the Resurrection and Parousia dramatically present.

Cross and Resurrection, history and eschatology express for believers the way and the terminus of human salvation, human flowering, to invoke an earlier image. That flowering image indicates the internal God-given power of human development in creation and its 'external' no less God-given and attracting forces in God's self-communication. In that flowering, humankind and cosmos discover and achieve their real and full identity. In the divine graciousness, God himself as Father, Son and Spirit emerges and flowers in human history, drawing it to its fulfilment. The most powerful link between liturgy and morality resides in their common and united capacity and call to let God flower in his own creation through redemption, resurrection and final fulfilment. Their greatest failures occur when they do not allow God to emerge and flower in his own world in this way. The life and death of Jesus Christ which constitute the heart of Christian liturgy not only express his development and flowering as Son of the Father but reveal in turn the emergence and flowering of God as Father, expressed in history by the sending of their mutual Spirit. This is what is at stake in liturgy and moral life: the emergence or obstruction of the real God in his own world. What liturgy attempts in seeking to admit God to his world, morality must also realise in the recognition and promotion of the in-breaking kingdom. Otherwise they collapse into idolising some human, historical achievement and are opaque to the in-breaking, challenging and flowering God of Jesus Christ. The risks of such failure have often proved too much in the past. They will continue to haunt Christians in the future. By holding liturgical experience and moral praxis in close, mutually critical and mutually supportive connection, Christians have a constant source of judgment, renewal and hope.

4

Moral Education

Shall We Dance?

For all moral theology's claims, at least in the Roman Catholic tradition, to be concerned with the practical living and growth of the Christian as a person, it has proven remarkably shy in engaging in any kind of dynamic interchange with investigations and theories of moral development. It might have been expected that the pioneering work of Piaget, first published in 1932, would have received some notice in subsequent textbooks whether of the unreformed manual kind or the reformed kind that appeared in the aftermath of Häring's *Law of Christ* (first German edition 1954). Yet I cannot find any serious notice of such work before Häring's new effort at a textbook, *Free and Faithful in Christ*,[1] published late in 1978. Similar contemporary attempts to produce comprehensive coverage of fundamental moral theology, such as O'Connell's *Principles of Catholic Moral Theology* or Böckle's *Fundamental Moral Theology*, do not appear to consider such work—from Piaget to Kohlberg— to be relevant to theological investigation of the basis and structure of morality for Catholic Christians. Of course Catholic educationists and moralists have taken some notice, as the Duska-Whelan book on *Moral Development*, the Böckle-Pohier (eds.) *Concilium 110: Moral Formation and Christianity*, and, more notably, Paul Philibert's 'Lawrence Kohlberg's Use of Virtue in his Theory of Moral Development'[2] testify. It would be difficult to characterise this belated and limited interest as manifesting or achieving the continuous and profound exchange which serious empirical exploration and theoretical interpretation of moral

1. Häring does not engage in critical dialogue with the work of the developmentalists.
2. *International Philosophical Quarterly*, Dec. 1975, pp. 455-479; cf. same author's slighter treatment in 'On Kohlberg', *The Living Light*, V/12, n. 4, pp. 527-534.

development demand of professional investigators and expositors of morality for Christians, even of the Catholic variety.

The first task of theologians, therefore, is to acknowledge their neglect in this area and accept the kind of collaborative reflection which this chapter proposes. Personally, I do not feel equal at this stage to any comprehensive theological or philosophical critique of the methods or results of the people engaged in moral development reseach in recent years. I have too much to learn to attempt that. Neither do I think it an entirely suitable starting point in any event. My heading for this section was not meant to be simply facetious. The image of the dance, the opportunity to get to know one another and above all the discovery of which steps we both know and approve, and which we find it impossible at present to harmonise, suggests something of the movement, the choice and exchange of partners, the rhythm and, I hope, the enjoyment, which may characterise our efforts.

Dancing to the Music of History

If I may be indulged in my image of the dance a little further, it is clear that none of us are actually taking first steps. Morality, moral philosophy, theology, psychology, and education did not begin with us or indeed with any of the illustrious predecessors we may summon to our aid in defining and defending our own particular dance pattern. As practitioners and theoreticians of morality we join the dance, we don't initiate it. However inventive we may prove to be, the dance has a history which we cannot ignore and a future in which we participate for a time but which we cannot finally determine or predict. The historical character of morality in all its dimensions of living, reflection, and communication not only encourages modesty on our part; much more importantly, it reveals the continuing chain or process within which we work. And it is a chain with many complex links and strands, much too complex to unravel fully here. Yet we cannot simply break the chain; we cannot totally step out of the dance into which we were in some sense precipitated by our entering the human community at a particular time and place, with a particular endowment and environment. The further course of our life and thought has made significant differences to us, we hope, but we have in some sense retained our identity and some of the shaping of that identity in our understanding and practice of morality as it swirls out of the past.

Perhaps the time has come to drop the imagery as it may be obscuring the centrality of history in the development not only of the person, as so many colleagues have recently underlined, but also of the community to which we belong, or more accurately of the communities to which we belong. As Americans and Europeans, as Christians and humanists, as Catholics and Protestants, as academics and people engaged personally in the art of living, as members of particular social and economic classes, even as women and men, we belong to a series of overlapping and yet distinct communities with tangled and intertwining histories. No serious attempt to understand our moral theory and practice can ignore that. A useful attempt may well begin right there. To which communities with moral ballast, as it were, do I belong? Which communities and which aspects of their historical formation have entered influentially into my moral formation in reflection and action?

These communities are for such a diverse group as this so wide-ranging that it would not be fruitful or indeed possible to distinguish and enumerate them. At least it is important that each of us bear in mind their reality and their influence, and that some of us endeavour to spell out more fully how certain influential historical communities enter into the shaping of our thought and behaviour. Perhaps the obvious way to confront that challenge is for me to reflect for a moment on the different communities and their traditions which entered into the forming of my moral theology. I am concerned here with my academic formation and not my personal moral formation, although clearly the two are interconnected.

The Shaping of a Moral Theologian

As a Roman Catholic theologian, I have grown to believe that religious commitment demands and shapes moral living and reflection on moral living. In that community and tradition, I have observed as central the attempt to relate and even integrate the way of life enunciated and above all lived out by Jesus Christ with the wider moral wisdom of the race. From the theological perspective the basis for such relationship was the doctrines of Creation and Incarnation; from the perspective of human wisdom or philosophy it was the doctrine of natural law as developed by Aristotle and reformulated by Thomas Aquinas. I would, however, have to acknowledge that the theological dimension, as found in Scripture and elaborated by patristic and scholastic theologians such as Augustine and Aquinas, reached the twentieth-century student in the very attenuated form of the moral theology manual which has for the most part disappeared in the sweeping revisions of the last twenty years. Its disappearance has not, however, led to any new agreed-upon and comprehensive understanding of moral theology within Catholic theology, although certain distinctive features survive. In philosophical terms also, the intrusion of new analysis and the reduction of the influence of the older natural law tradition have changed the dialogue between religious or theological approaches to morality and the fruits of human wisdom. And one of the unexplored dimensions of Catholic moral theology is how far Kant may have indirectly and unconsciously replaced or certainly modified Aristotle and Aquinas in the manuals and later.

Catholic and Protestant traditions of moral reflection cannot be readily translated into Aristotle-Aquinas versus Kant, into teleological versus deontological, or, above all, into absolute versus relative with the various approving or disapproving overtones attached to these. Furthermore, the impact of ecumenical dialogue makes it increasingly difficult to distinguish Catholic and Protestant moralists.

Having sufficiently muddied the streams of Catholic theological tradition which have washed over me, let me turn to a parallel stream which has become more significant with the years, both for me and for the renewal of Catholic moral theology. My early doctoral work dealt with Church-State relations. In the intervening years I have for practical and academic reasons found myself greatly preoccupied with social and political morality, nourished to a limited extent by the encyclical tradition of Catholic social teaching but more deeply and widely by the political tradition and needs of my home country Ireland and by an increasing awareness of, uneasiness about, and commitment to the deprived and exploited countries which constitute a large part of the world. The result of all this has been a series of attempts to articulate for my university students and ordinands an account of moral reflection that did justice to the Catholic-Christian traditions and which still provided critical insight into the meaning and structure of human life, personal and social, and into the fresh interpretations, structures, and claims which were continually emerging in the world about my students and myself. These attempts have naturally undergone important changes with which I will not bore you here. I believe, however, that some account of where I find myself now, with some of the background reasons, may indicate my readiness or unreadiness for joining in dance or dialogue with moral developmentalists. (How I do wish I had a more elegant name to describe them—one more in keeping with the elegance of their own work!) In any event this is all I have to offer as a prospective dancing partner just here.

Content: Structure and Basis

A distinctive feature of the Catholic moral tradition has undoubtedly been its attention to content in describing and prescribing a way of life for Christians. The origins of this content shared the complexity already alluded to in the relationship between scriptural and philosophical sources. The manner of presentation varied enormously through parable or story, direct command, exhortation and counsel to the system of virtues and vices of the Aristotle-Aquinas type and to the legal system of commands and prohibitions which characterised the manuals. In whatever fashion it was presented, it had clear and frequently precise and detailed directions on what constituted good moral behaviour in a range of areas from sex to trade to war. It would have been unthinkable in this tradition, therefore, to propose a programme of moral education which did not emphasise content. Catholic objections to the Piaget-Kohlberg method, fairly or unfairly, seized on the lack of interest in content which they claimed to find there.[3] This may prove a profitable area in which to practise some steps together.

Of course, the hard-nosed content of traditional Catholic morality has not survived unscathed in theory or practice in the developments which have been taking place. The concessions, as some read it, to a more flexible or liberal or vague understanding of content in sexual and other issues are not simply surrender to the *Zeitgeist*. Serious difficulties in defending the origins or argumentation or presentation of particular

3. Cf. Philibert, op. cit.; K. Ryan, 'Moral Formation: The American Scene', ed. Bockle-Pohier, op. cit. pp. 100–105.

64

problems have arisen and not always in the permissive direction. For example, the arguments justifying war and capital punishment have come under sustained and cogent criticism. Such difficulties in content have forced Catholic moralists to examine more critically the basis for particular ethical positions which for long had been unquestioned. Two of the more notorious of these, illustrating the precise problems of origin and argumentation and the interrelation between Scripture and Natural Law, are contraception and divorce. Despite such difficulties it would be a mistake to think that all interest in and practical certainty (as Aquinas might call it) about moral content have disappeared or been undermined by the new search for origins and for coherent defence of clear-cut ethical positions.

In discussing the more formal elements of basis and structure in relation to content, one of the more important items on the agenda for theologians, philosophers, and developmentalists is the meaning and role of virtues and vices. Indeed Professor Kohlberg explicitly rejects what he takes to be the traditional virtues approach to moral analysis and education, reducing it, it would appear, to some kind of Skinnerian reinforcement procedure and finding 'the bag of virtues' incoherent and arbitrary.[4] As my colleague Professor Hauerwas[5] has some important criticisms to make of that position and as it has already been effectively analysed and criticised from a more traditional Catholic viewpoint in the article by Philibert instanced above, I will try a rather different approach.

One of the points on which the defenders of the virtues and their developmentalist critics seem to agree is the goal of morality as development of the self, self-actualisation, (self) perfection or personal holiness. However these descriptions may intend important differences, and they do, they seem to me to focus on the individual person or moral agent as source and term of the development process. This I believe to be only half the truth. Moral behaviour is for me relational and communal as well as personal. Indeed I see the focus for each of us in learning morality and behaving morally as lying equally outside and

4. L. Kohlberg, 'Stages of Moral Development as a Basis for Moral Education', *Moral Education* (Toronto 1971) pp. 23–92. Other works by Kohlberg as well as Piaget's original volume are taken for granted in this discussion.
5. S. Hauerwas, 'Character, Narrative and Growth in the Christian Life', in *Toward Moral and Religious Maturity* (New Jersey 1980).

beyond the self in another person or community. Moral action is always interaction. The summons to respond and in my view, developed in more detail elsewhere, the empowerment to do so come in an important sense from the *other*. At its fullest, the summons and response are mutual at least to the point of demanding mutual recognition and response as human beings. This structure applies between groups of communities as well as individuals. It is that continuous interplay of summons and response, which occurs between people at every stage and in every context, which provides some general formal account of the structure of morality.[6]

In this account the virtues describe critical qualities of the responses or rather of the relationships which the responses at once express and create. (It may be that Professor Hauerwas's difficulty with Aristotle's circle may be more intelligible in a relational interpretation of morality.) The classification and enumeration of these virtues may not be as easy or as coherent today as in the time of Aristotle and Aquinas. Yet to dismiss such useful tools of analysis entirely seems foolhardy at this stage. However, my concern is a little different, deriving from a relational view of morality. In recognising, respecting, and responding to the other (individual or group), the complex reality of self and other calling for such recognition focuses the responder on different aspects, characteristics, and needs of the other in different, recurrent, and typical situations. These responses to typical situations are to some extent categorised by the virtues; for example, to the sexual situation by the virtue of chastity. This categorisation applies to the responses and the responder, agent or subject, but such responses are evoked by the other and her or his human endowment and need in the situation. Looking at it from the point of view of the evoking or provoking other, what typifies the situation is a value to be responded to or realised. Virtue and value analysis of morality come together in this way in a relational or interactional structure. Such analysis has the advantage of grounding value in existing human beings even if, like the virtues both in number and kind, they have been created by the community to describe and cope with the complex interactions in which the members of the community find themselves. They both, virtues and values,

6. My extended version of this occurs in *Gift and Call* (Dublin-New York 1975). For later developments, cf. *Doing the Truth* (Dublin-Notre Dame 1979).

form part of the complex dance which has been in motion since the dawn of history and which seems essential to the survival of human community and human person.

By that I do not mean to suggest that the particular concepts of virtue and value or any particular classification of them is essential to human and moral existence. Other moralists, including Catholics, operate and organise differently. The most obvious alternatives centre around duties, laws or rules or principles. It may be the Kantian influence of Catholic moral theology to which I referred previously, but I do not find any ultimate incompatibility between deontological and teleological approaches to morality, although admittedly certain examples of the one might exclude the other. In my earlier analysis, the person(s) of the other(s) are at once goal of my response in a teleological fashion and constitutive of my duty to respond in a deontological way. I find that a person comes before me as 'is' and 'ought' combined, not as a puzzle about that relationship. In the universe of moral development and moral education, I should think this fundamental to an understanding and justification of various stages of response as being truly, if incipiently, moral.

Another aspect requires consideration here. If values and virtues are rooted and relative to persons in the way indicated above, then duties, rules, and principles are no less so. Kant may well be invoked in support of such a position with his call to treat persons as ends and not means. The formal nature of this statement should not blind us to its fundamental significance.

Duties, rules, and principles constitute a further way of coping with human moral interactions, identifying, structuring, and classifying them as good or bad morally. Such a procedure has a long and honourable history, including a biblical history, but it is not the only possible procedure or necessarily the best one.

I should, for myself, be inclined to distinguish those rules or principles, however formal (in the sense of lacking material content), which seem to me to be properly based in human person and community from principles such as the universalisability principle or Rawls's original position or adopting the other's role, which seem to me sophisticated hermeneutical devices for illuminating or testing çertain ethical positions or rendering them more persuasive, but not for finally grounding or justifying them, still less for excluding others as equally or more central. Or is this the Catholic preoccupation with an ontological foundation for ethical positions rearing its ugly head again? And if it is, must we face those 'gory locks' and 'ugly head' if we claim a philosophical or theological justification for the morality we espouse in developmental research and moral education?

Persons, Communities, and the Great Moral Issues[7]
The basis for morality and its structural analysis centres on the person in the account offered so far. However, a little more attention must be paid to personal reality and its community context than has been possible so far. I did emphasise the role of the historical community in one's entering into, understanding, and living morality. The centre of call and response might, I pointed out, be individual or group. That this is so is clear from any consideration of the great moral problems of our time from racism and sexism to peace and war to population and starvation to conservation and pollution. These are problems which concern large masses of people. It is from such large groups or communities, varying in size from Three Mile Island and Harrisburg to the subcontinent of India, that the moral call or summons comes. And it comes to groups and can only be responded to by groups with the necessary resources, organisation, and moral commitment. A moral analysis which ignores such demands or a moral education whose contents are confined to one-to-one or small-scale and more manageable problems can hardly be said to be facing the moral needs of the time. It is clear that the problems exist but the 'how' of tackling them remains obscure. The 'how' includes more adequate analysis of the concepts of group responsibility and response, strategies for exercising that responsibility, and education in understanding the problems precisely as moral for us and in responding to them coherently and effectively. Too much of our moral analysis and education reduces to rearranging the deck chairs on the *Titanic* precisely because these problems are not faced. A consideration of them would, for instance, radically alter the general character of the dilemmas posed in some moral development exercises.

From the analytic viewpoint, moral philosophy and theology

7. A basis for Christian ethics or moral theology giving primacy or equiprimacy to the social is attempted in the author's *Social Ethics and the Christian*, Manchester 1979.

68

have been greatly impoverished by their concentration on individualist issues and on the moral behaviour and development of the individual in isolation from his or her communal existence. The individual can only become a person in and through a community. If one were to accept self-actualisation in one of its secular or religious forms as the goal or test of moral development, as so many do, even that is threatened if the close and unbreakable relationship between person and community is not attended to. In their anxiety for the welfare of their children, to take a homely example, parents frequently ignore the kind of community they are preparing or endorsing for their children in pursuit of what seems to them the necessary wealth to give their children a chance to go to college, to have the best possible chance in life. Their chance of fulfilment in life may be much more influenced by the kind of society such pursuit of wealth is promoting than by college education or any other family provision. The socio-economic structure of the national and international society not only is a source of some of the moral problems listed above, it also enters into how different people perceive and respond to these problems. And it may have an even more inhibiting effect on the conventionally privileged than on the obviously deprived. In the language of the Latin Americans, the deprived and exploited may be loudly or silently calling for liberation and this may be one of the great moral imperatives of our time, even if our moral analysis and education don't indicate this. Paradoxically, however, the privileged may also need their liberation from the self-centred, consumerist, and trivialised lives which their society offers them. And to be liberated in this way they may need the deprived because only in the new structures and relationships which a new society might offer could both privileged and deprived emerge as liberated and new people and, in the process of interactional morality, operate as mutual liberators.

Without in any way accepting either a collectivist or a positivist version of society and its relation to morality, I believe that adequate moral analysis and education must focus on both poles of person and community. It is important that Kohlberg's postconventional level reveals such a strong social awareness. I do not think that it may or can be ignored at earlier levels or that the Kohlberg form reveals the deeper dialectic between person and community which I have been seeking to articulate here.

The contractual or liberal versions of society do not take seriously enough its organic character and the destructive divisions of class and race and sex which may exist within it or the destructive relationships such a society may have with other societies. All are issues that must figure prominently on the agenda of moralists and educators.

The basic connecting links between form and content are more fully expressed as persons-in-community and community-of-persons with both their historical concreteness and their capacity to transcend themselves. But that is to anticipate.

Time Past and Time Future: Fulfilment or Destruction

The historical nature of morality enters intimately into its personal-community understanding and expression, as we have seen. The past supplies some of the resources out of which the agent (individual or group) performs moral actions. In doing so he forms or shapes himself. He develops morally, for good or evil. To borrow Hauerwas's word, the agent is building his 'character'.[8] This way of expressing it overcomes the atomistic emphasis on individual actions which bedevilled the Catholic manuals for example. I am not altogether sure that some accounts of moral education escape it, if exclusive attention is given to hypothetical problems as a method of promoting cognitional growth. The holistic development of the person is neglected. Moral development in the perspective of this chapter is not increased moral understanding of particular dilemmas or even the simple translation of these solutions into action. It is the growth of person and community through time, of course by activity based on some understanding but set in the appropriate personal and community context.

I say *some* understanding because as moral activity takes one into the future, no one properly understands what he has done until he does it. By this I mean not only that the consequences of his action are not predictable but that the very activity itself is properly understood only in the doing. This element of learning through *praxis*, which reflects the openness and creativity of moral activity, must play a role in any tests devised to explore moral development and in programmes designed to promote

8. This movement in recent moral theology from focusing on actions to focusing on agents or subjects is traced by James A. O'Donohue in 'Moral and Faith Development Theory', *Toward Moral and Religious Maturity*, op. cit.

moral education. Otherwise the creative nature of our moral lives is totally ignored and little more may be at stake than highly sophisticated marble-playing.

The role of the future in relation to moral development of person and community carries its shadow side also. We have seen too many people and communities destroy themselves not to recognise that the moves we make into the future carry a high risk of failure and destruction for self or others. This destructiveness is not usually simply initiated by us. We live in an ambiguous world. The ambiguity of the destructive and the creative characterises the moral community within which we hope to become moral beings. The ambiguity is deeply rooted in our persons and activity. The best of our moral responses will be predominantly but not exclusively good or creative. Moral development consists from this point of view in promoting the creative at the expense of the destructive. Moral philosophers and theologians seem curiously loth to discern and affirm this ambiguity; they present their natural law or other moral principles as if they were derived from and intended for a world basically unmarked by evil. True, they measure failure against the virtues or rules or principles they enunciate. But this anaemic failure derives from the weakness or the malice of the particular agent. It is not the rich prevailing failure of seemingly ineradicable evil in person and community, failure which everyone endorses or augments, but in which everyone is also trapped. Clearly there is great scope for those engaged with morality as philosophers, theologians, educationists, psychologists and social scientists to give, if not the devil, at least the evil, its due. Thereby conservatives and progressives might enjoy a more realistic view of a past which the former so easily romanticise and of a future which the latter so readily idealise. Perhaps the point is to change the world rather than understand it, but some developing awareness of the creative resources of person and community and of their destructive limitations seems essential to the task.

Self-actualisation: Transcendence and Conversion

I have already expressed my reservations about an understanding of morality and moral development that centres on the actualisation of development of the self on the grounds that morality is relational, interacting with other persons, and communal, understood and exercised in community structures. I wish to pursue a further aspect of this by observing that the call of the other(s) which evokes moral response is first of all their very presence seeking recognition as other(s). The recognition of them as constituting worlds of their own who may not be regarded as extensions of my world, or manipulated by it or incorporated into it, takes me out of myself to be aware of this finally other world and by the very same act of transcending self, as I would call it, enables me to discern and distinguish myself. It is the transcendence to others then that is at the heart of growth of self. Recognition of, respect for, acceptance of others in the mystery of their otherness help achieve at the same time an awareness and acceptance of the mystery of the self. I do not use the word 'mystery' here lightly or in any mystifying sense but as calling attention to the inherently rich character of person (self or other), which makes our exploration never-ending and the ultimate meaning and structure inaccessible to our conceptualising and verbalising.

It is the presence of the other which calls forth at least the response of recognition. In a true sense that presence not only calls, it enables. It is a gift presence which we cannot command or create and which in its gift-character draws us out of ourselves, enables us to transcend ourselves, sets us free to respond. Moral life is, in that sense, gift and not achievement.[9] It is not possible to ignore the achieving and striving dimension of moral response, but it must be balanced by and indeed subordinated to this gift dimension.

A number of obvious connections with Kohlberg's work occur to me here. The line of development, provided it is not interpreted in a too narrow sense, suggests to me growth in our recognition of, respect for, and response to others. The first level of avoiding punishment or seeking reward reveals typical reactions to people by people at very different stages of their chronological development. I would find it, therefore, rather difficult to accept the irreversibility which is claimed, knowing, as I do, how people regress in critical situations and fail to transcend themselves maturely in recognition of and response to others. The rich young man in the New Testament bears thinking about here.

A somewhat different feature, not peculiar to Kohlberg and

9. See Hauerwas, op. cit.

72

his colleagues, stresses the value of entering into the roles of the others. As a device for increased understanding of others, particularly in face of the dilemmas presented, I can only approve. However, if it is presumed that one can really probe the mystery of others in this way, even for the purpose of moral response, I would be very wary. I am still more wary of the implied suggestion that there is only one mature response to each dilemma or that responses can be so easily classified as Stage 3 or 5 or indeed that there may be any satisfactory response at all, given the ambiguous world in which we live. This, of course, suggests some connections with later stages and my unwillingness to give the universalisation device the critical role which Kant or Kohlberg do. I believe it has considerable value in certain areas which might be traditionally described as dealing with distributive justice, but it cannot really cope with a great deal of moral life ranging from trust and love to personal vocation. And of course it removes or at least greatly impoverishes any notion of both the creative mystery of the human being and the pervasive reality of evil in its myriad forms.

The summons of higher stage reasoning which Kohlberg presents so persuasively I would want to anchor also in persons and communities where one is engaged in actual living and not in classroom discussion. It connects with the summons to transcend oneself and one's condition in the awareness of the other. However, the strictly cognitional limits of the experiment prevent this from fully emerging. The change to another level of moral reasoning, which this precipitates, has overtones of intellectual conversion as explored by Lonergan and others. (I could not avoid the impression of close parallels between Kohlberg and Lonergan[10] in the stages, the invariance in sequence and cross-cultural claims. This is an impression which may be unjust to both thinkers.) My view of the transcendence necessarily involves the whole moral agent and again is embodied in his turning to the other. Conversion is to the others, perhaps through the medium of ideals or values but as finally grounded in the others. Conversion then is an apt description of the historical moral life. It is so first of all because we must continuously recognise, know again the others, whether already known or swimming into our ken for the first time. Their mystery summons us again and again, their needs for love or

10. Cf. Lonergan, *Method in Theology* (London-New York 1973).

73

food or education or simply recognition as persons constitute a permanent task. In attempting to fulfil it we are ourselves converted, changed, if not 'utterly' at least partially. And that change is as much their gift as our achievement. The conversion I speak of is not first of all provoked by evil or given religious significance. Of course, our need to turn and turn again to the other is rendered the more urgent and the more difficult by our being enmeshed in evil or sin, entangled in self and in fear of the other. The presence of the other is never merely gift bearing the promise of conversion or liberation. In his ambiguity and mine his presence is also threat or potentially destructive. Only the predominance of gift over threat in the mutual recognition of gift or the restoration of that recognition where it has been lost can provide the appropriate conversion and liberation. In this evil world I and my brother or the other also carry the mark of Cain. But it is the turning to the other, not some abstract turning from evil, that makes for real conversion. The implications of such transcendence and conversion in social rather than personal terms are even more urgent today, as I suggested earlier. The consciousness such conversion will demand, the political will necessary, and the logistics of carrying it out, even partially, almost induce despair. How moral education will face the problem is not just the concern of moral educationists. The survival as well as the growth of all may be at stake unless radical conversion through social, political, and economic structures occurs between people now a threat to one another on a nationalist, racial, sexual, or class basis.

Morality, Love, and Faith

The apocalyptic overtones of the previous paragraph are not the main reason for introducing the discussion of faith at this point, as if, to quote Brendan Behan, I were a nighttime Catholic, the fear of the dark inspiring belief in God. I have perhaps sufficiently emphasised the dark side of human living and its relevance to moral analysis. I do not wish to invoke faith or God as literally *Deus ex machina*. For all the secular pattern of my particular dance, I am well aware that this secular pattern cannot be taken in isolation and that much of what we enjoy as purely moral steps in our world has a religious history, played a role in that dance we call Judaeo-Christian tradition, and can only be fully understood in its origins and development within

74

the history of that tradition. I do not conceive developing that understanding as my precise role here, although it is a task that may not be ignored in this kind of discussion.

In most human traditions, religion and morality have been in interaction. This is particularly true of the Judaeo-Christian story. The interaction may be viewed and described in diverse ways. Many view it in an exclusively deductive fashion. From faith in Yahweh or the acceptance of Jesus Christ as historically recorded one can deduce a whole pattern of life or morality. Even if this view is not espoused in an exclusivist fashion, it plays a role in the way most Christians derive and justify their moral stances. On no less solid historical grounds one can say that Jews and Christians have viewed the relationship between their faith and morality in a more dialectical way, with the one challenging, confirming or condemning, and finally transforming the other. From the Decalogue in its Covenant setting to the dialogues of the Book of Job and the moral diatribes of many of the prophets, one can discern these dialectical relationships between faith in Yahweh and moral response to the neighbour. The character of your God is revealed by your treatment of your neighbour; commitment to the God of Israel demands very specific responses to the neighbour. The dialectic is no less evident in the New Testament and reaches tragic proportions in the failure of the guardians of the faith of Israel to recognise their own God in the person, life, and teaching of Jesus Christ. Unable to break out of their own self-righteousness, they cannot truly recognise the human other and so are blind to the Ultimate Other, the one true God in whom they profess to believe. Moral blindness bespeaks a deeper blindness in faith and they destroy the disturber of their ways lest his light dissipate their now comfortable and comforting darkness. In the subsequent history of Christianity this dialectic has been at work in the entire Christian community and in the individual believer. If, to adapt Aristotle, only the just person can do just acts, only the good can know God. Must we complete the circle and say only the one who knows God can be good? It may be more instructive to cast it in different form, the form beloved by prophets in preaching, by Jesus in his teaching, and by Saint John in his theologising. Recognition of the neighbour in her mystery, response to her in her need is not only demanded by Jesus, and imitative of him, it is response to Jesus himself as his express teaching in Matthew 25

75

reveals and as the reflections of the author of the Johannine epistles confirms. In systematic reflection on the doctrines of Creation and Incarnation we begin to sense the inner dynamism of response to neighbour as it encounters image of God now transformed into adoptive daughter or son and mediator of the absolute mystery which Jesus called the Father. If recognition of the neighbour is deficient, as in this ambiguous world it will always to some extent be, then recognition of the Father shares that deficiency and ambiguity. Yet the distinction of the two traditions of morality and faith, and the ability of person and community to discern the distinction, provide the challenge to mutual condemnation and correction as well as mutual endorsement and illumination.

For Christian moral educators the distinction and dialectic are of critical importance. How far may they separate what they distinguish? How free are they to embark on moral education programmes which abstract entirely from the commitment of faith? How valid are formulas and programmes explicitly designed to restrict the moral in a way that does not breach state school policy on religion, for people for whom such separation is not finally acceptable? I do not pretend to know the answer to these and other questions which might be posed along similar lines. I do believe, however, that if the work of the moral developmentalists were expanded to take account of what I believe to be a richer although still primarily secular expression of morality, Christians would be considerably more helped in their work of moral education. Indeed it may be that it is the individualist, liberal character of the underlying philosophy rather than the dismissive attitude to the religious dimension which is the greatest obstacle to the effective cooperation of Christians with the very remarkable achievements of Kohlberg, his predecessors, and his colleagues. One may illustrate this by recalling the pre-eminence afforded to justice in this work, practically to the point of the neglect or rejection of the other virtues. How extraordinary that academics should find so little room for discussion of truth as a central social virtue and not as an antidote to cheating at exams but as a dynamic force summoning men to seek, speak, and even die for the truth. In conventional Christian terms the passing over of love or charity seems more remarkable. The rational and liberal thrust of the participants may have made them unduly suspicious of the vagueness and pliability of these terms. In the approach to morality outlined here as in many other approaches, love can be a very hardheaded term. The recognition, respect, and concrete response demanded by the presence of the other are at once the test and expression of the love, which takes account of the whole person in appreciative recognition and turns that into service in feeding or clothing or education or whatever. In the larger-scale and more structured relationships operative in local, national, and international society the same appreciative recognition must find expression in the sensitivity of the provisions made and of the people who implement them. Without such human fullness people are degraded by our service rather than enriched and liberated and we in turn fail to break out of our protective, calculating shell, fail to transcend ourselves and be liberated. Perhaps the final rational—but to me absurd—conclusion of such a situation would be that one would feel called to the supreme expression of loving, by laying down one's life, without in fact having any love at all.

Moral Theology and Moral Education: Notes of a Would-Be Choreographer

Even if the particular specialist is still unable to say, 'I could have danced all night,' one may at least try a few hesitant, awkward steps with a cooperative and learning partner. The choreographer's suggestions outlined here derive from the sometimes slow and patient, sometimes fast and furious exchanges which took place as the nightingales sang at the Abbey of Senanque.

1. The continuing tradition of the Natural Law, treasured by moral theology, has clear affinity with the respect for the moral reasoning process and the importance of justice in the work of Kohlberg and others. A broader and deeper understanding of that reasoning process as involving the biological, psychological, social, and spiritual unity called person would provide for richer exchange, and fewer '*faux pas.*' The tendency to isolate justice and rights and claims in conflict does not convey the sweep of morality in the Natural Law at its best or as incorporated in the Christian tradition of the West. Other issues and attitudes, virtues and values have to form part of any programme of moral education and its scientific investigation.

2. Moral philosophy and theology as well as moral education

77

have been predominantly individualist. One becomes a person only in community, thereby changing the community of family, school, neighbourhood, city, nation, world. Community is in turn formed and reformed by persons. Moral educators, like moral philosophers and theologians, are faced with the difficulties of maintaining in creative tension the poles of person and community. The experience of Senanque suggests that they try to face them together.

3. The community dimension of all morality assumes almost apocalyptic urgency as one contemplates the global moral problems confronting mankind: war, actual and potential; starvation; waste of diminishing resources; pollution of the atmosphere and beyond. Only community awareness and response can cope with such problems. Only effective moral analyses and education can enable a community to achieve that awareness and response.

4. Analysts and educators cannot ignore the darkness that dogs their steps, the evil that lurks outside or even within the patch of light in which they have chosen to practise their steps. The evil is structured into both person and community, not necessarily as a prevailing force but always as threatening. The moral task involves a struggle that the good may prevail over the evil. The best results will always retain some ambiguity. The struggle is never finally resolved. The threat continues and must be carefully identified in analysis and education.

5. The historical sense, so clear in moral development programmes, provides further help for the philosopher and theologian in understanding the moral agent. In the contexts of both community and evil, of moral action as interaction and of good action as also overcoming some evil, the development takes the form of conversion. It is in the traditional senses a conversion *from* (evil self-centredness) and a conversion *to* (good and the others). It should be a conversion of person and community.

6. Such conversion is only partly understood in anticipation of moral activity, which at its best and deepest is a creative venturing into the unknown. It is in the doing that full moral understanding is achieved. Programmes of moral education require opportunities for such doing by persons in community and by communities of persons.

7. The relationship between morality and religion is perhaps best understood as one of creative interaction. Distinct but

inseparable for Christians, they provide mutual challenge and correction as well as illumination and confirmation. The conversion to the human other (person and community) which characterises moral activity encounters also the mystery of the Ultimate Other as mediated by the human. The further reach of moral activity is prayer. The turning to the Ultimate Other demands and empowers the recognition of and response to its incarnate presence in the community.

Theologians, philosophers, psychologists, and educators have their own patterns and rhythms. They can and must enrich and extend them together, if their efforts are not to resemble some individual *danses macabres*.

5

The Holy Spirit and Human Identity

Introduction

The original topic proposed for this chapter, 'The Holy Spirit and Anthropology', seemed to me too broad in its scope. My own refinement and confinement of the topic to 'The Holy Spirit and Human Identity' may overlook some of the underlying possibilities for exploration which the original title promised on the relationship of divine power and presence to human existence and aspiration, achievement and frustration. As my thinking on this new topic developed, I felt the urge to redefine and further confine to 'Holy Spirit and Christian Identity'. That would certainly be to betray the spirit of the original suggestion, although it might look like a more manageable theological project. The first and most important difficulties with relating Spirit and human/anthropological reality focus on the danger of reducing one to the other, so Spirit becomes a dimension of human, or human simply an expression of Spirit. The refinement of identity poses the difficulty of whose theological area this is. As with so many questions posed for a theology seeking to respond to questions new at least in their intellectual, cultural and practical contexts, no easy answer is available. The traditional specialisations do not comfortably or adequately cover such questions. In particular, that recently refurbished warhorse, systematic theology, even when it tries to combine doctrinal/dogmatic, historical and moral theology, is too amorphous in approach and diverse in content, in a word unsystematic, to form a definite specialisation. We may have to rest content for the present with theologians, within the general context of systematic theology or outside it, addressing related questions as they occur with all the resources they can command, without the designation of particular specialities. On a personal note, I find the renewal of moral theology has, to a large extent, lost its impetus because of a failure to take seriously the broader resources and questions of Christian tradition and contemporary Christian and human experience. Yet in any authentically renewed version of theology as a study of the Christian way of life, required of Christians and model for others, human identity as discerned and shaped by the Spirit would surely figure.

Structure

The structure of this chapter is relatively simple. What is built on that structure is more complex, obscure and almost certainly more disputable. I move from an analysis of human identity, or rather of particular features of it, to a discussion of the Spirit, in relation to Jesus and so to his disciples in their search for and achievement of identity. I attempt to complete the circle by moving on to the particular human practices of prayer and politics in concrete situations. In this way I hope to explore some connections between the Holy Spirit as he comes to us as Spirit of Christ in the New Testament and in the life of the Church, and human identity as I discern some of the more significant features of the latter. By attempting to test this understanding by the characteristic activities of prayer and politics in actual situations, I will, at least, have seen the experiment through, although with what success must be left to others to judge.

Features of Human Identity

The choice of features of human identity for discussion here is not simply arbitrary, nor, I hope, personally eccentric. The features would, I believe, be significant, if sometimes differently labelled, in any serious discussion of human identity. The justification for this rests primarily with the fuller exposition of each feature. These particular features, I believe, offer helpful ways of connection with the activity of the Spirit of Christ, the main task of this chapter. Again, the justification for that belief must await the later performance of the task itself. Finally, the features do reveal some personal interest, as all such discussion must. There are features that have become important to me in the intellectual and personal struggles in which a Christian is inevitably involved as he tries to live and understand his faith in the world. However, I doubt if my struggles are simply eccentric or that the features arising from them and presented here are peculiar to my reading of human identity.

Differentiation

In the search for human identity differentiation might seem to be an end as well as the beginning, and the question 'Who am I?' reducible to 'How am I different from others?' The difference from others has a clearly biological or material base, at least this side of cloning, and originates as a *given* which may be subsequently discovered, appropriated, developed and even transformed. The prospect of discovery and appropriation, development and transformation, indicates that while the biological base provides certain limits as well as resources of human identity, it is not exhaustive of it. The various other dimensions of human existence which progressively emerge in individual consciousness and social relationships, in the priorities and activities of historical human living, at once express and construct personal identity as a biological, psychological, sociological and historical reality. Recognising somebody, even a face in the crowd, is not just discerning a biological pattern, but responding to a person with whom one shares some common world, directly or indirectly.

The differentiation of an individual person then enjoys that paradox shared by most human phenomena, of being both given and achieved, and the paradox extends into the apparently most achievement-oriented of people and their apparently most spectacular achievements. The receiving may be greatly obscured by the achieving of the world's fastest miler or of the Nobel Laureate in science or of the candidate elected as the President of the United States. A little reflection will reveal how far athletic prowess or scientific or political success depends at every stage on the originating gifts, e.g. biological, intellectual or familial, which the achiever received and more significantly still, on the continuing help of family, educators, coaches, collaborators, supporters, organisers, of the athletic or scientific or political communities within which and in dependence on which the achiever reached success. Of course, there were obstructions and probably obstructors in the way also, and the personal dedication, effort, industry made a critical difference to the achieving performance which took advantage of and transcended the receiving. The paradox would disappear if due

82

weight were not given to the irreducibly personal and achieving contribution of the achiever and the achievement.

These rather dramatic instances of human receiving/achieving illustrate the more complete and complex, if less newsworthy histories, of human identity in which we are all engaged. (The identity of the athlete or scientist or President of the United States may not be equiparated with their athletic, scientific or political differentiating roles and achievement, although the temptations for themselves and others to do so may be great.) In historical terms, the receiving and achieving which constitutes differentiation is never simply complete; the fullness of differentiation is a life-long task. The task-reference stresses the call to achievement which is sometimes rather remotely and aggressively understood as self-assertion. Self-assertion suggests a range of actions and attitudes which are not all necessary to or even compatible with the concept of differentiation being explored here. The thrust to survival with its biological origins may not at the human level operate as a drive for survival at any price, e.g. the price of the existence of other human beings, without radically calling in question the value of that which one wishes to survive, human existence itself. The self-assertion which issues in the search for personal space to grow and flourish, may easily intrude on the space and growth of others. When personal initiative and enterprise develop or rather decline into self-aggrandisement in the pursuit of money, power and pleasure without any consideration for the needs and rights of others, the self-assertion becomes self-destruction. Differentiation as aspect of human identity has to take account of the others in search of and entitled to human identity, if it is not to involve self-contradiction and indeed eventually self-destruction. Differentiation occurs within a set of historical human relationships with other people, who may not be simply used as resources for the self but demand response to and engagement with their struggle for identity also. Solidarity with the others must balance and complement the thrust towards differentiation of the self.

Solidarity

A person is born into a particular historical community, sharing not merely the biological heritage of father and mother, but the wider heritage of a history shaped by geographical, climatic, economic, political and religious conditions and predecessors' response to them. The given of the total human heritage is a given in community, in solidarity with which the new member is both enriched and limited, from which he/she must begin to discover a personal identity. Personal identity, however, demands a commitment to and not just captivity by the community given. What that means is that in the search for development and identity the person will draw appreciatively, but not uncritically on the riches of the giver community, will endeavour to overcome its limitations and seek to contribute to the riches in turn. Solidarity with the community as partly inescapable involvement with and predominantly free commitment to it, focuses first of all on the other members of the community, their gifts and wishes, needs and limitations. Appreciation of and commitment to them constitute the primary component in human solidarity. In the exercise of that appreciation and commitment, the new member discovers and establishes his/her own resources, patterns of behaviour and personal characteristics.

The community of solidarity may not, indeed cannot, be artificially limited in space or time. In the contemporary world above all, with its potential for instant and universal communication, the geographical range of solidarity stretches with varying degrees of identity and effectiveness around the world. The people of Kerry can and do rejoice or suffer with the people of Kerala. Presidential elections in the USA evoke hopes and fears in the USSR. The success or failure of grain harvests in Eastern Europe, East Africa and the American Midwest are at least potentially interlinked and fateful to the survival of so many otherwise barely connected people. Solidarity at multiple levels is today worldwide.

Limitations in time are no less artificial. The influences of 1690 and of 1916 on Northern Ireland 1980 are one small indication of that. Concern for the environment in terms of pollution and wastage of scenic resources reflects people's sense of solidarity with the people of 2080. In time, as in geography, solidarity focuses on people past, as with William of Orange and Padraic Pearse, and future, as with the coming generations who may be affected by pollution of the atmosphere or shortage of resources. To ignore the past or future generations in the name of establishing our own identity is again to call in question the very goal of our endeavours. To be captive to them by allowing

84

the aims and slogans of 1690 or 1916 to determine our thinking and aspirations in the very different world of 1980 or to sacrifice a present generation to a future is equally destructive of the genuinely different, free and valuable in human identity in the name of a false solidarity. Solidarity needs the balance, distinctiveness and freedom of differentiation no less than differentiation needs the resources, context and continuity of solidarity. A fresh perspective on their mutual dependence emerges in the consideration of the two closely related features of memory and creativity.

Memory

Without entering into the philosophical debate about how far memory as distinct from body constitutes human personal identity, it is clear that memory performs a significant function in the identification of person and community. The given of the past and the continuous retrieval and remoulding of that given deeply influence identity in the present and set parameters for its development in the future. People as individuals and groups may try to suppress their past as shameful and guilt-provoking. They try to rewrite it to meet the requirements of their new status and aspirations. Yet the silt of time, of past human achievement and fortune, cannot be simply dispersed and forgotten. For that past and those memories to play a positive rather than a negative, obstructive and destructive role, they must be acknowledged and appropriated. Insofar as they are guilt-provoking or otherwise imprisoning, they must be transcended. They cannot be simply evaded. So much we might learn from the confessional, the psychiatrist's consulting room and from the dramatic political eruptions which finally challenge a long history of oppression and discrimination. How memory and memories provide the fuel for violent conflagration or restorative celebration is the stuff of history and poetry and religion, of the deepest dimensions of human identity and existence.

Creativity

Uncritical enthusiasm or hopeless apathy in submission to the past as remembered is no less enslaving than attempts to evade it. The memories that matter are themselves of free, innovative, creative achievements. Their creativity usually incorporated and transcended memories of earlier achievements. Their current thrust of remembering is not towards the embalming of the past but the transformation of the present and creation of the future. Only in that way are the deeds and people remembered duly honoured for their own creativity. So far from restricting creativity and innovation, remembering at once inspires them and provides some criteria for assessing them. By the very nature of creativity such criteria cannot be exhaustive. Creative innovation is not the result of computerised pre-programming or of the precise calculations of consequences. It involves the genuinely new and hence unpredictable. The search for it involves risk, the risk of being wrong, of being hurt, more seriously still of others being hurt. Such risk may not be lightly undertaken. Yet it cannot be totally avoided if human beings are to harness their resources from the past and present to meet the challenges of the future. Through that search and with that risk human identity, for person and group, develops in living fashion.

Jesus Christ, The Spirit and Human Identity

The close association of the Holy Spirit with the person and achievement of Jesus Christ in his life, death and resurrection is the immediate foundation of all Christian understanding of the Spirit. The prehistory of the Spirit of Christ which Christians may decipher in the deeds and words of the Old Testament provides a background for the prophetic anticipation and the final giving and recognition of the Spirit in the end-time which the coming of Jesus and his final exaltation inaugurate. Holy Spirit as Spirit of God is also Spirit of Christ, even Spirit of Jesus for the New Testament believers. The subsequent spiritual and intellectual struggles which issued in the great conciliar definitions from Nicea to Chalcedon and beyond turned on the being, personal character and salvific role of Jesus as pivotal, but in so doing also clarified the being, personal character and salvific role of the Spirit. The historical eclipse of the Spirit in the theory and praxis of the Church may have been due to the exaggerations of a Christomonism as the historical emphasis on the Spirit may have seemed at times to obscure the specific nature and uniqueness of Jesus' achievement. Yet our whole Christian tradition insists on the indissoluble bond in divine origin and historical human activity between Jesus and the Spirit. Any

86

understanding then of the relationship between Holy Spirit and human identity must take account of the relationship between the Holy Spirit and Jesus' own identity as understood by the first disciples and the subsequent tradition.

It will not be my task, here, to follow the New Testament and subsequent teaching through the various stages of development which historical analysis reveals. Awareness of this analysis must shape our discussion of the Spirit because of the mediating role assigned to Jesus Christ in attempting to relate the Spirit to human identity. This mediating role may be summarised by recalling that Jesus was himself endowed with the Spirit, that he promised the Spirit to his disciples on his departure (death) and conferred it directly at Easter (Jn. 20) or indirectly at Pentecost (Acts 2). It is the relationship of this endowment, promise and conferring to Jesus as authentically and fully human which enables Christian believers to explore the future relationship of the Spirit to their identity as authentic and completely human beings.

However one critically evaluates the infancy narratives in Matthew and Luke, it is clear that these New Testament authors/redactors highlight the role of the Spirit in the conception of Jesus as another way of indicating his divinely assigned role as Messiah and Saviour. Despite the precedents from Abraham and Sarah to Zachary and Elizabeth, the context and content of the angel's request to Mary, her eventual acceptance and the promise of the overshadowing Spirit suggest a significant distinguishing and discontinuity of her Son from previous prophets and heralds of Yahweh. The stories surrounding Jesus' birth and the reactions of Simeon and Anna in the Temple confirm their author's insistence on the continuing work of the Spirit in the differentiation of Jesus while maintaining his solidarity with Israel and the human race through immediate origins, ritual presentation and anticipated destiny. The differentiation and solidarity merge with memory of Yahweh's deeds as basis for the creativity of his promises in the words attributed to Simeon, speaking under the inspiration of the Spirit (Lk. 2:22–38).

The accounts of Jesus' baptism by John the Baptist contain clearer indications of historical basis. The reference to the descent of the Spirit, as a dove, on Jesus together with his recognition by the voice from heaven as 'my beloved son' at the outset of his public ministry provide a critical stage in the development of Jesus' divine and personal identity. John the Baptist's preceding testimony to the one mightier than himself who will baptise with the Holy Spirit as recorded in the synoptics (Mk. 1:7–8 par.) is expanded in the Johannine reflection to explicit recognition of him by the Baptist as the Son of God (Jn. 1:32–4). The symbolic sequel in which Jesus is led by the Spirit into the desert and is tempted by Satan completes Jesus' preparation for his mission (Mk. 1:12–13 par.). The interaction between the mission/ministry of proclaiming and manifesting the inbreaking Kingdom of God which now begins and the person of Jesus forms the core of the continuing gospel story, leading to his execution on the Cross and his ultimate vindication by God in Resurrection. In that interaction the differentiation of Jesus within his self-proclaimed solidarity with Abraham, Moses and prophets takes shape in his attitude to the Temple, to the Law, to established religious practices, teachings and leaders of the time, in his works of power or signs as John prefers to call them, in his confrontations with and triumph over the demons, in his prayer as expressing his solidarity with God as Abba and in his table-fellowship as expressing his solidarity with the marginalised, the tax collectors, prostitutes and sinners. The emerging identity of Jesus provoking the inevitable opposition of those whose interests were threatened, calls again at critical times on the Spirit. The Spirit of God is the source of Jesus' power over the demons and so the definitive sign of the presence of the kingdom (Mt. 12:28). The Isaian gift of the Spirit of the Lord (Is. 61:1) which Luke claims for Jesus in the synagogue at Nazareth (Lk. 4:16–30), or Luke and Matthew in response to John's disciples (Mt. 11:2–6; Lk. 7:18–23), is the source of the messianic blessings which Jesus' mighty words and deeds accomplish. This presence and activity of the Holy Spirit in and through Jesus reflects the critical role of Jesus' own person in inaugurating God's rule or kingdom. It renders inseparable the acceptance of Jesus, of the kingdom and of the Spirit. It renders, therefore, more intelligible the rejection of Jesus as rejection of the Father and as the underlying significance of the enigmatic phrase about the sin against the Holy Spirit. The evangelists' interpretation of the Jewish charges against Jesus as blasphemy fit into this pattern. Jesus in his person and ministry embodied, under the sign and by the power of the Spirit of God, the new era of God's relationship with humankind.

This basic personal identity as Jesus of Nazareth, son of Mary and Joseph, is attested by the Scriptures. It was more fully analysed and confirmed by later Church controversies and their conciliar resolution. That basic identity, given and yet achieved through his mission and ministry, may be analysed, as has been already indicated, in terms of differentiation and solidarity, memory and creativity, with advertence to the shaping role of the Spirit in each instance. This shaping role of the Spirit in the case of Jesus reveals a level of God's activity and presence that was definitive not only for him, but for his disciples and humankind. The human identity of Jesus with the four characteristic features of interest here was not only formed in response to God under the influence of the Spirit. It also mediated and re-lived the presence of God in a way that shaped the identity of that presence, the way we call the Son second person of the Triune God. In Jesus, God himself established a new identity in human history through the differentiation of the Son while deepening his solidarity with the Israel and more clearly and effectively extending it to all human beings so that there is no longer Jew or Gentile. This new identification of God recalled and fulfilled the memory of his earlier deeds, covenants and promises in a new creation which constituted Jesus as new Adam. Jesus became new head of the human race, brother of all people, who by the gift of the Spirit were enabled to say Abba Father, as adopted sons and daughters of the Father. The total impact of the divine initiative in Jesus was the establishment of a new covenant, a new basic relationship between God and humankind. Through this covenant the identity of Jesus emerged as fully and wholly son of Mary, son of Man and son of the Father, as the Messiah or Christos, as suffering servant and Risen Lord, as new Adam and Logos. More profoundly still the identity of God in human history became more fully differentiated while remaining in continuity or solidarity with the God of Abraham, Moses, David and the prophets. This fuller differentiation recalled and fulfilled the promises of the new covenant (Jeremiah) and the outpouring of the Spirit (Joel) while transcending all previous covenants in a new creative activity. Central to this was the emergence of Yahweh as Father to Jesus and so to humankind by the gift of the power and guidance of the Spirit.

The new historical identity of God in relation to humankind inevitably involved a new historical identity of humankind in relation to God. The daughterhood and sonship of God as Father, the sisterhood and brotherhood of Jesus the Christ available to humankind through the Spirit create a new context for human identity at its deepest which shapes and seeks expression in human person and human community. The pattern of that basic identity has been established in Jesus just as the power of it has been provided by the Spirit. The summons to discipleship, to the following and imitation of Jesus as Son of the Father and brother of all people respects the basic features of differentiation, solidarity, memory and creativity within the covenant traditions of Israel as critically established in Moses but reaching back through Abraham and Noah to the creation stories themselves and forward through the prophetic discernment of a new divine initiative.

The newness of the new covenant in Jesus was sadly to provoke a break with many people within the covenant tradition of Israel. The rejection and death of Jesus and the subsequent refusal of many in Israel to recognise that he died for 'our sins and was raised for our justification' led to a definitive breach between Jew and Christian, with eventually some of the horrific historical consequences which haunt us today. Yet human identity in its Christian shape remains indissolubly bound to its Jewish origins just as Jesus for all his differentiation and creativity developed religiously as well as humanly in solidarity with his Jewish origins and was nourished by their memories. Jewish-Christian dialogue, so belatedly begun in our own time, provides the occasion at least for Christians to recover some of the original strengths of their own identity by recognising appreciatively and appropriating discriminatingly what that Jewish heritage offers. The promise of the Spirit which was to lead Jesus' disciples into all truth may find fresh fulfilment in this Christian return to their Jewish origins and to their historic God.

Such a return, involving that biblical dimension of *Shub* or metanoia or repentance offers one illustration of the quest for identity to which Christians as disciples of Jesus are summoned. The pattern of that discipleship has, as I have said, been basically and normatively established in Jesus. The way of it as in sonship/daughterhood and brotherhood/sisterhood was summarised by him in love of God and love of neighbour. Further facets of discipleship were revealed by Jesus' teaching in the parables of the kingdom and the Sermon on the Mount as well as in the Pauline discussion of the gifts of the Spirit. Central to all this was the life-and-death style of Jesus himself. His self-giving in love, to the point of dying for his principles and his friends, charted the road to complete identity for himself and his disciples, anyone who would come after him. The overall pattern of identity then involves a living and dying out of love, the primary gift of that Spirit poured forth in human hearts.

Disciples answer the call of Jesus. They follow his way, imitate him. They die with him and are raised to new life in him. They live in him, are members of the body of which he is head. This intimate and all-involving relationship with Jesus enters into and influences every aspect of human identity. Yet all disciples enjoy their own uniqueness, their own differentiation and distance from Jesus as well as from each other. The maintenance of distance in this fashion is critical to the personal identity of the disciple, but also to preserving the uniqueness of Jesus. The tendency to a kind of Christic imperialism, something issuing in narrow uniformity in life-style, must be resisted out of respect for Jesus and for his disciples. In this the Spirit plays a dual role. Not only does the Spirit provide the disciples' unity with Jesus as brother/sister, but the distinction of Spirit and Son manifests the distance and differentiation. In the more conventional distinction between objective standards of human living and subjective efforts and achievements, Jesus and his life-style offer objective challenge and pattern, while the Spirit provides the subjective enlightenment and capacity to respond to challenge and attempt the pattern. It is the enlightenment and capacity provided by the Spirit which enables the disciple to find his own differentiated and creative way while recalling and remaining in solidarity with the historical achievement of Jesus and his pattern.

As St Thomas Aquinas (*S. Th.*1:II, 106) says, the new law of our behaviour then derives from our participation in the person and achievement of Jesus by the presence of the Holy Spirit. The objectivity of the 'law' of Christ (Gal. 6:2) combines with the discernment and creativity of the Spirit in a never-ending dialectic and so shapes the identity of disciples as human beings. The universal mission of Jesus and the infinite range of the

91

activity of the Spirit suggests that in other fashion, and through the different religious and human conditions, the interaction of Jesus and Spirit enter into the shaping of human identity. The paradigmatic way of their influence on human identity remains that of explicit discipleship. Through discipleship we learn of the reach and direction of their influence on all human beings. The concrete examples to be discussed in the next section will centre on the gifts and demands of discipleship in the characteristic human activities of prayer and politics.

Worship and Human Identity

Current theological wisdom, confirmed by the Second Vatican Council, maintains that the Church, the community of disciples, is most fully and properly itself in its performance of the liturgy, in its worship. Clearly at the Eucharist the community of disciples identifies itself with Jesus in his characteristic action of identification, his death and resurrection, and so identifies itself to its God whom it addresses as Father. All this occurs through the transforming power of the Spirit as expressly recognised in the prayer of Epiclesis. At the same time the community identifies itself to itself in the discipleship of the sons and daughters of the Father, the brothers and sisters of Jesus. Further identification to the world, to humankind as the distinctive and differentiated group of Jesus' disciples, is accompanied by identification with the world and humankind as recalling and sharing in the salvific solidarity and commitment of Jesus. The Church exists in response to Jesus' call for the sake of humankind. The call to discipleship is a call to serve God's humanity. The activity of the liturgy reveals and renews this commitment. Without this commitment and the effort to live it, the liturgy involves a self-contradiction, the community of disciples is engaged in eating and drinking judgment on itself (1 Cor. 11:29).

By placing human beings in the presence of their ultimate reality, prayer or worship enables them to differentiate themselves at this deepest level. The absolute otherness of God transcending all human possibilities and attainments evokes the recognition and reverence or awe called worship. At the same time it grounds not only the differentiation between God and human beings, but in the Judaeo-Christian tradition the differentiation of human beings themselves. As human beings are created in the image of God and called by Jesus to be sons and daughters of the Father, their human otherness reflects and participates in the divine otherness, making them in their differentiation from one another focuses of recognition and reverence. The worship which is response to God has its correlative at the level of inter-human relationships as response to the irreducible otherness expressed in the differentiation of human identity. Failure to recognise and reverence divine and human otherness expresses a tendency, readily indulged, to use God and other people as furnishings in one's own world of which the ultimate reality will be mere projection of the self in power or wealth or pleasure. The creation of such idols, ever a threat to true worship and frequently a reality, may replace the genuine otherness of God directly or indirectly by distorting genuine human otherness. Such idolatry is the climactic destruction of human identity. In Christian understanding it is cast out only by the power of the Spirit (Mt. 12:28)

Otherness and response to it are complemented by solidarity and communion. Within this communion difference may be enjoyed and celebrated. Without it difference deteriorates into fragmentation and non-communication. The celebration of otherness within communion and its realisation in worship express in joy and play the mutual enrichment of our differentiation. Such joy and play may issue in music, dance, poetry. They provide a counterpoint to the harshness of an alienated and sinful world, an alternative and challenge to the utilitarianism of so much relating with God and human beings. In directly religious contexts the playful Spirit bearing a rich variety of gifts releases in the community the joyous energies which occasionally characterise our prayer-lives. It is in this context perhaps that the gift of tongues associated with Pentecostal Charismatic prayer groups is best understood. In non-religious contexts, for explicit disciples and other human beings, the celebration of others and the re-creative play of which humans are capable may be understood in faith to be fruits of the same playful and creative Spirit. Where there is play, there is, in however implicit fashion, worship or prayer. Human identity continues to bear the mark of the prayerful and playful Spirit.

Celebration in religious and non-religious contexts involves remembering and inspires creating. Without repeating the points already made in regard to the roles of memory and creativity in human identity, the identity of Jesus and the structure of the liturgy, it is clear that in both religious and non-religious contexts the faith understanding of celebration embraces these features of human identity. The thrust of the argument is to reinforce connection between celebration and worship in their functions of expressing and promoting human identity for all peoples, whether explicit disciples or not, in both religious and non-religious contexts, and to recognise in this connection the work of the Spirit.

Politics and Human Identity: The Case of Northern Ireland

The features of differentiation, solidarity, memory and creativity assume particular shape in the social organisation and activity called politics. As peoples and communities seek to organise themselves, internally and externally, under the law and by international recognition and agreement, differentiation with the respect it evokes and solidarity with the commitment it requires, draw on shared memory and diverse creativity to provide the institutions and inspiration of an enriching common life. This may be most easily seen in a situation where memory and the creativity of diversity are employed to obstruct solidarity and where differentiation is fragmenting and destructive. Northern Ireland offers a classic instance of such a situation. There are numerous other situations past and present where memory divides and 'creativity' destroys human identity or where the identities accepted or aspired to are politically incompatible. In Northern Ireland the political incompatibility of the identities of Unionist and Republican have long and bloody histories. The bloodiness with its intermittent intensity, its past and prospective duration, is reason enough for depression. For Christians the depression is deepened by the failure of the express Christian espousal of faith by the opposing groups to transcend and transform the alienations of history as the saving power of faith in Christ might be expected to do. Indeed the ready translation of Republican and Unionist into Catholic and Protestant suggests that the faith-application of both has helped to reinforce rather than to overcome the incompatibility and hostility.

This is not the time to rehearse past culpability of the Churches. Pertinent to the discussion here is how far the conflict in Northern Ireland is a conflict of human identity between the opposed groupings and, given the explicit Christian application of so many people there, how far light and power might be expected from the Holy Spirit in overcoming the difficulties. Differentiation at ethnic, cultural and economic levels combines with political and religious differences to promote group-identities which tend to be exclusive of one another. The Anglo-Scots ethnic background as opposed to the Celtic, and the British cultural traditions as opposed to the Gaelic, seem indissolubly intertwined with economic division (east and west of the River Bann, for example), political commitment (to Unionism and Republicanism) and religious affiliation (Protestant and Catholic). The role of the Spirit in establishing radical solidarity between Jew and Gentile, bond and free, Protestant and Catholic on the basis of sonship/daughterhood of the Father and brotherhood/sisterhood of Jesus Christ is largely frustrated. Yet the historical limitations to the identity of groups and individuals in Northern Ireland, where potentially enriching differentiation has become destructive fragmentation and the memory of 1690 or 1916 has led to a kind of enslavement rather than inspiration, must be challenged by the presence and demands of the Spirit which so many on both sides acknowledge.

The hostility and violence in Northern Ireland diminishes the identity of all in addition to maiming and killing so many. Republicans and Unionists, neighbours' children, sharing a geography and history rich in potential have to find ways of enriching rather than destroying one another. Some new creative solidarity is called for. And called to promote this are in particular the communities which claim to be led by the Spirit and the human leaders who aspire to mediating the Spirit. The present situation is for all the explanations and excuses a judgment on us as Christians. Response to the Spirit who transcends the boundaries of Catholic and Protestant demands solidarity and creativity of an unusual kind. Response derives from the gift already on offer, if we did not refuse to recognise it. Until such recognition takes place effectively, the Christian will continue, however reluctantly, to be party to the destructive divisions. Catholic and Protestant Christians, as individuals and communities, will be impoverished and frustrated in their Christian and human identities. Irish Catholics need Irish Protestants and Irish Protestants need Irish Catholics to achieve and enjoy the identity they so frequently and ardently proclaim by means which too often frustrate their desires. Only surrender to the one true God of Jesus Christ under the guidance and by the love of the Spirit can fully release from the idolatries which have now intruded into political and cultural contexts of their Christian faith.

PART II

Social and Political Tasks

6

Prayer and Politics

In a series on Church and Politics the title Prayer and Politics sounds at once proper and puzzling. Proper because prayer is at the heart of the Church's life; it could be properly described as a praying community. Puzzling because prayer raises the Church above the level of politics. However it might relate to political life in its teaching and social service, the Church at prayer and particularly in that category of prayer regarded as at once most sublime and normative, worship of the Father, transcends the petty concerns of political and social activity. Prayer for help with these concerns, of sorrow for neglect of them or for too great preoccupation with them to the neglect of the Father may in this way bear on our political lives. But real prayer in which the Church realises itself as Church in recognition and praise of the Father expresses the transcendent nature and vocation of that Church, in the world but not of it.

Yet as so many popes, bishops and theologians keep reminding us, the Bible is full of warning about our neglect of the neighbour on the pretence of attending to God. Jesus' own teaching and life is a perfect example of attention to Father and neighbour. The example has continued to inspire the Church in its concern and care for the sick, the poor and the oppressed. The range and depth of this concern has expanded over the centuries. With today's global communications and increasing interdependence the boat-people in the South China Sea become neighbours to those along the Irish Sea. And it is not just that our neighbour now really is all humankind, extending over the whole globe but that our responses when called for have to operate in an organised way that involves laws and resources controlled or harnessed by various state authorities, laws of immigration, for example, if we are to take some of the boat-people into Ireland, or the cooperation of the Seventh Fleet of the American Navy in rescuing those at sea, or the cooperation of Malaysia and other countries in providing transitional refugee camps, not to speak of the ultimate cooperation of the Vietnam government in providing for their own people in their own country. The Geneva conference organised by the UN showed how political love of neighbour has become. But one does not have to go so far afield to realise the inescapable political dimensions of love of neighbour. The provision of work, of proper pay and conditions and the honourable discharge of work, which the Irish bishops have stressed more than once recently, have, in our mixed economies, increasingly political implications. That is, they affect the total Irish *polis* or society and have to be regulated by the social authority of the State. The presence of Ministers of State at the opening of new factories is one small indication of that; the impact of a strike such as the postal strike a much larger one. In the broad sense of political, then, as concerned with the welfare of the community as a whole, and indeed in the narrower sense of expressing that concern through the organs of state, love of neighbour has taken on political colour we scarcely noticed before. The promotion of justice in society which the 1971 Synod of Bishops described as 'a constituent element of preaching the gospel' will have inevitable political repercussions in the broad and narrow senses. The further clarification of that remark will be treated later.

Given that concern for the neighbour has a political character, is it still true that prayer as the Church's most characteristic activity touches only indirectly on these political needs by petitions for help with them? Without denying the sincerity of such prayer where it is accompanied by genuine efforts to help the neighbour, it hardly sheds any fresh light on the nature and value of either prayer or political activity. Some people will undoubtedly be inspired by praying about these matters to deeper understanding and commitment. Others may substitute prayer for action and fall into the trap of using their religion as an escape from life and their God as an escape from man. Others may take the line that the important thing about these issues is not to pray about them but to change them and drop all prayer in favour of action. The extrinsic connection provided by a prayer of petition approach does not touch the

100

real heart of prayer and does not effectively connect with the concerns of politics.

Prayer as Liberation of God

A return to the simple but profound view of prayer offered in the school catechism as 'a raising of the mind and heart to God' could provide a more profitable way into the discussion. It has the advantage of focusing us immediately on the centre of prayer—*God*. And it is focusing *us*—human beings. That relationship whereby we contact God in prayer involves us, our human activity and really depends on us. However, the availability of God for contact and our ability to take advantage of that availability, derive from God as his gift or grace. The creative receptivity which we bring to prayer characterises our human living as a whole but is at its most intense in our creative reception of the Father of Love. The active-passive nature of our prayer emphasises both the initiative of God and our own contribution. It enables us to understand the reach of the divine graciousness in that he waits upon our invitation. He stands at the door and knocks, seeking entry into our hearts and lives. Without our consent and acceptance he cannot be fully present in his own creation. The awesome request to the peasant girl in Nazareth is repeated to us as God seeks to become flesh in our lives. We are his point of entry into the richness of creation. We allow, even enable him to be at home in his own world. We let him be himself as Creator, Father and Redeemer. By our prayer, by raising our hearts and minds to him, by letting him enter into us in that way we set him free. We are the liberators of God. It sounds crazy that the all-mighty God should have put himself at our mercy in this way, that he should depend on our wayward prayer for the time and space to be himself in human history of which he is the Lord and Creator.

This dependence on human response for his emergence as God of Love in human history may be traced through all of his covenant relations with humankind. It naturally achieved its critical and normative form in Jesus Christ. Here God took on fully the human condition. In the life and death of the man Jesus he was admitted in the fullest way to the very centrepiece of his own creation. He was finally and fully at home in his world. The *kairos* had occurred. The reign of God was at hand, in our midst. Through the response of Jesus the creative receptivity of all was

101

ensured although God would still wait upon our exercise of it in faith and prayer.

God's Self-identification in History

In seeing the mystery of the incarnation and the activity of Christian prayer as allowing God to be himself among men, we are carried a step further into witnessing the identification of Yahweh as the Father of Jesus and of Jesus as the Son of Yahweh. The God of Abraham and Moses and the prophets identifies himself more precisely in and through the history of Jesus. He relates to Jesus as Father to Son, only begotten Son, and then relates to us as Father because we are now adopted sons, brothers and coheirs with Jesus. The self-identification in history reaches completion with the sending of the Spirit whereby we cry Abba, Father. The differentiation of God into Father, Son and Holy Spirit in and through the life and mission of Jesus draws us into the historical task of God achieving and expressing his most intimate identity in our lives and our history, his own creation. In the explicit reltionship of prayer we are letting the differentiated God of Christian faith express himself as Father, Son and Holy Spirit; we are permitting him to achieve his tri-personal identity in that which is other than he is as his creation.

The Coming of the Kingdom

The entry of God into human life through Jesus, faith and prayer is described in an old biblical tradition and in Jesus' own words as the coming of God's kingdom or reign or rule. It means that God is present to human history in a definitive saving and transforming way asking for our response, for our reception of him as he has come to us finally as human in the person of Jesus. The kingdom or rule of God has been inaugurated. It is in the process of realising itself but it is not yet complete. Our history is the vehicle of its realising itself. In that history our prayer is the clearest and the normative expression of recognising and accepting the presence and rule of God. By being set free to be himself in the world, by expressing and realising in human history his trinitarian identity and now committing himself by power and presence to the final salvation and transformation of humanity and the world, the God to whom we raise our minds and hearts is in turn setting us free, enabling us to express and realise our true identity as sons and daughters of the Father, brothers and sisters of Jesus and one another by the gift of the Spirit, and sharing with us his power and the transforming task of promoting and realising his kingdom. It is only on the completion of that task, when the kingdom is fully realised, that God and ourselves will be fully liberated to one another, achieve together the fullness of our identity and rejoice in the fullness of presence. At that totally intimate stage we will no longer need to lift our minds and hearts to God and he will no longer have to wait upon our permission to enter and be at home.

Prayer into Politics: Realising the Kingdom

All this discussion of prayer appears to leave us a long way from the boat-people and unemployment and all the other concerns of politics. The kingdom which comes to us in prayer as God's power and presence directed to transforming us and our world, offers the most immediate prospect of fruitful inquiry. The rule of God is not for our hearts only, but our whole lives. It is not for Christians only but for all humankind. The values of the kingdom, so often presented in the Old Testament as characteristics of God himself in his loving kindness, in his justice, in the peace and fulfilment to be available to all, received more concrete expression in the life and teaching of Jesus. Gospel values or kingdom values may be summarised as the complete fulfilment of our human condition as it came from the hands of our creator, was assumed into his own life in Jesus and is destined for the intimacy of divine life itself. They involve therefore respect for, development and fulfilment of the human potential of each of us, to be inaugurated and pursued in history and receive completion in resurrection. Clearly our responsibility is the inauguration and development in human history. And that is not an individual task or achievement. It is the brotherly and neighbourly task of and for all. Kingdom values draw us out of ourselves to all the others in whom the kingdom must be inaugurated and developed, in whom God's power and presence are at hand. To raise one's heart to God is to be open to his coming not only in oneself but in all the others. That coming is inhibited and obscured by their privation and our neglect. To pray is to seek the coming of the kingdom, the achievement of its values in the society in which we live. It is to accept our political vocation to help transform that society.

Church and Kingdom: State and Society

To refer briefly to an earlier difficulty, I would point out while I use politics for the most part in a broad sense of organised activity for the welfare of society or particular groups in society, I distinguish society and state. Society I take to be the whole set of human relationships and structures by which a particular people is constituted. State is the set of statutory or legal instruments including parliament, administration, laws, whereby that people governs itself. Society is a broader and looser concept. It is often difficult to know how the distinction is to be drawn or maintained. Yet if society is reduced to state so that the whole of its life is expressed in and directly subjected to state authority, citizen is reduced to unit of state and personal freedom is lost. In this connection religious freedom plays a significant role because it claims that the human being and his freedoms are not defined and circumscribed by the state but transcend it. The point of this digression is to indicate how the Church exercises its political role in promotion of the kingdom without usurping the role of the state. In preaching and acting out kingdom values in society the Church is doing its part to ensure the transformation of society. In alerting people to the injustices in society, in calling attention to and taking the side of the deprived and oppressed, it may well be accused of interfering in politics. Yet its prayer-life will not allow it to escape this call to witness and service of the kingdom. In this fashion the Church acts in part as conscience of society. But such a description is inadequate. Sometimes the society has to be conscience to the Church, in its leaders and other members because it has been insensitive and blind. Prophetic calls to society do not always originate with the Church. It would be a mistake to give the impression that the Church may issue stirring calls to conscience and leave it at that. There must be service as well as announcement of the kingdom and its values. This is what social justice as a constituent element of the gospel means.

God's Self-identification and Politics

The relationship between prayer and politics mediated through the kingdom may still seem somewhat extrinsic. It might appear to be merely the application of prayer for the coming of the kingdom rather than any intrinsic connection between prayer itself and social-political action. This difficulty, in so far as it is one, may be clarified later when we discuss the reverse move from social and political action to prayer. Just now it is necessary to consider the other elements of prayer already discussed in their relationship to politics.

The most difficult of the three to grasp in itself or in its relation to politics may be the self-identification of God which occurs in and through prayer and is explicitly adverted to in liturgical prayer. All prayer is to the Father in Jesus Christ by the gift and power of the Spirit. We consciously structure our liturgical prayer in this way. The identification of God relevant here is not the internal trinitarian life in itself, of which we might say that the persons are identified as distinct in their internal relations. We are concerned with that identification as it emerged in human history, as God became drawn more deeply into relation with his people. This growing relationship involved growing identification on both the human and the divine side. He became more clearly and distinctly their God; they became more clearly and distinctly his people. The identity of both sides developed, The climax to this development in Jesus Christ had as we saw enormous consequences for the divine identity within history, consequences which his people were not for the most part able to accept. It also had consequences for human identity which we are only gradually recognising and realising.

In our prayer critical aspects of our identity as human beings are revealed and developed. As we pray 'Our Father' we acknowledge that all walls of separation have been broken down in Jesus Christ, between Jew and Gentile, slave and free, male and female. The identity of each of us is bound up with the identity of all. To exclude from our prayer and social concern particular classes or races or religious groups is to inhibit the emergence of our own identity, to prevent the growth of the persons we are really called to be by the Father. It is to contradict the thrust of our prayer.

Our identity is developed in history over time. We become who we are called to be. We are at once given and have to achieve that in the divine plan by gradually growing in community with the others, taking charge of our own history, assuming responsibility for our own destiny. Our prayer life expresses and reveals our personal responsibility for living as subjects of our own history and not just as its enslaved objects. That is an inescapable demand of our prayer for ourselves as individuals and as members of society, ecclesial, national and universal. To raise one's mind to God in prayer is to raise one's person to respond to him in the whole of our history and to affirm that as the universal human vocation in which we participate and to which we contribute. Our prayer is only complete when we and our neighbours, in the fullest range of neighbour, are engaged in becoming subjects of our own history and so enabled to respond of ourselves and by our own names to the divine summons. Those who in James Baldwin's phrase 'have no name in the street', who are absent from history because they have no control over their lives and destiny, limit our prayer also and call to us at prayer to release them into the presence of the summoning and liberating God. In so far as they are lacking in identity, in name and personal opportunity to become themselves, the identity of God as their Father, of Jesus as their brother and of the Spirit of Truth and Freedom, are unrealised in human history. The social and political task becomes the task of facilitating human identity for the deprived and so facilitating divine identity in history for the God who has made their privation his very own.

While insisting that we achieve our identity in and through history and society, it is clear that our identity or that of our God cannot be reduced to historical development and social relationship. And this for the very good, and to the believer obvious, reason that the divine identity with which our human identity is now inextricably bound up, transcends all such social and historical limitations. The roles of Father, Son and Spirit in our becoming ourselves, realising our identity, do not invalidate our historical and social existence. In fact they confirm and support it. Yet they also open us up to that which is beyond history and society and creation itself. In a scarcely credible way they enable us to transcend our created condition without destroying or negating it. That transcendence occurs here and now, although it is only properly realised with Jesus Christ in the resurrection.

Such identity is known to us in faith. It is expressed at prayer, particularly and explicitly at liturgical prayer. Yet it has to be worked out in daily living, in the shape of our personal relationships: the task of politics in the broad sense. The faith affirmation can at times be anaemic, lacking the impact which such an exciting and demanding concept of human identity should have. In the search for deeper awareness of such impact we must at least occasionally seek a more intense experience of the trinitarian dimensions of our own personality or, better, open ourselves more fully to the trinitarian presence and structure in our lives, prepare ourselves to receive that divine presence and power more creatively. The search and need for this is not always or easily met in our liturgical celebrations. So many people today look to more intense or, as we might say, more emotional prayer experiences. In the Catholic Church these people frequently find help and inspiration in charismatic prayer groups. Others prefer less dramatic or overt forms of group or individual prayer. And there has been an important return to emphasis on contemplative prayer and hermit life, temporary or permanent. Because the Western Christian tradition had lost some of the trinitarian awareness which ought to permeate its prayer a number of western Christians are seeking it in the Eastern Christian tradition and still more are experimenting with Eastern (non-Christian) religions. Some are even experimenting with drugs or other artificial non-religious phenomena in an effort to restore to their personal experience some sense of the transcendent.

This is in no way intended to be a complete survey of the range of activities which human beings now and in the past have undertaken in search of the transcendent within their lives. Still less is any comparison or evaluation of their respective merits intended. The first point is to emphasise yet again to those who too easily reduce prayer to an intellectual experience or fideist affirmation, that it enters into our very identity. For all its elusive mystery it should impinge upon our felt experience of ourselves at times. At least openness to that experience should be prepared for and encouraged. Otherwise the deepest structure of our existence and identity will not enter into the conscious formation of that identity in a dynamic way. The second point, which may escape some of the searchers and achievers in experiencing this dimension of prayer, is that it is not an isolated 'God and me' phenomenon. It is always 'God and us'. It carries us beyond ourselves not just to the Father but to all his sons and daughters with whom our identity and destiny are intertwined. The expansion to the transcendent which prayer involves is an expansion to the transcendent as it is present in history and society in the brothers and sisters who share the same Father, the

107

same brother Jesus Christ and the same Spirit by which alone we can all say Abba. If we do not say it together and address it to the presence of the Father in all human beings we do not say it properly at all. There is no such thing as individualist, private prayer as there is no such thing as an individualist, private Christian. Even the prayer of the hermit has an inescapably social dimension. It too plays a role, sometimes a very powerful role, in enabling people in the wider society to find and express their divinely given and structured identity in richer forms of prayer and human living. The mediation of the contemplative and the hermit, like the mediation of Christians generally, realises and witnesses to the explicitly divine dimension of the identity of all but it must take flesh in the social structures and relationships as well as the personal historical development of all. To ensure that these two aspects are continually recognised and realised is a primary task of the Church.

Liberating God in Prayer and Politics
Central to this exposition is the recognition that in prayer we allow God into our lives; we allow him to be at home in his own creation. This liberation of God reaches into all the dimensions of human life, that part of creation in which he has put himself at the disposal of his creatures. He is not to be, indeed he cannot be, set free in my religious life alone, or in the history of my individual life apart from the familial, professional, local, national and international relationships which enter into and form a constitutive part of my total life. He is my God in the totality of my life and so in all the overlapping structures and relationships which make up that life. Through that life I am part of the whole people, their structures and relationships of which he is also God. For my prayer to have its due liberating effect on God, it must look outwards to a whole web of human society and history with which I am intimately bound up. The liberation of God cannot be accomplished in times of prayer only but demands expansion into personal and social living. In particular it demands expansion into the areas of my own living which cannot yet accommodate God, in which he cannot feel at home. Our personal conversion and development is a requirement of our prayer as we are called to admit God more and more into our lives, as he seeks the freedom of our inner city. The personal is not, as we know, a separable part of us. It comes into existence

and develops in and through history and society. God's search for freedom through our prayer moves on into that history and society. Where we fail to reach out to the others in love and service, God is restricted in his freedom. Where persons, groups, classes, races or nations are excluded from proper relationships with their fellow-humans, where through discrimination, oppression or poverty and the structural maintenance of these, sons and daughters of the Father are deprived of freedom and growth, his freedom to be himself in his own world is unduly restricted. And it is restricted not just in them in whom his creative redemptive power cannot have free rein, but even more in us who have the awareness and the resources and so the responsibility to enlarge the range of God's freedom by transforming the unjust structures and sharing ourselves and our goods. Prayer and politics are both about the liberation of God, allowing him to be more free and more fully at home in his world. They are in their different ways two sides of the same commitment to which we are summoned in Jesus Christ. To play one off against the other or to evade one in the name of attending to the other is to put asunder what God has joined together.

From Politics to Prayer

This chapter has sought to explore the meaning of prayer in search of its connection with social and political activity. It may be helpful to treat briefly of the reverse move from the meaning of social and political activity to prayer. It is clear that not all those active in the promotion of social and political good derive their inspiration from prayer. It is perhaps even more clear that not all who take prayer seriously consider social concerns and activity as more than occasion for prayer for help in hard cases. Yet the character of attention to other human beings which such activity involves has something to tell us about the character, meaning and even necessity of prayer.

Social and political commitment is based on awareness of people in need. That awareness develops into a moral commitment because we recognise their value and worth as human beings with the same rights to life, freedom and fulfilment as ourselves, including the basic needs implied by such rights. More deeply we see their recognition as bound up with our own. We see our survival and development bound up with theirs. We see their treatment by others or ourselves as a statement about our claim to similar treatment. It is in interaction with, recognition of and response to these others personally and structurally that we affirm and protect our own humanity, our own value and worth. That interdependence may be frequently obscured and its active implications often ignored. We are all thereby reduced. When we do recognise our interdependence and consequent obligations, when we do pursue a socially and politically just society, we are opening to the value and dignity of these human beings that inspire awe before their mystery, humility and gratitude before their diverse talents and achievements, often won against great difficulties. We begin to sense some of the remarkable richness, diversity and mystery of mankind. We may and should feel more than ever that we should remove our shoes for we walk on holy ground, that trodden by the mysterious entity we call human. When such awe is accompanied by a love that is born of service, we feel further the puzzles and paradoxes of the world. How can love possibly exist in our world? When that love breaks down or competitiveness and hostility over human needs reassert themselves we discover anew the possibility and reality of sorrow, forgiveness and reconciliation. The prevailing reports of the social and political horrors of our or any time should not blind us to these creative and transforming realities. In so far as we enter them in our social and political work we are being extended beyond our petty, self-centred concerns into the world and mystery, transforming mystery of the others, just as they are drawn into the mystery of ourselves which apart from this exchange would not be accessible. These attitudes of wonderment, awe, humility, thanksgiving and forgiveness are characteristic of prayer. It is only in so far as they come alive for us in our relational and social lives that they will have vitality in our prayer life. Much of our prayer life is dull and boring because we do not have any vital personal life in which we are open to, creatively receptive of, the human others. Effective expression of that personal vitality and openness is to be found in our social engagement, our political commitment.

These attitudes arising out of political activity are not just characteristic of prayer. In an important sense they are the stuff of prayer. The creative receptivity of the human others involved in politics does not stop short at the human, whatever may be

110

our conscious intent. In the light of creation and incarnation the human other is a mediation of the ultimate other we call God. Our openness to and movement to the human other by its own inherent (but God-given) dynamism reaches on to the divine reality of the Father, Son and Holy Spirit. Social and political activity, where it is genuinely attentive and responsive to the human others, transcends its appointed sphere in prayer.

The limitations of individual or group agents in political activity hardly need to be emphasised. How much of it is really self-seeking in the search for power, money or prestige provides the common (perhaps too common) material of politics bashing. Like every other human engagement the political in the broad and narrow senses will be ambiguous, a mixture of good and evil, of real attention to others and sheer promotion of self. Prayer activity does not escape that ambiguity either. It can be self-absorbed, a way to security or power or prestige. Jesus was well aware of that weakness in some of his contemporaries, even in some of his disciples in their desire for places at his right hand and his left. The transcendent or prayer dimension of politics does not undermine its meaning or independence. It guarantees meaning and independence by opening to the fullness of the meaning of human existence in the mystery of God, and by recognising its role as the direct mode of historical and social liberation for humanity and so for God. In recalling and seeking to respect this transcendent dimension, it may escape in part the worst temptations to which politics and politicans are exposed— the divinisation of a particular ideology or programme, people or leader. Prayer without the challenge and channel of politics cannot fulfil its tasks of liberating God into his own world, enabling him and us to achieve identity in human history and society and gradually establish his kingdom, which it is the Church's duty to preach and promote.

7

Love, Power and Justice

Love, power and justice are three of the most significant, yet most elusive words in theology and in many other realms of discourse. The richness of meaning and the variety of use preclude any recourse to settled definitions as starting-point. Paul Tillich, in his book, *Love, Power and Justice*, has made an attractive and perceptive analysis that will undoubtedly influence the shape of this chapter, but I do not think that it makes either an apt starting point or satisfactory framework in the present context. The more politically orientated work of Weber, his predecessors and successors, from Marx to Marcuse, or the cumulative insights of the psychoanalytic tradition, offer rich resources for investigation and reflection in any thorough discussion of love, power and justice and their relationships. However, I prefer to exercise my theological reserve and commitment by attempting a primarily theological discussion in which the range of meaning and usage appropriate to these words emerges in a faith-reflection on the relationships between God and the human race and between human beings as these relationships are understood in the Judaeo-Christian tradition. I do not have in mind a pursuit of the words or their equivalents in usage and meaning through the biblical and theological tradition, Kittel-fashion. My strategy is rather to examine theologically the overall relationships and see how these words might be applied and understood with due regard for biblical, philosophical, sociological and psychological scholarship.

Love

The centrality of love in the Christian tradition provides a useful starting-point. Given the elasticity and elusiveness of the word some clearer indications of how I am using it are necessary.

112

I do not think that one should or indeed can oppose Old and New Testaments or Covenants on a basis of love. The suggestion that the God of the Old Testament appears predominantly as a God of justice while that of the New Testament emerges as God of love, however one interprets those words, does not correspond to the records we have. There is no need to labour the point. It would not be adequate to my purposes, as I said earlier, merely to investigate the word and its immediate contexts. The whole range of divine-human relationships, as recorded and reflected on in the biblical tradition, illustrates and illuminates the loving initiative, creativity and persistence of the God who is summarily and climactically described as love. The impact of this divine initiative and creativity on humanity is, as the records show, mixed but the mixture could be well analysed in terms of loving, non-loving or indifference and anti-loving or hating. The first task of this chapter is to discern some of the critical elements of loving which the biblical relationships imply. Such discernment by us must take account of existing praxis and theory of loving in Church and broader community, which interact with the biblical data in an inescapable, but not necessarily vicious, hermeneutical circle. The mutual challenge, critique, possible confirmation and occasional transformation that such interaction and interpretation involve, are laden with difficulties which can be barely noticed here. One's hope is that overcoming some difficulties will carry the excitement and satisfaction of real discernment.

In biblical tradition and human experience, and also in systematic reflection on both, considerable emphasis is given to the unitive character of love. For many theologians, philosophers and psychologists, unity or community constitutes the primary characteristic and supreme expression of loving. The models of loving usually considered at the human level in terms of friendship, marriage and family, at the divine level in terms of trinity and unity and at the divine-human level in terms of the relationships between God and Israel, Christ and the Church, Jesus and his friends, all concentrate on this unitive character. It is clearly essential to a proper understanding of love. Yet the kind of unity is very important. Human experience of friendship and family life underline how unity can easily become domination, possession and so destruction. Some understanding of God and faith might suggest a similar tendency to absorption

113

either by a loss of human self in quietist surrender or by the domestication of God in self-centred possession. The attractive unitive vision of de Chardin or the powerful thrust of Tillich's analyses of love as 'the urge for the reunion of the separated' could mislead the unwary into confusing the unity of love with absorption or possession. The biblical data and human experience suggest that difference and differentiation are as important to loving as unity and communion. In personal discourse, where 'love' is properly used, without differentiation there is no possibility of loving. And genuine loving confirms and extends real differentiation. It might be helpful to express in formal terms the extent of loving as deeper differentiation in greater unity and apply this to relationships between God and humanity as well as to human relationships themselves in face-to-face or in more mediate and structured contexts. To appreciate the significance of this formal and summary description of loving and its effects it is necessary to distinguish certain elements in loving as it occurs between personal beings.

There is a close connection between loving and knowing in the Old Testament tradition. To know one's wife means to love her, in the full creative sense. This connection between knowledge and love enters into the New Testament understanding of the relationships between Father and Son, Jesus and his disciples, God and humankind. In the subsequent theological tradition the connection takes various forms with the priority going to love or knowledge as one follows Augustine or Aquinas, but neither is ever taken in isolation from the other. In our own time the dialectic goes on with greater emphasis on deeds of love as ways of knowing but it is a dialectic and not a series of psychological or chronological or even ontological steps.

In focusing on recognition by one person of another as an essential element of loving. I am not reducing it to some merely intellectual awareness but thinking in fuller human terms which include Tillich's urge to unity and his realisation of it as well as the distinguishing and the distance essential to the other as the other. For the moment I wish to concentrate on the distinction and the distance, while acknowledging that appreciation of the distinction and distance can only occur within some unity or community. To recognise Jesus or Mary as particular people and as different from oneself one has to accept implicitly something of what unites and is common to all three. Without

114

that kind of community, however unreflected on or unacknowledged consciously, recognition of them as different would not be possible. On the other hand conscious differentiation is basic to personal community as distinct from organic or other sub-personal unity. In the family, the local community, the Church, the nation and the international community, between individual persons and groups of people, real recognition is the fruit of this interplay of unity and difference. The crucial role of Jesus Christ in the mutual recognition of God and humanity is further emphasised by the unity and difference which he personally embodied as both human and divine.

The recognition of the other as other is of course simultaneously a distinguishing, recognising and identifying of the self. Without that kind of interaction the self is not discovered, identified or realised. An examination of the process of self-discovery by Israel, by Jesus, by the historical and contemporary Church and believer, discloses the role of the divine other in human self-identification.

The creative action of God is of course a loving action. In that creative action God causes, enables to exist, recognises as distinct, a created otherness. Created human otherness constitutes not just an exercise in divine initiative or a manifestation of divine power. It includes a quality of otherness to which God must react in loving recognition. Humankind is not God's plaything but his partner in loving. The creative recognition of God completes the movement of creation through friendship with the divine. Human distortion of that in sin, and persistent divine attempts at restoration reaching their climax in Jesus Christ, illustrate the recognising love of God for humankind.

The differentiation of creator and creature, of God and humankind is so obvious and radical that it presents particular difficulties for the unitive dimension of loving both as basis and as goal. Aristotle considered it impossible to speak of friendship between God and humankind because friendship demanded equality. Equality of course implies certain common bonds. The mystery of divine-human friendship which is characteristic of Christian faith emerges in the history of Israel and is fully realised in Jesus Christ. Through him differentiation, recognition and unity are made available to all human beings and in a way that their love and friendship with God implies and these qualities are realised in their love and friendship with one another.

115

The recognition by God or human being of the other, as an aspect of loving the other, takes the other fully seriously in her otherness. In the fuller dimension of respect for the other, one does not intrude but waits upon her self-revelation. Recognition and respect do not seek to dominate or control, to manipulate or possess. They let the other be herself, give her space, freedom, to be herself. So much at least is required by the recognition and respect of love between persons, unique centres of knowing and loving, of accepting and creating, of self-possession and self-disposition. The creative and redemptive activity of God confirms the best insights of our psychological, social and political traditions in acknowledging the uniqueness and freedom of each human being and the respect which that implies.

Letting the other be is not, however, some kind of theological, sociological or psychological *laissez-faire*. It does not reduce to the indifference of an attenuated liberalism. That could certainly not be predicated of God's creative recognition and respect for humans, which provide the model for their recognition and respect for one another in turn. The 'letting be' in the fuller sense intended here, means not only providing space and respecting freedom but also providing the context of encouragement, stimulus and assistance in which somebody becomes more fully her true self. Loving as letting be means loving people into their fullness. It means enabling people to become more fully their true selves, to realise their true potential. This is the story of God's love for humankind, and of his success and failure as great lover or great 'letter-be'. John Macquarrie makes effective use of this idea of God's activity in his *Principles of Christian Theology*. Once again God's activity provides the model and the criterion of human activity, particularly as that divine activity is manifested in Jesus Christ. The space which parents give their children, which teachers give their pupils, which society provides for its members, must, in diverse fashions no doubt, express something of the loving care of God for his people with the accompanying encouragement, stimulus and support. How this is to avoid the extremes of indifferent tolerance and suffocating paternalism if not downright repression in the different contexts, demands thoughtful analysis and sensitive praxis. Such analysis and praxis are closely related to the understanding and practice of power, the second significant and perhaps most elusive of our three words.

116

The move from recognition and respect in the analysis of love to letting be as enabling to be has already reached the threshold, if not the inner sanctuary of power. Power could in its polyvalent usage be described as the ability to be (oneself) or as enabling to be (of the other). Tillich centres on the ability to be, as involving first of all resistance to non-being and then assertion and expansion of one's own being. This kind of ontological analysis connects with psychological versions of willing to be and self-assertion and with sociological understanding deriving from Weber's 'chance of a man or a number of men to realise their own will in a communal action even against the resistance of others who are participating in the action'. The thrust of these and other analyses of power is to stress the ability of the self *to be*, even at the expense of others, by asserting and achieving its own will. Power relates closely to influence, domination and control while power-struggles reflect the inevitable conflict between different wills. The longest shadows are cast by Nietzsche's will-to-power and Acton's judgment on its corrupting influence.

Without ignoring the importance or realism of such analyses, I should like to continue the line of thought provoked by my previous investigation of love as recognising, respecting and finally enabling others to be. The 'almighty God' as he is known in Judaeo-Christian tradition clearly possesses power. The exercise of this power in the creation of human beings resulted in the possibility of personal love. Its further expression in redeeming friendship took the way of loving recognition and respect, of inviting, attracting, and enabling through the power of love. The success and failures of that project are readily available to the believing reader of the Scriptures. Despite the awesome distance between creation and creator, between history and its lord, to which the Scriptures abundantly testify, the overall impression is not one of a God simply and arbitrarily asserting himself but of a patient, sensitive search for the loving response, and so authentic fulfilment, of his human creatures, as individual persons and as peoples. The kingdom or reign of God in which his power will be fully manifest, is shaped by and dependent on his recognition of and respect for the personal character of human beings and their freedom to respond in love or to retreat into self-centredness. His own surrender in love in Jesus Christ is directed to attracting their love in return, to liberating them from the vicious circle of self-enclosure. This description of the power of God may suggest weakness rather than power. Such an understanding would be reinforced by concentrating on the surrendering, not-turning-the-other-cheek, victim-like dimension of Jesus in his life and death. It would generate on our part what Nietzsche has so cruelly criticised as the morality of slaves and underline the Marxian criticism of Christianity in its domestication of critical and revolutionary impulses. It would seem to leave us with a Jesus, meek and mild, who put up with everything because he had not the courage and the strength to protest, to refuse and to revolt.

The objection illuminates the difficulty Christians and others frequently experience in trying to reconcile love and power, practically and theoretically. The creative strength of God in fashioning human beings in his own image, and in recognising and respecting them in their freedom as he drew them into loving relationship, has its awesome, even sometimes terrifying, expressions in the historical accounts of the Old Testament. The people of Israel were left in no doubt about the power of Yahweh, corrective as well as creative. In Jesus the signs of the kingdom were naturally signs of power—the healings, the nature miracles and more profoundly the forgiveness of sinners. The teaching was of one with authority, with divinely bestowed power and in its content it presumed both to confirm and transform the law. This authority of person, teaching and activity inevitably provoked a power-struggle which, however, Jesus resolved in the totally surprising and paradoxical way of loving surrender unto death and creative transformation in resurrection. The power to renounce the power of physical force and social establishment, the power to enter fully into solidarity with the socially powerless, the power to meet in love the vicious response of a threatened establishment and the power to forgive his enemies at the very end, all this evoked the definitive show of divine power we call the resurrection. That power in weakness overcomes for Jesus, by way of the Cross, the weakness of conventional power, and Christians must wrestle with the same power in weakness as they seek the liberating power of Jesus' redemptive activity.

Justice

In seeking to mediate between love and power the third

118

element in our triad, justice, plays a key role. It should not however, in Jewish and Christian tradition, be treated as simply some kind of derivative concept helping us to reconcile those great independent ideas of love and power. Justice or righteousness (*sedaqah/dikaiosune*) enjoys an independent significance of its own in Old and New Testament literature, an independence and significance that came from its author and origin, God. For some commentators justice is the basic characteristic of God's relationship with humankind. As such it must be understood in its full biblical significance as the quality or qualities of God which enter into his covenant dealings with Israel and humankind, and focus them, in sensitivity and fidelity to that covenant with God and with one another. The full religious, personal and social due which human beings owe to their God and one another embraces the whole range of religious and moral values with all their personal, social, political and economic implications. It was in this tradition that Jesus preached the kingdom with its values and implications and that Paul elaborated further on the justifying justice of the Father available through Jesus Christ whereby we are set free for freedom, to be fully and authentically ourselves.

It would be no distortion of the biblical tradition of *sedaqah* and *dikaiosune* to see it in terms of the respect shown by God to the people of his creation and choice. His regard for their freedom, the detailed expression of his concern for their genuine development, his judgment on their failure, and his fidelity to his commitments, provide the basis, the model and the capacity for their respect for one another. That respect translates into justice as the form of loving which refuses possession but overcomes indifference. In structuring love in this way, the justice of respect, concern, fidelity and commitment gives content to the enabling power of love by restraining its thrust to domination and oppression while harnessing its energies to the authentic work of enablement. Such justice must also reflect the clear-sighted judgment of God on the failures and distortions of human love and power. It can thus provide the insight and commitment to overcome these failures and distortions on the model of the persistent and transforming activity of Yahweh and Jesus.

The justice in recognition and respect due to all, in which love must find expression and power be exercised, could be given appropriate historical expression in the emergence of each and all as subjects in history and of their history. It is only as historical subjects that human beings can respond to God and to one another, that they can become disciples of Jesus, sons of the Father and participate in the inbreaking kingdom. The task of discipleship is to provide and promote this historical subjecthood and to do it after the example of Jesus by attending primarily to the socially marginalised and historically invisible. The victims of social and historical oppression in the categories of race, sex and class now so familiar to us and in categories still to emerge and to be identified, constitute the primary manifestation of justice as judgment upon our discipleship and the primary challenge to our communal and personal responses. It is in their interest and on their behalf that the unitive urge of our loving and its enabling capacity in power must be primarily exercised. In that exercise love and power merge fruitfully and effectively in the promotion of justice, in the emergence of new and fuller human subjects in history and so in the realisation of the kingdom or reign of God.

At this point numerous concrete problems of how love, power and justice are to be realised in the innumerable instances where they are now so obviously and painfully lacking, clamour for attention. I can deal with only a few of these and, even with these, much too briefly.

The current interest in liberation with its theological and political dimensions connects clearly and closely with the understanding of love, power and justice presented here. The focus of that liberation is the oppressed as indicated above. Their plea, spoken or unspoken, for freedom from various oppressive forces enters for Christians into the call "Come, follow me", the call to discipleship. Their eventual liberation as subjects of their own history will constitute some historical realisation or anticipation of the final, eschatological kingdom. In their liberation lie the possibility and the need for the liberation of their oppressors. Without the liberation of the oppressed, the oppressors remain in the enslavement in which Jesus found the established political and religious leaders of his own time. One of the great insights of the Mahatma Gandhi in the struggle for the liberation of India was into the need of the British colonial regime for liberation also and into the liberation of India as the only means to that liberation for Britain. In the new liberated relationship both peoples could be recognised and respected in their authentic self-hood and could hope to achieve authentic fulfilment. The divinely given righteousness of the covenant relationships of Old and New Testament could assume historical and political form in the relationships between British and Indian governments and peoples. How far such political goals with their theological significance were really achieved in the case of Britain and India need not detain us here, except to invoke as counter-point the relationship between Britain and Ireland.

I do not propose to rehash the historical and contemporary problems of Northern Ireland as the focal point of still unresolved political, social, psychological, economic, cultural, even racial and religious difficulties between British and Irish governments and peoples. Despite the fruitful relationships that have existed and still exist between these peoples and governments, the failure of the 1920/21 settlements between the countries after the tumultous preceding decade has left both unliberated in significant ways which find murderous expression in Northern Ireland just now, but were already evident and festering in the previous sixty years of Northern Ireland's existence. It was there that the non-liberation in both sides was most concretely experienced and is still most deeply entrenched. I am not offering another solution to this complicated situation but calling attention to two sometimes neglected aspects of it. Firstly, there is need of liberation for the British as well as for the Irish governments and peoples. Unless the British recognise that—as they did, however implicitly in India, subsequently in most other colonies and most recently in Zimbabwe (Rhodesia) —they will not attain insight, will and energy or the love, power, and justice to tackle the problem fairly and fully. I have no wish to diminish Irish responsibility in the matter; however, I do believe that the British, who enjoy the immediate governmental and military power, have a responsibility and a need for their own liberation which is simply overlooked.

The second and less encouraging point is that they may go on overlooking it or even if they do take it up, they may not find a way to liberation by disengaging in acceptable fashion as they did elsewhere. In other words there may be no satisfactory solution in our life-time or the foreseeable future. It is essential to the Christian vision that we go on looking for a solution, for the

121

historical liberation that will properly express the values and the coming of the kingdom. It is not part of that vision to believe that we will easily, soon, or indeed ever, find it.

Such a depressing prospect serves to remind us of another critical difficulty in the search for justice through the loving exercise of power. How far can such exercise invoke force, violence, the destruction and killing of other human beings?

The scope of the discussion here is enormous. I have tried to tackle it more fully a number of times in other contexts. I will confine myself therefore to a number of crucial points.

In the world in which we live, force and violence are pervasive and, it would seem, ineradicable. Order and peace are preserved in any society by the threat and usually the exercise of some forcible restraint. Most of these societies came into existence through some group imposing its will forcibly on others. Most liberation movements involve the threat or the actual exercise of force in attempting to overthrow the oppressive regime. The continuing fact of violence is undeniable. That need not make it any more moral than lying but it at least demands the attention of moral analysts and leaders. In particular it demands the attention of Christians concerned for love, power and justice as historical manifestations of the kingdom. Elsewhere I have referred to Christians as kingdom-spotters. They would be poor spotters if they could not identify and did not attempt to evaluate the violence prevalent in our history.

Force and violence as expressions of power are obviously disabling rather than enabling for the people subjected to them. By definition they restrict and restrain if they do not destroy and they do so against the will of their victims. They are *prima facie* therefore opposed to the respect for and enabling of others which has featured so largely in this discussion. So if they are to be acceptable to Christians and not just endured *faute de mieux*, they require further explanation and justification. Such explanation and justification can only derive from that respect for and enablement of others which those subjected to forcible restraint are themselves violating, whether as conventional criminals, political revolutionaries, apparent guardians of the law, or masters of an oppressive regime. The first consideration therefore, given the fact of violence, is to ask what is its basic thrust, to establish or maintain oppression, to establish or

122

maintain liberty and liberation. The latter kind of violence must continue to retain as its normative or controlling principle, respect and enablement for all others. To examine the complexities of this, the temptations and dilemmas which those engaged in violence, implicitly or explicitly, must face, would far exceed the limits of this chapter. My purpose is to indicate an acceptable if rather traditional way into the moral analysis of violence by both guardians and opponents of the given social order or disorder. The final appeal in justifying any such exercise of violence is to the overall reduction of the violence done to the people at large.

But is this the Christian way? For all the sophistication of moral and political analysis in terms of reducing violence, can Christians committed to loving their enemies and to taking up the cross to follow Jesus, really engage in the cold-blooded killing of their opponents or enemies? How can one reconcile the political violence of revolution or war or, for that matter, of self-protection and security forces, with the example and teaching of Jesus Christ? It is important that each generation of Christians agonise over these problems. It is not enough that they appeal to traditional moral analyses of just war, just revolution or justified self-defence by person or society, given the evidence from Jesus Christ. Given the pervasiveness of violence and oppression it is not enough that Christians proclaim that violence is not for them, at least not without offering alternatives that can protect the weak and liberate the oppressed. In the search for alternatives, for more human and ultimately more Christian ways of protection and liberation, Christians have a particular responsibility to the pursuit of love, power and justice as experiences of the kingdom in history. Their overall task is multiple, deriving from their obligations to the weak and oppressed, to the persistent reduction of violence and to its continuous replacement by ways that are truly liberating for both sides of the oppressor-oppressed relationship and of the power struggle.

The Case History of Zimbabwe

My summary discussion of love, power and justice in relation to violence may be illustrated by a reprise of the history of Zimbabwe and its liberation in relation to the local Christian communities, particularly the Catholic Church. The missionaries who came north of the Limpopo River with the Pioneer Column in 1890 were both ministering to the conquerer-settlers and in search of new peoples to whom to preach the gospel. The gospel of salvation through love was beholden to and qualified by the military conquest and settler context of the new masters of what came to be known as Rhodesia. In that situation the message of love reached out to the African population by bringing the gospel message of loving salvation hereafter, and certain loving care in terms of the benefits of 'European', 'white', 'Christian' civilisation. Such benefits as education, medical assistance and agricultural development took little or no account of the traditional ways of the Africans and sometimes seriously disrupted them. Besides, the missionaries were not allowed to interfere with the vital interests of the European settlers whose continuing deceit and violence totally undermined the traditional patterns of African life. The love which so many missionaries experienced and expressed for the Africans and for which they sometimes spent themselves heroically was so narrowly channelled and structured in thought and deed that it posed no threat to the violent power of the conquerors, although it had some mitigating influence in concrete situations.

The real awakening of the African people and of the Churches took place in the 1950s. With the pastoral 'Purchased People' issued personally by Bishop Donal Lamont of Umtali in 1969, after he had failed to get the approval of the Rhodesian bishops as a group, the moral and Christian debate shifted decisively from love to justice. Love was given authentic form and content in justice. This shaped the debate over a decade as 'the reasonable demands of simple justice', to use a phrase from a subsequent episcopal document, were more sharply defined and more strongly demanded by and for the African people with the growing support of the Churches, particularly the Catholic Church. But the demands were even more strongly denied by the increasingly oppressive white regime led by Ian Smith. By its unilateral declaration of independence in 1965 this had become a formally illegal government and lost international recognition. In this period many white Christians, almost all laity, and in the Catholic Church up to 50 per cent of the clergy and religious, opposed the position defended openly by the Churches.

By the end of the decade the failure of the call to justice was obvious. Internal protests, economic sanctions, international pressures of various kinds and seemingly endless negotiations led mostly to greater political repression and economic privation for the Africans. Smith and his supporters were not about to yield one iota of their power and it was exercised in an increasingly dictatorial and oppressive way. Symbolic of the failure of the appeals to justice and of the arrogance of white power were the new Constitution and Land Act introduced in 1969. The Catholic Church opposed both. Provisions of the Land Act in particular forced on the bishops a direct confrontation with government power. This act divided the country formally into European and African land, with 50 per cent for 250,000 Europeans, including all of the good land, and 50 per cent for more than six million Africans. Europeans were not permitted to frequent African land, nor Africans permitted to frequent European land. 'To frequent' included attendance at school, clinic or church. The government ministers could grant permission in special circumstances, but it must be sought by the interested party, in many of the cases by the Church. With this control of who could attend Mass where, for example, the Church was directly subjected to state power and it reacted strongly and loudly. In the subsequent interchanges much of the protest was blunted and an uneasy compromise worked out in practice, whereby the Churches would be deemed by the government to have asked and received permission. In the government's mind this 'deeming' could be withdrawn at any time. To some churchmen at least, it was a purely governmental fiction.

The clash over the Land Act exposed the Church clearly and fully to the conflict in Rhodesia as a basic power struggle which could only be resolved by a shift of power from the European minority to the African majority. As all other means seemed to have failed over a considerable period, the African nationalists reckoned that only force could bring about this power shift. So by December 1972, the guerrilla war of independence became the centre of the African struggle. This came to an end after the Lancaster House Agreement of December 1979, the subsequent cease-fire, elections and then independence for Zimbabwe in April 1980.

The shift from love to justice to power which Churches and churchmen gradually recognised as critical to understanding the situation in Rhodesia was achieved slowly and for the

125

Africans very painfully. The effective leadership of the Catholic Church through its bishops in the period of the search for justice is also significant. Its role in the violent power-struggle is more complex.

The goals of the revolutionaries were very much in line with the developing message of the Church on justice. The goals of the European security forces were not. What became difficult and almost paralysing for the Church leadership was its inability either to accept the war as a legitimate means to achieve the valid revolutionary goals or to suggest effective alternative means. Church criticism of particular violent incidents and methods had little effect although through the newspaper *Moto*, and later through the Commission for Justice and Peace, the Catholic Church had important influence at home and abroad in exposing, for example, the terrorism of the security forces, and the oppressive conditions in the so-called 'Protected Villages'. Many priests and religious laboured heroically, some at the cost of their lives, to help the poorer Africans caught between opposing forces. It could be said that in the sixties the Catholic Church provided effective leadership in pursuit of justice and that even in the traumatic events of the seventies it showed its devotion to the oppressed African people in many important ways. Given the previous history and the confusion of contemporary events the Church may have done all it could. And it would be unfair to simplify, even caricature, the line which led from close association with colonial regime to dissociation and justice for Africans now through the failure of all attempts at negotiation to decrying the violence as 'that is not what we meant at all', as an acceptance of the fruits of violence in an independent Zimbabwe. Yet there are harsh elements of truth there which will have to be reflected on anew in South Africa, for example, and in dozens of countries around the world from the Philippines to Argentina.

The Church

The role of the Church in the promotion of love, power and justice as illustrated by the case of Zimbabwe, is greatly complicated by its previous and present associations with unjust political regimes. It is also complicated, as the Synod of Bishops in 1971 indicated, by its own exercise of love, power and justice. As a herald, a partial realisation and explicit promotion of the kingdom and its values, the effective witness of the Church depends greatly on its own structures and practices and how far they embody these kingdom values. Without attempting to evaluate the long historical record I prefer to ask Catholic and Christian communities two questions: (1) How far are we perceived as recognising, respecting and enabling our own members to achieve their authentic fulfilment through the exercise of their freedom and how far are we perceived as dominating, controlling and restricting our freer spirits? (2) How far in response to criticism of particular incidents and structures do we become immediately defensive, resort to elaborate justifications, even cover-up, and how far are we open and frank, committed to getting at the truth so that the love and power may be seen to assume the concrete form of justice?

God's Shaping of Human History

The source and norm of love, power and justice as exercised by human beings must be God himself in his self-communication to humankind. The recognition, respect and enabling to which we are called are not simply to reflect or be measured by these divine standards. Our task as Christians is to discern and promote the kingdom, the coming reign of God. It is to take responsibility for the divine shape of human history. This is the trust he has given us. To fail in this is not to undermine human fulfilment simply; it is to distort or hinder the divine presence itself. Letting God become himself within our history is the ultimate significance of our Christian exercise of love, power and justice.

8

The Dignity of the Undignified

Where is God now?

'The SS hung two Jewish men and a boy before the assembled inhabitants of the camp. The men died quickly but the death struggle of the boy lasted half an hour. As the boy, after a long time, was still in agony on the rope, I heard the man cry again, "Where is God now?" And I heard a voice within me answer, "Here he is—he is hanging here on this gallows . . ."' (Elie Wiesel, *Night*, New York: 1960 pp. 70ff.)

We need to be continuously and forcibly reminded that Golgotha is a far cry from the beautiful music and liturgies of our solemn assemblies—the far cry of (near) despair at abandonment by the victim and of disbelief of the onlookers. Where is God now? Let us see if he will come to save him? These are questions seeking an answer from Gulag to Robben Island, from more conventional and accessible slums and shanty towns across Asia, Africa and Latin America. And they surface persistently and acutely in millions of typical cases in the 'affluent' and 'Christian' West; cases like Chris in Dublin, homosexual, rejected by his family, unemployed and by now unemployable; or like Liz tied to an alcoholic husband who beats her while her six children are gradually abandoning their impossible home and 'inadequate' parents; or like Seamus who was picked up by the police, beaten and sentenced although protesting his innocence and then went on the 'blanket' in Long Kesh prison, i.e. living in his own excrement; or like Hazel whose husband, a prison officer, was shot before her own and her daughter's eyes, or . . . One could go on and on listing the griefs and degradations that are all about us, just around our own corner or stretching across the globe in a chain of terror and oppression that defaces and obscures the image of God in man, oppressed

128

and oppressor, that inevitably and reasonably if often despairingly or hostilely raises the final question, 'Where is this God now?'

For the alert and alive Christian the question is both inevitable and painful. Too many of us are more alert to the pain of the question for us, than to the suffering of the boy on the gallows. So we ensure by our sleeping pills and tranquilisers that we are not awakened by sight or sound of suffering human kind. The defaced image on the gallows is carefully excluded by concentrating on the pretty and prettified faces with which we surround ourselves. The cries of pain from the ubiquitous torture chamber, political and domestic, cannot penetrate the media-centres we call our homes. Only the great exclusion of the degrading and disturbing enables us to enjoy life or even to survive. There are people to take care of these things. Pilate's hand basin is invisibly at our side. Besides we pay our taxes and so contribute to all kinds of welfare projects at home and abroad. We even make voluntary contributions to several programmes designed for the needy. We are never consciously unkind to the deprived; we just don't want them around us.

So much of Western Christian living for laity and clergy seems to be bounded by the limits just described, the limits of the 'Great Exclusion'. And so much of the reflection on Christian living which in its systematic presentation we call Moral Theology takes no more than a few halting steps outside these limits, that we may be faced once again with a *trahison* not just of the *clercs* but of the *croyants*. At least reflecting believers, professional theologians and others, have to consider how far the 'Great Exclusion' may be the ultimate exclusion, the exclusion of God, and how far the question of where God is now, may be more appropriately raised in the circles of the privileged than among the 'Wretched of the Earth'. At any rate there is the awkward difficulty of reconciling the God of the privileged and oppressing peoples with the God of the deprived and oppressed. For the moral theologian, description and analysis of the Christian way of life must return to the life and example of Jesus, his search for and finding of God ultimately on the Cross, but along a route that took him to seek out and befriend the outcast and 'undignified' of this world, develop a community of disciples from them and then experience their betrayal and desertion at the crucial time. Rejected by the leaders, the masses and even his friends, he prayed to be spared the final indignity of

129

criminal crucifixion and cried out as the possibility of final abandonment, suggested mockingly by his enemies, came crowding in on him. He might well have been waiting on the Godot of Beckett's tramps, Didi and Gogo, but for him the only tomorrow possible was in the transformation of the Resurrection, the Father's response to Jesus in final recognition and acceptance. This person, life, death and resurrection form the heart of Christian living. They must also form the heart of Christian theology, Christians' fumbling attempts to recognise, explore and express the nature, relationships and activities of the God of Jesus Christ. To make any significant progress in this daunting task the 'Great Exclusion' which Jesus overcame in his personal relationships and most profoundly in his sufferings and death, must be in turn overcome, at least partially, by believer and theologian. The searching question about God's absence and presence must be honestly and courageously faced. Evasion of these preliminary tasks invalidates the whole exercise and with particular ignominy for the moral theologian

The Image of God and Moral Theology
    The structure of the Christian life and so of moral theology might well be described as the call to unveil, discern and recognise the presence of God as he has communicated himself in the covenants of creation and incarnation. The recognition involved is no mere doffing of the hat or nod of the head to be accompanied by 'polite meaningless words'. It is a recognition that constitutes a way of life and a life's task, for the 'terrible beauty' of the living God demands total human response and is constantly in danger of being obscured by the false beauties of gods created in our own image. In so far as moral theology is a Christian theology, its structure and method of analysis must reflect on the paradigmatic unveiling of the presence of God as it occurred in Jesus Christ. His focus of interest on the poor and the outcast and his own acceptance of the role of the suffering (and rejected even unto death) servant, provide moral theologians with an inescapable starting point in their analysis of the pursuit of God as he is mediated through his created human images and finally through his own son.
    To begin one's moral theology by seeking God within the rejected and apparently deformed images of the outcast, the suffering and the handicapped, poses immediate and difficult

problems. How can it be reconciled with the traditional understanding of creation reflecting the *vestigia Dei* as the heavens proclaim his glory, the glory of God in humanity fully alive and the created world charged with the grandeur of God? Whether morality is conceived in terms of the coming to fulfilment of the work of the Creator and indeed Redeemer God or in the other classical Christian tradition of the Natural Law, it seems almost perverse to attend first of all to the deformed images, the failures of creation or society, in search of the summoning, empowering and guiding presence which a theological analysis of morality might ascribe to God. It intensifies the very problem of seeing God as source and terminus of morality by underlining the very aspects of human existence, the handicap, illness and degradation, physical, mental and spiritual which constitute the difficulty of seeing God as all-powerful and yet moral or loving creator. Yet however one attempts to explain the evil in the world, at least the physically, mentally and socially and even spiritually deformed human beings may not be overlooked or excluded in any Christian contemplation and response to the image of God in the world. If one is to take as critical the example of Jesus himself, one will turn first to these as truly mediating as well as needing God, and as ultimate test of our ability to recognise and respond to the supreme mediation of God in Jesus himself. 'As long as you did it to one of these least ones. . . .' (Matt. 25)

It is important to the true recognition of their mediating role as images of the divine and to the moral value of response to them that they be recognised and respected as valuable in themselves, divinely valuable with all the dignity that goes with that and not merely as recipients of our or even God's special care and above all not as occasions for our moral activity. The real disrespect and indignity would be to make the deprived into stepping stones for the privileged on the way to God.

The Unity of Human Kind

Part of the difficulty in discerning the image and presence of God in the least ones derives from the sharp individualism which dominates our thinking. Image of God is for us to be associated exclusively with the individual. The other individual, and particularly the individual with a difference which is by our standards impoverishing, is alien to us in a host of ways which may easily exclude that individual from our consciousness and certainly from our consciousness of him or her as locus of God's presence and as manifesting God's nature and glory. When the deprived are institutionalised or living far away or even just the wrong side of the tracks, the exclusion is easier and more effective. But the individualism is not overcome by attending to other individuals including deprived ones, essential as that is. A deeper shift of consciousness is demanded whereby I think primarily in inclusive 'us' terms rather than in 'me' and the 'others' terms or in an exclusive 'us' and 'them' terms. When the unity of humanity begins to be thought and felt and acted upon, the real locus of the divine image becomes evident to us in the human race as a whole, its historical members at any particular time, taken both in their irreducible individuality and in their unbreakable unity. Until that kind of image of humanity prevails, humanity as image of God will be partial and fragile. The understanding of the Church as sacrament of the unity of humankind, to which Pope John Paul returns a number of times in his first encyclical *Redemptor Hominis*, reflects this basic Christian truth. Each one's imaging of God and its moral implications are inseparable from the total imaging and mediating which form the origin and criterion of human dignity and indignity. The dignity of the 'undignified' cannot be separated out, leaving the dignity of the rest intact. Averting one's eyes and ears and minds from Chris or Liz, from the victims of thalidomide, poverty or torture does not eliminate their significance for one's own dignity. It merely impoverishes the meaning and living of that dignity.

Becoming Human

Given that it is the whole of humankind which properly reflects and mediates God according to Christian understanding, it must be further recognised that humankind is only partially realised in any particular era or group or individual. Participation in humankind is a historical, developing and always incomplete process. In that sense no total participation is available in history even for the most gifted individual. We are always incomplete, partial, handicapped and deprived, without of course our basic human dignity as mediating and reflecting God being destroyed. Our relativisation undermines much of the muddled thinking that colours our attitudes of superiority and

132

inferiority. It could be easily transposed into the offensive 'There but for the grace of God, go I' or some other patronising expression and attitude. That is not the point at all. The other whom we are tempted to patronise for some supposed inferiority is equally God's gift and grace and a necessary reminder, better, revelation to us of the diversity of God's gifts and of our necessarily limited sharing in them. Lord and Lady Bountiful's slumming bears no relation to the recognition and response which characterised Jesus' behaviour; his response to the physically ill, the socially outcast and the evidently sinful from the paralytic to the publican to Mary Magdalen is our norm.

If we are not allowed slumming and do-goodery in face of conventional illness and poverty, perhaps God is. Some traditional interpretations of both saw them as an opportunity for discipline and development on the human side and testing, eventual caring and love on the divine side. Both elements create difficulties. Some of the more awful physical or social suffering appears to reduce rather than enlarge the human character of the victim, while its canonisation as divine test easily leads the non-victims or social agents to hypocritical resignation on behalf of the victims—a truly opiate effect. The suggestion of a sadistic God trying out his experiments even for our ultimate reward seems incompatible with the God who empties himself to assume the human condition of the suffering servant. It is precisely here that the Christian experience of God uneasily harmonises with the all-powerful, impossible deity, remote in his transcendence and apathetic if not sadistic in his experimentation.

Without presuming to offer any satisfactory, much less definitive answer to these classical difficulties, I consider that two factors, one anthropological, the other theological, have a bearing on how we address them. Becoming human is not just an individual but a social task, not merely in the sense that one becomes human in community over time, but that the human condition emerged gradually and is still struggling towards some richer achievement. In that evolutionary-historical development it is possible to observe the slow struggle for and of the human species in which all of us with our various gifts and limitations are engaged. The struggle to become human, at first a strictly evolutionary one and then a historical one, remains a permanent task with its historical, as well as its evolutionary

133

triumphs and failures. Triumph and failure characterise the lives of all of us in their biological, psychological, social and other dimensions. The 'undignified', as they appear to us, are a critical part of that struggle, frequently in their very conventional failure and indignity pointing the way to new possibilities and triumphs. Our forward thrust as a human race is as much dependent on the apparent failures as on the successes. This is reinforced for us in remembering that our criteria of discrimination between genuine success and failure are very crude, invested with self-interest and blinkered by the social, cultural and personal conditions in which we are formed.

God and the Human Struggle

But where does God stand in such a struggle and how does it concern him? What kind of God emerges from this struggle to achieve humanity? The preposition 'in' is not carelessly invoked. The God of Christ is so intimately bound up with human origins and destiny that in the struggle toward humanity he must be both involved and discernible. For it is the image of God which emerges as humanity emerges, to reach its culmination of sonship in Jesus. Across the spectrum of human gift and achievement broods the spirit of the living God. In the combination of gift and achievement which issues in the struggle towards fulfilment for individual, group and race, the image of God finds its fitful, fragmentary and partial expression. Even in the historical Jesus the expression was not such that one could not be mistaken. Yet that historical Jesus underlined the sources of mistake in seeking the image and realisation of God among the powerful and successful of this world. The suffering servant has more potential for humanity's basic task and dignity in revealing the true God than the mighty on their thrones or the geniuses in their laboratories or studies or studios. The God we confront, as the creation and resurrection narratives reveal, is the source of might and genius, but the crucial revelation of him occurs in failure, suffering and crucifixion. His part in humanity's struggle towards fulfilment is not primarily that of firing the pistol shot to start the race and presenting the laurel wreath at the end, to invoke Paul's image. His primary presence and involvement is in the struggle itself, taking on humanity's burden and pain, suffering with humanity through and beyond all the natural and historical failures and sufferings to which human flesh is heir. It is a suffering towards and not a simple surrender. Physical suffering engaged much of Jesus' time and energy as a healer and in his own as well as his prophetic predecessors' message and example, the sufferings of the oppressed cry to heaven for vengeance. A Christian God suffering in and with his people is not a recipe for medical or social neglect but rather a profound indictment of both. Whatever you do or do not do to these is done to this suffering God who reigns from the gallows rather than a throne and emerges in the efforts of the paralytic to find health and yet live and love without it rather than in the success of the athlete in breaking world records. The God engaged in human struggle and suffering provides the inspiration and the power for moral response as well as the basis for human dignity—above all in those engaged in the most difficult struggle and in the most painful suffering. The charter of the moral life which moral theologians attempt to draft for the guidance of Christians should look somewhat different if devised from the angle of suffering humanity, the angle preferred by Jesus and his God.

A Moral Theology of Caring

In the struggle towards fulfilment of a single people, each person with his individual, relative and sometimes complementary strengths and weaknesses, the concept of caring for one another is indispensable. Caring relationships and caring professions are clichés of the time. In that mutual caring the struggle is made meaningful as well as tolerable for many. The distinctively divine involvement finds its appropriate expression. Some clarifications and qualifications are however in order.

The caring by the self-styled strong can easily become self-indulgent and patronising, revealing the slumming attitude or using of others for one's own goals. Caring rests on recognition and respect above all. It must involve for caring and cared a reverence for the dignity, privacy, and the mystery of the more vulnerable and exploited. Properly and fully, the caring relationship is reciprocal and dialogical but one party, individual, group, class or even nation may/can be easily maintained in a dependent and exploited role, thereby maintaining the other in an exploiting role. This defeats the whole point of the caring relationship and frustrates the positive advance to which the human struggle is directed.

135

Of course, in infancy and old age, in personal and social sickness, some people and groups will be more dependent and require sensitive and prolonged caring. Impatience, with the effort needed, may lead those providing care to take the easier course of regarding the dependence as one-sided and unalterable or to press for a 'normalisation' which may not be possible. In both situations, the true dignity and gifts of the 'dependent' are ignored and violated. The real dependence of the 'caring' is obscured. Human solidarity is violated. Divine engagement in the total struggle is reduced to the paternalism of the 'strong'. Until we learn our need of the Chrises and the Lizes, of the physically and mentally handicapped, of the poor and exploited classes and races, and enjoy the skills required for dialogue and mutual caring as partners, we cannot hope to be effectively helpful after the manner and by the power of Jesus Christ. We thus continue to frustrate the divine design of allowing his image in humankind to grow and be transformed into the image and participation of the only begotten Son of the Father. We are not yet in a position to proclaim our universal brotherhood and sisterhood in Christ.

Solidarity and Mutual Liberation

The source of our being sisters and brothers in Christ is the sharing of the human condition to the point of self-emptying which God in the person of his Son undertook. It was his definitive entry into the human struggle, his climactic expression of his solidarity with all humankind. Such solidarity is the way of human salvation, pioneered for us in Jesus, offered to us as gift and task in the concrete relationships of our lives. Evasion or rejection of that solidarity is the way of damnation, of destruction. It cannot remain a solidarity of good intentions, of remote benevolence or paternalistic doing good. Solidarity demands sharing, being side by side, engaged as equal partners in the night-battle. So fleeing to the suburbs or offering them cake or employing others for that kind of thing in order to escape personal involvement will not entitle us to say 'Lord, Lord' or validate our claims to be sons and daughters of the Father, because we refuse the demanding task of being brothers and sisters of one another. Our exclusiveness becomes our exclusion. Our efforts to be free of it all, or rather of them all, result in our enslavement and imprisonment. We are rapidly engaged in constructing our own Long Kesh or Robben Island.

Without Jesus Christ and the God of Jesus Christ there is no salvation, no liberation. Without these least ones there is no access to Jesus and the Father. In Christian perspective we need them more than they need us. At any rate, if we are the escapers and evaders, we are also the rejecters of sonship and daughterhood. The solidarity of mankind, illuminated and given final significance by divine engagement in its struggle, provides the way of salvation as the way of effective brotherhood. That salvation is a mutual liberation into the freedom wherewith Christ has set us free. (Gal. 5:1)

Letting God be Himself

The difficulties of understanding and accepting suffering in creation and human life as deriving from a loving God, are not entirely removed but at least easier to live with if God has shown his willingness to share them with us as he has in Christ. A fuller Christology recognises Jesus as no isolated and aberrant intervention by God to clean up the human and cosmic mess. Jesus the Christ is central to creation as well as salvation, to the cosmos as well as humanity. This engagement of God with the human struggle originated in his creative engagement with the cosmos which was created in and through Jesus Christ, the first born of all creation which is now reaching out for, struggling towards the fulfilment which is his in Resurrection. God's involvement in the cosmos and human history has taken on the character of a drama which exceeds the merely human and cosmic. It is a divine drama, in which in a sense the destiny of God is at stake. More accurately (although our expressions are all so crude in this discourse) by his work of creation-salvation, God has entrusted the fulfilment of his plan to his creatures. Without their recognition and acceptance of it, in however anonymous a form, the plan cannot be fulfilled. But he did not entrust just a plan, however far-reaching, he entrusted himself. Personal relationships always involve such entrusting. God initiated personal relationships with mankind. In loving them in personal fatherhood terms, he placed himself at their disposal. Would they respond as sons or daughters or no? The sacrament, effective sign and guarantee of that entrusting was Jesus Christ. What is at issue is not just the salvation of mankind but the fulfilment or betrayal of the divine trust.

137

In a different idiom, enjoying the authority of Jesus, what mankind has been offered by God is a share in the building of his kingdom. His involvement in the human struggle is directed towards the final achievement and the transforming fulfilment of the kingdom. The kingdom as presence of God's loving, healing and transforming power is already at work among us. But it has yet to reach its fulfilment. For that he depends on our cooperation, our solidarity with him and above all with those whom he has indicated to us through Jesus as primary locus of his presence, the 'undignified'. In acting out this solidarity and so promoting the kingdom, we are responding to the God who is coming as well as the God who is already with us. We are preparing the way before him. In a true sense we are letting God be himself in his own world, with his own people. The ultimate measure of our sharing care of the neglected and rejected is the liberation of God so that he may complete his loving transformation of his world, so that he may be fully at home in it. Only when that work is completed will we no longer need to ask, 'Where is God now?' For he will be self-evidently everywhere.

9

The Future of the Business Corporation

Complexity, Involvement and Interest

There is some point in wondering what a moral theologian, 'nice guy' or no, is doing at a conference on the business corporation. Is he expected to give it his blessing, meanwhile reproving the peccadilloes that all are heir to and that undoubtedly occur in the conducting of the best regulated businesses? Or is he to adopt a stern and prophetic role, denouncing the 'necessarily exploiting' character of such enterprises? The temptations either way may be overwhelming and not just as a sop or a scourge to a particular audience but because the complexity of the structure, the activity, the motivating forces and the social role of a large business corporation today may prove too difficult to grasp, analyse and confront morally. Self-indulgent sops or scourges offer an easier way and a more certain return from some constituency or other. Yet the 'complexity' clause may not be invoked to evade the moral challenge which the power and pervasiveness of business corporations constitute for all of us, including those of us who have never been in an executive suite and can barely distinguish a savings from a current account. For all of us interact with the companies at least as consumers of their goods and services, as integrated into an economic system which they dominate, as inhabitants of a world whose resources they transform, consume or pollute, and even as members of universities and churches which may be financially dependent on them.

I labour this rather obvious involvement of all, including the moral theologian, in order to insist on the moral responsibility of all, and particularly of the moral theologian, to assist in clarifying the moral issues which derive from the reality of business corporations and which affect everybody in various ways.

139

Involvement always creates an interest for or against, and interest is a notorious influence on moral evaluation. The moral theologian is no more immune than anybody else to the dangers of interested knowledge or the conflict of interest, for example, between moral evaluation of corporate activity and personal or institutional dependence on corporate financing. With everybody involved and therefore interested, 'interest' is no more an excuse for evading the moral challenge than is complexity. It is, however, a more subtle and incalculable influence both because it cannot simply be shed, however many layers of the onion are peeled off, and because there is no finally adequate formulation of how it enters into our moral understanding. Some identification and clarification of interest is essential to moral evaluation in this as in other areas. And it will form part of the inevitable but not arbitrary simplification which moral analysis of such complex issues involves. Clarifying interest and justifying simplification are continuing tasks for the moral analyst. They cannot be undertaken in any comprehensive way in the moral notes presented here.

Wealth

Wealth and poverty are concepts that are central to the complexity, interest and confusion which surround the moral analysis of economics, business and the corporation. The Christian tradition in particular has continually displayed, in understanding and practice, an ambivalence towards both these concepts that still affects theological, moral and even political discussion. Acknowledging the blessedness of the poor and the difficulties of the rich in entering the kingdom of God combine uneasily with condemnations of poverty, the promotion of a greater share of the world's goods or wealth for all and the persistent if disguised belief that the good are industrious and thrifty and so likely to be reasonably wealthy. This ambivalence may account for the Christian, particularly Calvinist, influence deemed to be at work in the development of capitalism, and the current Christian, particularly Catholic, engagement with the development of socialism. Without presuming to undertake a critique of such grand theses, I will confine the first of my notes to a more modest consideration of the meaning and role of wealth.

Wealth, as generally understood, ranges over the broad range

140

of valuable human realities from land and natural resources through human artefacts and artistic creations to human institutions, including the familial, educational, political and medical, to human beings themselves, their talents, achievements and traditions. It is in this broad context that papal encyclicals, theologians and some economists speak of integral human development or the development of the whole person. And it is in this broader context that the translation or reduction of wealth to money appears clearly inadequate and yet, because of its fluid and diverse character, dangerously seductive. The interchange between money and wealth in the narrower sense of material resources, goods and the capacity to produce them seems more obviously defensible until one begins to consider incalculables like labour, management, risk and social cost and the arbitrary nature of the calculating mechanism from the invisible hand of the market to the heavy hand of the bureaucrat. In the first significant simplifications I concentrate on wealth in its material senses and leave aside the complications of translation into money. Justification for these simplifications will emerge, I hope, in some clarification of the moral and Christian confusion surrounding the topic.

Christian Tradition

Within the Christian tradition of creation, human beings are seen as material or bodily beings, in continuity with, in need of and in charge of the earth and its resources. The 'in charge of' or 'stewards of', as one theological expression has it, reveals the discontinuity between the human and the cosmic without destroying the continuity or reducing the need. The 'image of God' which distinguishes men and women within the cosmos is the source in biblical terms of their responsibility to God for the goods of his creation and for one another. In that primary sense the earth's goods belong to all, are to be developed and used for the benefit of all. The thrust of this primary divine intention has persistently surfaced in the religious and moral tradition of Judaism and Christianity—in an Amos denouncing the neglect of widows, orphans and deprived by the rich and powerful; in Jesus contrasting Lazarus, the poor man, with Dives, the rich man, among a host of other parables and admonitions; in the early Christian experiments of community of goods; in the patristic recall and development of the message of Jesus and the prophets; in the scholastic teaching of the reversion of goods to communal ownership in extreme need; in the long practical tradition of Christian provision for the poor; in the witness intended and often achieved in monastic and religious life, brilliantly exemplified by St Francis of Assisi and Mother Teresa of Calcutta; in the recent papal insistence on justice as the real name for peace; and in the growing Christian sensitivity to the injustice of the current distribution of the world's goods.

That by divine intention, the earth's resources are for the survival and development of all; that in the Judaeo-Christian tradition all have a responsibility to contribute to and as far as possible to ensure the survival and development of all: these truths provide perspective and a standard of evaluation for any system of controlling, developing and distributing material goods.

They provide perspective by indicating the broad goal of the system, its structures and activities, which must offer some coherent and dynamic approach to enabling all increasingly to benefit from these resources and their developments. That 'all', in biblical intent and current global interdependence, transcends class, race and even nation to include human beings everywhere. Objections to such a wide scope as unrealistic or irrelevant in the conduct of business or national economic life do not dampen business enthusiasm for access to new and remote markets like China or national dismay at the selfishness of OPEC in raising prices once again. Our sense of global opportunity and of global reverse is not always matched by a sense of global economic responsibility. The biblical perspective on the goods of the earth for all is not adequately realised by opening up new markets for Coca-Cola or resisting any price rises for primary products that happen to affect us. It would be relevant to our topic, but distracting in its complexity just here, to trace the involvement of American oil-companies in the recent price increases and how far they took advantage of the OPEC initiative. Their recent huge increase in profits recorded has not to my knowledge been given any other plausible explanation.

At this point we are moving from perspective and overall goal to systems, institutions and performance and their more strictly moral evaluation. Without entering into such detail as the recent performance of the oil companies, it is possible to see how the responsibility of development and distribution of the earth's resources for the benefit of all may suggest criteria at both the organisational and the behavioural levels. The moves from the general biblical and traditional Christian criterion to particular historical systems and activities cannot be seen in terms of either logical or historical necessity as if a single system and pattern of behaviour could be clearly and irrefutably deduced from the biblical premise. Many and complex historical forces enter into the development and distribution of the earth's resources. The various stages of the technological revolution from the agricultural revolution more than five thousand years ago through the industrial revolution some two to three hundred years old in the west to current technological transformations clearly affect the development and distribution of goods and their systems of organisation. Concurrent changes in social and political awareness and organisation, and the interaction of all of them with moral understanding, have compounded the task of providing economic moral guide-lines. The history of moral attitudes to usury reveals how complicated such interactions can be and how often moral analysis and theory limps behind actual practice. What appears to be simply opposed to the biblical intention may on further analysis prove in the concrete situation to be less simple and at least arguably if ambiguously directed to the general purpose of overall development and distribution. Such analysis will take account not only of the concrete situation and the general biblical injunction but also of some further Judaeo-Christian truths that affect all human relationships and activities.

Integral human development demands development and distribution of earthly resources as a necessary but not sufficient condition. At the level of the necessary it is already qualified by the sinfulness of human beings. The very Genesis story, which establishes human stewardship, also records human enmity arising in Chapter 3 between husband and wife and leading to fratricide in the Cain and Abel story in Chapter 4. A cosmic enmity involving struggle between human beings and the earth's resources constitutes a further dimension of the fallen condition of humanity which enters so deeply into Jewish and Christian anthropology. The promise and achievement of Redemption which characterise Christian faith do not simply remove the threat and realisation of that sinfulness in history. The gift and call to a new life in Christ are still affected by the

143

weakness and selfishness of the *simul justus et peccator*, the justified
person who is also still a sinner. In fulfilment of the call to
develop the gifts of this world for the benefit of all, sinfulness will
continue to qualify even the best-intentioned efforts and
sometimes issue in the worst-intentioned. For that reason no
particular system of development and distribution will be ideal,
free from sin in its structures and activities. All systems will need
some devices to restrain the strong and protect the weak. But it
should still be possible to assess in the concrete how far systems
and practices carry an unnecessary and remediable burden of
human sinfulness as expressed in the excessive possession and
consumption of some and in the privation and exploitation of
others. The evaluation of the corporation and of the system it
symbolises turns at least in part on such excessive and privative
practices and on the restraints and the protections which the
system possesses or lacks.

Freedom

For the material development to move beyond the necessary
condition of human development it must express and respect
that basis of human responsibility, that discontinuity with the
rest of the cosmos symbolised in the image-of-God talk, human
freedom. To enjoy and exercise any measure of that freedom a
human being must be able to satisfy certain basic material needs
such as food, shelter and clothing as necessary condition. The
dialectic between the material and spiritual dimensions of
human existence is thus clearly identified. Taken a step further
into recognition of development and availability of material
resources to meet human needs and responsibility in freedom to
ensure this, the dialectic relates the two moral values of justice
and freedom. In a world qualified by human sinfulness these
values exist in a dialectical relationship that may not be able to
transcend their particular historical opposition. Such is the
nature of a sinful and unredeemed world. In the sinful but
redeemed, a provisional transcendence of the conflict and a
limited historical synthesis become possible, although they will
never be a proper realisation of the transcendent synthesis of the
coming kingdom in which righteousness or justice and freedom
or liberation emerge in their God-promised and true character
as different aspects of the same integral human fulfilment or
salvation. A simple opposition of freedom and justice and the

pursuit of one to the almost total exclusion of the other reflect the sinful and unredeemed character of economic and political systems as evidenced, for example, in some capitalist and socialist systems and in the writings which reflect the interests of their apologists. They are not adequate to the redeemed if sinful vision of Christians with their sense of the gift, the promise and the summons of the kingdom values of justice and freedom.

Justice

Here it is necessary to expand my previous use of the terms 'justice' and 'freedom' and explain the simplifications involved. Justice I confined to the value inherent in developing and distributing the world's material resources for all its peoples. Fair distribution has become a conventional description of justice at large or social justice as it is commonly called in distinction from commutative justice which concerns one-to-one relationships of exchange and the like. Such distribution is not calculable in any mathematically exact way, and inevitably much less so than the apparently more confined and controllable just price. And it is not some fixed unchanging state of affairs but both a historic goal and provisional and approximate achievement while the approximation of it may vary. The goal demands at any particular time a sharing in the basic necessities by all human beings as human. Systems, enterprises and activities that are opposed either in their objectives, structures or actual management and performance to such sharing of the basic necessities do not meet this minimum standard of justice which emerges from the Judaeo-Christian tradition.

Fuller Christian Vision

The development of the resources to meet the needs I take to be part of the same moral responsibility. How the responsibility is shared and discharged requires more detailed discussion than is possible here. The existence of it, however, reflects elements in the Christian tradition about human celebration of, gratitude for and stewardship of earthly goods, human participation in the creative activity of God, human solidarity and responsibility to and for one another, the moral value of work and of a caring and thrifty, as opposed to a wasteful and self-indulgent attitude to God-given resources. The traditional Puritan virtues of industry and thrift find their due place in a more comprehensive

145

Christian vision with celebration, thanksgiving, creativity and sharing. A justice which includes the dynamic dimension of development will be open to these richer aspects of the tradition, particularly as it is symbolised and concentrated in the sacramental life. In Christian sacrament as in earlier Jewish tradition critical material goods and events like food, meals, water and washing provide ritual expression for grateful celebration and community sharing of the creation and re-creation of humankind and cosmos in the Mosaic and Christian covenants. The deeper, fuller and ultimately divine significance of justice as the righteousness of God making humanity in its cosmos righteous, emerges for Christians in the Eucharist above all, expressing the reality, the hope and the summons of the kingdom yet to be and already inaugurated. To ignore this significance and its moral implications while attempting to celebrate the Eucharist is to eat the body and blood of the Lord unworthily as Paul indicated to the Corinthians.

The fuller implications in our tradition of a justice of distribution and development exceed demands for a bigger slice of the cake or even for making a bigger cake. Useful as these images may be in conveying the harshness and urgency of material needs they omit all reference to the further human and religious dimensions of gratitude, celebration, solidarity and creativity. It is only when response to the harsher needs is joined with these that human freedom too finds its proper expression in development and distribution.

Development leading to growth of material wealth, a bigger cake, may offer a wider range of certain goods to certain people and in that sense increase freedom of choice. That greater freedom of choice may be extended to more and more people, by more equitable distribution, thus enabling them to escape the confines of purely basic necessities. Freedom of choice of material goods cannot claim very high ranking in the realisation of human freedom *tout court*. Indeed a multiplicity of goods of a particular kind may be a wasteful deployment of energy for the producer and an unnecessary distraction for the consumer. Where the goods are increasingly trivial and the needs artificially stimulated by elaborate and seductive advertising, freedom of choice may easily turn into consumer enslavement to continuously stimulated, artificial and insatiable need. The sinful condition of humanity finds ready outlet for the exploiting producer and self-indulgent consumer of such goods. How and by whom and to what extent the restraints and protections are operated may be highly disputable but some need for them to protect human freedom even at this level of supply and choice of material goods may not be ignored on the basis of interest.

The further exercise of human freedom in economic enterprise, innovation and organisation is sometimes hailed as the grand achievement of the capitalist system and as the essential economic base of liberal democracy. Without trying to assess such grand claims it may be said that human freedom finds a natural expression in the economic as in other fields. And the Judaeo-Christian responsibility to develop cosmic resources and so provide for humankind presumes that human beings themselves freely undertake this task. The value of any enterprise and operation will depend on how far in the concrete historical circumstances it is a genuine exercise of freedom and a genuine harnessing of the world's resources for humankind. Such moral value is not simply undermined by the need for profit to fuel further expansion and engage more effective skills. Yet there are more freedoms to consider and more benefits and profits to respect than those of the entrepreneurs or managers. There are the freedom of the work-force to organise and negotiate; the freedom of the consumers to protest and their protection against fraud and exploitation; the freedom of competitors. All these freedoms will need careful and perhaps strong regulation so that in particular the weaker elements in the system may not be exploited by the powerful. In the current situation it is difficult to see how these freedoms can be protected and reconciled without some legal and governmental control directed to the overall community good and freedom and operating at national and increasingly international level. Where business enterprises such as the large corporations transcend so many national boundaries and exceed in resources so many nation states within which they work, protection of freedoms for others will demand internationally agreed standards and control.

The words control and particularly governmental and international control have largely heretical overtones for defenders of certain interests. Freedom, they feel, is being undermined. To assess this charge more fully it is necessary to turn to another key concept in the debate, that of power.

147

Power

Power is clearly related to freedom, to one's own and to other people's. It is the capacity to achieve certain results. In this context the power to harness the earth's resources and human energies and so provide various goods and services for people has been evaluated as basically good and a part of Christian responsibility. That enterprise however, involves not only the capacity to produce goods and services but also creates an impact on the lives of a whole host of other people. In manufacturing industries that would include people who produce and supply the raw materials as well as the employees, the consumers, the competition and the general public in so far as certain consequences of the product such as pollution of the atmosphere affect everybody. In the range and manner of people affected and in the restraints and protections needed power and freedom are correlatives.

The control of resources, supplies and even markets which large business concentrations can achieve makes for easier and perhaps more efficient management and up to a point at least economy of scale in production which ought to benefit the consumer. It is no great secret that such concentration and control carries its own temptations for sinful people to exploitation of primary producers, workers, competitors, consumers and the general public. The power of OPEC and other primary producers, of unions, of consumer bodies and of competitors act as important countervailing forces but with varying thrust from the strong-arm measures of OPEC and certain unions to the weakness of small businesses and most consumer bodies. Legislative protection and governmental regulatory agencies must try to compensate for weakness but are exposed to the powerful lobbying of the large business interests which may succeed in emasculating legislative proposals and even 'capturing' the regulatory agencies.

The power struggles between various interests need to be continuously monitored morally. But there is a deeper human and Christian significance to the power question, deeper than simply the moral niceties of fairness or even the promotion and protection of freedom in economic affairs. In so far as it includes control over resources, including the non-renewable, over opportunities and conditions of employment, over availability and cost of products, over the condition of the environment, economic power controls

148

the lives and destinies of masses of people. Such control reduces and may even destroy the basic freedom of the human subject to participate in the pursuit of her or his own destiny. The power wielded by large-scale economic enterprises may in its own way be more subtly but no less inimical to human freedom than that of political dictatorship. At this stage it becomes equally irreconcilable with the Judaeo-Christian vision of human person and society.

It might appear at this stage that the moralist has succumbed to the temptation of moralising instead of analysing and clarifying. The line between moral analysis and moralising or moral exhortation and condemnation is a very thin one. Indeed it is hard to see how the moral analyst can go beyond clarification to evaluation without approving, disapproving, exhorting and condemning. Yet there is an easy moralising that indulges in easy simplifications and reflects unexamined interests. It would be too much to expect that I have entirely avoided that here. Yet the purpose of these notes is to raise certain questions and problems which the current economic world and its great symbols the business corporations must confront if they are to receive some positive moral and theological evaluation.

More Strictly Theological Notes

This paper has so far been largely concerned with some of the key words and concepts associated with corporations or at least the economic system within which they have developed, words and concepts such as wealth, power and economic freedom. Admittedly the system and the concepts were related to the Christian perspective of creation, sin and redemption and confronted with the Christian meaning of the values of justice and freedom. Yet there remains a lingering suspicion that Christian beliefs and values are tangential to the real world of the business corporation and that economic systems and business activities have a practical logic of their own that is unrelated to Christian faith. At any rate it seems to me necessary to reflect on certain Christian words and concepts to see how far they speak to the activities, structures and people of the business world.

Discipleship

The most obviously related of such concepts is that of

discipleship. The Christian authenticity of this concept is unquestionable. And in particular times and climes it offered and offers a way into both Christian faith and Christian living that is illuminating, empowering and radical in its reach. In the main-line Churches, as they are called, it could, did and still does become obscured for larger numbers of people as Church becomes coterminous with society, and faith and morality as much cultural as religious phenomena. Even then discipleship continues to exert a disturbing and transforming influence on ideas, movements and people, disrupting the easy collusion of established religion and established culture (including economic life) and confronting all Christians with less acknowledged demands of the Gospel.

In Jewish and Christian tradition faith and conversion initiate and sustain the life of discipleship. Whether one emphasises the initiation in radical conversion, in justification or in the continuing conversion in sanctification (including the need to overcome persisting sinfulness), the acceptance of Jesus (Yahweh in Judaism) and, through Jesus, the Father in faith, offers new life and calls for a new way of life.

The new way of life is of course personal. It must be accepted, appropriated, and lived out in personal fashion that involves both personal response and responsibility, and affects every facet of that response and responsibility. In the light of the Gospel call, it is impossible to exclude from the reach of discipleship any facet of responsible living. Discipleship as way of life then embraces the whole moral character and behaviour of the disciple. To treat a particular dimension of the moral life as if it were unaffected or unqualified by one's Christian faith is to introduce a division into discipleship which has no evangelical legitimacy. Whatever one means by saying there is no specifically Christian economics or politics or even morality, it cannot be, given the evident sense of discipleship, that these dimensions of living are entirely independent of one's Christian faith.

One possible way of reconciling the demands of discipleship with the relatively autonomous character of economics or politics, is to concentrate on the personal character, virtue and behaviour of the disciple. The moral dimension of discipleship is confined, for example, to the personal honesty, integrity and fairness of the business person in business dealings. The overall structure of the business world or even of a particular large business corporation is not regarded as a matter for discipleship

150

evaluation, decision and response. This approach has considerable attractions and impressive historical precedent. Its attractions include urgent personal demands and manageable criteria of performance which would make business life trustworthy within the system. The acceptance of the system or at least the judgment that the system in general is not a matter of Christian concern has the further economic attraction of providing stability and predictability. The historical precedents include both acceptance of political, economic structures as the given within which Christians must work out their salvation and also rejection of them by more radical groups, Churches and subcommunities like religious orders, as corrupt and irreformable. More pervasively a strong tradition of salvation as personal and so individual reinforced by a strong tradition of morality as also personal in that individualist sense, has tended to isolate discipleship from such social or stuctural concerns.

For all the individualist indications noted above, discipleship is a community reality. One becomes a disciple by joining the community of disciples. In Christian terms there is no such entity as a purely individual disciple. This should alert us to the dangers of interpreting discipleship living in individualist terms. Yet the reality and significance of community for disciples introduces new complications into this discussion, arising from the tensions between diverse communities demanding the attention and response of the disciple. If discipleship is a community reality and a complete way of life, has the disciple any alternative but to opt out of unbelieving communities, whether cultural, economic or political, which may have hitherto claimed his attention and are all about him? Attempts at such a response have a long Christian history. Although they may never have achieved any absolutely pure form, they persist and recur in Christian history in ways that challenge and judge other attempts at resolving Christian tension in this world.

Other attempts to resolve or at least reduce tension in belonging simultaneously to believing and other communities have sought a unity of Church and society that originated with the Constantinian liberation or Theodosian establishment. This took a particular 'international' form in medieval Christendom and the Holy Roman Empire and a 'national' form in post-Reformation Churches, eventually formalised in the principle, *cujus regio, ejus religio*. While ecclesiastical authority and community officially constituted the dominant partner in the medieval unity of believing and political economic communities, the political authority tended to dominate in the post-Reformation unity, even in those nations which remained Roman Catholic.

The Enlightenment and its fruits, the American and French Revolutions, political and economic developments in the nineteenth and twentieth centuries, have made any formal unity of believing (Christian) community and politico-economic communities increasingly unworkable. (The prospects for Islamic countries and for countries with dominant religions other than the Christian will not be considered here.) However, in practice, thinking and structure, discernible and significant residues of the unity solutions remain, reinforced for many believers in politico-economic terms by the apparently clear choice between a capitalism which at least accepts God and a socialism or marxism which denies him. The unity solution which arises from this choice may be informal but no less potent than some of the formal solutions of the past in the western world (or of the present formal unity sought in some Communist countries by denial of Christian belief).

Discipleship and Kingdom

In seeking to understand and maintain the social distinctiveness of the believing community and Christian discipleship in history and in the world, their relationship to the kingdom which Jesus preached and inaugurated is critical. This kingdom he took to be in continuity with that proclaimed and promised in Jewish tradition. Discipleship involves recognition, acceptance, proclamation and promotion of that kingdom. The kingdom is inaugurated and partially realised in history but its completion lies beyond history. Completion is, as the technical word puts it, eschatological. Total fulfilment of humanity and cosmos lies in the future, beyond history and all historical achievements. Within history the kingdom has already begun, and emerges fitfully and partially. The community of disciples attests to this already and future kingdom. It does this in mystical fashion by recalling, realising and sharing more widely in its worship or prayer the experience of God's presence in power and love which Jesus enjoyed. It attests in prophetic fashion by discerning and promoting the values of the kingdom in love, justice,

152

forgiveness and peace as they emerge within and without its own structures and confines and by denouncing and opposing the countervalues and countersigns of the kingdom which hatred, indifference, injustice and destruction embody. The community of disciples further bears witness to the eschatological dimension of the kingdom by insisting on the relative and incomplete character of all historic achievements, on the equal transience of all human destruction and on the call for openness to the God who is coming in power.

The disciple in community is called to service of the kingdom in its mystical, prophetic and eschatological dimensions. The kingdom itself, however, is not discerned or realised just within the confines of the community of disciples but across the broad reaches of all human communal living and achievement, including the economic and political. The challenge to discern and serve the kingdom and its coming in the economic context and community, demands of the disciple both a sense of the moral values of the kingdom at stake in economic activities and structures, and the power and perspective provided by the mystical, prophetic and eschatological awareness of the community of disciples. Successful interaction between discipleship and economic activity in a way that respects their distinctive characters and their personal and social dimensions requires the mediation of the kingdom and its values. Such interaction will not attempt to canonise any particular economic achievement or prospect as definitely that of the kingdom. Yet it will not ignore systems and settle for individual values. The conditions set by certain systems at particular times may be so opposed to and destructive of the kingdom and its values that radical change is called for, even though the disciple recognises that any new system will carry its own limitations and anti-kingdom elements.

By using service of the kingdom to relate economic activity and Christian discipleship, it is possible to maintain the necessary distinction and tension. The translation of kingdom values into economic activities, priorities and structures or the evaluation of economic life by kingdom standards calls for fuller ethical and theological discrimination. I would like to call attention to two further theological aspects even at the risk of breaking down the distinctions and tensions or else appearing to dabble further in theological irrelevancies.

153

Cross and Crucifixion

Discipleship in Gospel terms is inseparably related to cross and Crucifixion. How and in what way a particular disciple must bear the cross in life cannot be described or prescribed in any general terms. Yet as indicated in our earlier discussion of discipleship it would be false to the Gospel message to confine this aspect of discipleship to some private and individual area of life such as personal health or family responsibility. The surrender which discipleship demands in imitation of Jesus and in service of the kingdom can reach into any area of life, including the economic and business area. So the exclusion in principle of one's business life from such a challenge or the refusal to contemplate such a possibility of surrender, in order to defend one's own or even others' power and wealth may expose the inauthenticity of one's discipleship. Some of the defences of particular systems and practices as well as attempts to enlist Christianity in service of one's own economic interests have this inauthentic ring about them.

Which God?

The full extent of the inauthenticity is only exposed when the final theological question to be asked here or anywhere is honestly confronted. What is the final and deciding principle of one's life to which all other principles are adjusted however subtly and sometimes unconsciously? Where lies the treasure for which a person will give all that he or she has? In the crucial situation and in the general pattern of behaviour, what ultimate and dominant principle is revealed? In economic as in other areas of life, what is in Christian terms known to be relative and is even affirmed to be such in so many words, may be really ultimate. The truly ultimate and absolute God of Jesus Christ, the God of the incoming kingdom, the God who subverts our human pretensions, ambitions and achievements may be replaced by a god of our own creation in terms of wealth and power and growth. The critical Christian test of the business corporation in the future will be how far it fosters the creation and worship of such false gods among its shareholders, managers, employees and consumers and how far it leaves people open to the inbreaking, disturbing and transcendent God of Jesus Christ.

PART III

Tasks for Local Churches

10

Redemptor Hominis and Ireland

The publication of *Redemptor Hominis* (The Redeemer of Humankind) on 4 March 1979 provided the first extended statement of John Paul II's approach to the papacy and leadership of the Church in the last fifth of this century. He showed himself very conscious of the historic significance of the completion of the second millenium of Christianity. This attitude to the future and to the concrete demands of history on Christian faith and practice indicate something of the Pope's vigorous commitment to a genuinely incarnate Christianity. Yet it was Christ in his role as redeemer, and the mystery of redemption rather than simply that of incarnation, which he chose to place at the centre of his thinking and direction.

Redemption, or at least this particular expression, has faded somewhat from the forefront of Catholic and Christian thinking and writing. There is, for example, no article on redemption in that standard summary of contemporary Catholic theology, edited by Karl Rahner, the one-volume edition of *Sacramentum Mundi*, published as *An Encyclopedia of Catholic Theology*. The term does not figure prominently in the Council documents. Of course the basic doctrine is described in the Bible and Church documents by a variety of other terms such as salvation, very much the mode-word of the sixties in such phrases as 'salvation-history' but increasingly replaced in the seventies by their own mode-word of 'liberation'. There are many such biblical words describing the achievement for humankind which God accomplished in Jesus Christ. They express different nuances of that achievement and would find some eras more congenial than others. All of them insist on the futility to which humankind is subjected, as the encyclical expresses it (§8, quoting Rom. 8:20), the condition of human weakness and sinfulness, and the divine initiative and power by which humankind is rescued from this futility or enslavement. The changing expressions for the divine rescue activity in no way diminish the sense of human weakness and sinfulness. It would be fair to add that Pope John Paul II shows a more realistic grasp of the pervasiveness and depth of the evil affecting humanity than say Vatican II's exciting and visionary Constitution on the Church in the Modern World (*Gaudium et Spes*) from which he quotes so frequently and so approvingly. It is, no doubt, partly this awareness which influenced him in his choice of the sobering view of Christ as redeemer to shape his first programmatic statement to the Church.

Despite the very precise title, the Pope does not attend, even in the briefest fashion, to the conventional dimensions of redemption and redeemer, deriving from their linguistic background of buying back. He leaves aside such easily misunderstood language and debate for other biblically based models with greater potential for helping contemporary Christians and others to grasp more clearly and more fully the heart of this mystery of redemption. Such images and models as new creation and human fulfilment offer better hope of recognising and understanding the divine activity of redemption through Jesus Christ, which is at work in every person and every society today.

The concern of this reflection on the encyclical is not as universal as all that. Irish people and Irish society as they are in need of, open to, and receptive of God's redeeming activity, constitute more defined, if still very elusive, subjects for analysis in the light of the encyclical. Increasingly theologians are beginning to learn the lesson, which John Paul also emphasises (§11), that the Christian mysteries must be related to concrete, historical people; they are not simply to be accepted and somehow applied but have to find their own particular incarnation and understanding. A simply universal, trans-cultural, non-historical theology would not be genuinely Christian theology. The universal dimension of Christianity is founded on the concrete historical particularity of a single person, Jesus Christ. Jesus of Nazareth must become the Jesus of Maynooth or Miami if he is to be understood, accepted, lived with and lived out in authentic discipleship in diverse places and times. The challenge to maintain continuity within such discontinuity, unity within such diversity, remains permanent for the Church. The attempt here to mediate between a statement directed to the universal Church, at least of a particular time, and the very particular situation of Ireland at this time is a partial response to that challenge and part of the continuing task of theology.

What is intended, therefore, is not a complete commentary on a complete text, even from an Irish perspective. It is more an attempt to initiate a dialogue between papal thinking and the Irish situation. It hopes to have the encyclical question and challenge Irish people in their situation and let the Irish situation in turn question and challenge the papal message. It is this kind of interchange and dialogue (§4) deriving from particular human experiences (§13) which promotes development in faith and understanding in both the local and universal Churches.

Redemption as New Creation

In chapter two of the encyclical (§§7–12), Pope John Paul expounds 'The Mystery of the Redemption'. Paragraph 8 in that chapter is entitled 'Redemption as a New Creation'. The theme of new creation, explicitly derived from Paul's Epistle to the Romans (Chapter 8) and Vatican II's *Gaudium et Spes*, permeates the whole encyclical and seems to me a very accurate formulation of the Pope's thinking. He indulges in no Manichean rejection of the world but dwells on and rejoices in the goodness of creation. Creation, however, including humankind, has been subjected to futility, a futility revealed even more effectively by the progress of modern time as illustrated by 'the threat of pollution of the natural environment in areas of rapid industrialisation or the armed conflicts continually breaking out over and over again or the perspectives of self-destruction through the use of atomic, hydrogen, neutron and similar weapons, or the lack of respect for the life of the unborn. The world of the new age, the world of space flights, the world of the previously unattained conquests of science and technology—is it not also the world "groaning in travail" that "waits with eager longing for the revealing of the sons of God" ' (§8).

It is through the life, death and resurrection of Jesus Christ that this futility has been overcome. A transformation of the poisoned and destructive relationships within humankind and the cosmos has been achieved so that one can speak of a renewal of creation, a re-creation or a new creation. For in him the Father found 'the fullness of justice in a human heart—the heart of the first-born Son—in order that it may become justice in the hearts of many human beings' (§9). This is achieved by the unity of Jesus Christ with each and every man so that all may become children of God. The God of creation who is 'faithful to himself' and so 'to his love for humanity and the world, which he revealed on the day of creation' develops 'a love that does not draw back from anything that justice requires in him', a love 'greater than sin, than weakness, than "the futility of creation . . ."' In human history this revelation of love and mercy has taken a form and a name: that of Jesus Christ' (§9).

The new creation of humankind in love reveals the true meaning of the human, its worth and dignity in daughterhood and sonship of the Father. Such revelation issues not only in 'adoration of God but also [in] deep wonder at humanity'. 'The name for that deep amazement at [human] worth and dignity is the gospel, that is to say: the good news.' It is also called Christianity. This amazement determines the Church's mission in the world and, perhaps even more so, 'in the modern world' (§10). But without love the human person remains incomprehensible. The futility to which the unloving intellect is subject becomes meaninglessness or absurdity. The new creation in redemption is also a creation of new meaning, significance and truth of and for humankind (§10).

In meaning, in personal relationships and in structured social existence, every person is re-created through Jesus Christ and his Spirit which has been given to us. Divisions and barriers of all kinds within persons and societies and between them have been overcome. The Church, as the explicit community of Jesus' disciples, becomes, as Pope John Paul repeatedly quotes from Vatican II's Constitution on the Church (*Lumen Gentium*), 'a sacrament or sign and means of intimate union with God, and of the unity of all mankind' (§3, §7).

New Creation and Irish Divisions

The richness of Christian themes such as new creation and the ultimate unity in the one God of all the divine redemptive mysteries is apt to become overwhelming, no matter how one tries to confine one's reflections. All this immensely complicates the task of establishing dialogue between the Pope's exposition

160

of the theme and the actual Irish situation. The complexity of the situation further compounds the difficulties. Stark choices have to be made; drastic simplifications endured. It is the way of all dialogue, all verbal exchange. The power of the word is undeniable but it rests partly on its capacity to focus experience or thought, and so simplify it. It suffers the inevitable limitations of its strength.

Choosing to focus on Irish divisions in the context of Christian redemption is scarcely a major surprise. Although it is important not to allow revulsion against the latest atrocity to obscure one's judgment, the decade of strife born of Irish divisions which the island has endured reveals very powerfully and very particularly the futility to which Irish people and Irish society are subjected and from which they are in urgent need of redemption. I cannot think of a more suitable phrase for that redemption in current Irish terms than 'a new creation'. Unless there is a new creation, the chaos will continue and the Spirit will be ineffective. 'Chaos' seems a strong word but again it is hard to think of one more appropriate to the increasing disarray in the attitudes, patterns of behaviour and structures of relationship, personal and social, of Irish society. The attitudes of republican and unionist, Catholic and Protestant, politically interested and politically apathetic, include elements of fear and distrust, hatred and rejection of the other, despair at the continuance of all these, and recurring, if diminishing, hopes of breaking out of them. The unpredictable and terrifying violence of the paramilitaries in which the republican brand has clearly taken the lead, as well as the more predictable but frequently discriminatory response of the military and police, foster the chaos in feeling and attitude and in any thoughts of a political solution. The structural relationships within Northern Ireland continue to reflect the siege-mentality of the more powerful and privileged unionist and Protestant groups and the resentful, rejecting mind of the more-deprived republican and Catholic groups. The introduction of direct rule and the abolition of Stormont have contributed to the unionist sense of inferiority and dependence, to resentment at the English precisely because of their own perceived loyalty to and need of Britain. The official British response to the situation that Ulster or Northern Ireland is an integral part of the United Kingdom is seriously weakened by a sometimes barely concealed contempt for the barbarity of these Irish who insist on fighting among themselves. The low priority which the Irish question holds in British politics confirms this.

Relations between Northern Ireland and the Republic, and between the Republic and Britain are no less confused and chaotic. So many people in Northern Ireland dismiss the Republic as a backward state dominated by the Catholic Church. Yet they tend to visit the Republic much more than citizens from the Republic go north, enjoying the more liberal and friendly atmosphere of Dublin and various Irish holiday resorts. They identify strongly with the Irish rugby team and whether they are Catholics or Protestants of republican or unionist background are often confused about their identity and ambivalent about their Irish and British loyalties. People in the Republic are appalled at the violence and yet at least some of them in some secret part of themselves do not really feel totally condemnatory of the killing of British soldiers. Many, perhaps all, would at some abstract level welcome a united Ireland and yet fear it and are frequently unwilling to take any self-sacrificing steps to promote it peacefully.

The Republic's relationship with Britain is no less confusing. The image of 'ancient enemy' has never entirely disappeared from the Irish mind and it tends to find certain English attitudes overbearing or patronising, exhibiting the 'Paddy' syndrome. Yet the cultural, economic, political, legal as well as geographic bonds are enormous. Free movement between the two islands, which amounts in many practical ways to dual citizenship, a large Irish-born population living and working in Britain and a significant if small British minority living in the Republic make for easy and generally friendly contact between the peoples of the two islands. However, in times of stress the old antagonisms and distrust re-surface. The residual Irish feeling of having been oppressed and of being still to some extent despised, as well as the English feeling that the Irish tend to be drunken, lazy and scroungers off the generous British social welfare system, contribute to the ambivalence and confusion which have been reinforced by the events of the last ten years.

Of course the Churches have not escaped the confusion and chaos. Although Irish people and a more informed wider audience do not identify the struggle in primarily religious terms, much of world opinion does. In terms of damage to the witness of Christianity and to Irish people's missionary involvement and aspirations, the home Churches may not dismiss such an impression. This is all the more applicable in that Church affiliation or identification plays a definite role in the origin and continuance of division and strife. The Churches, which claim to be mediators of redemption and new creation, are at least partially responsible for the 'subjection to futility' and 'chaos' which affect Irish people, north and south. In so far as they do, they are themselves in need of redeeming and re-creating. Instead of being signs of the unity of believers and of all humankind as this encyclical insists, they have for too long been signs and even realisations of the disunity and destructive division of the Irish people.

The need and the urgency of a re-creation of hearts, relationships and structures in the historical situation, of the redemption of Ireland in history, must first be discerned and accepted before the creative and redemptive process can begin. A major part of the human difficulty in finding redemption is the unwillingness to recognise the need for it. While unionists can blame republicans for refusing to accept Northern Ireland as part of the United Kingdom and for attempting to change things by force, and while republicans can blame unionists for holding on to exclusive power and using it oppressively, and while both can blame Britain for refusing to face its responsibilities to govern or to withdraw, and Britain can blame both for refusing to agree on a solution, hopes of a political re-creation are nil. This is reinforced by the failure of the heralds and bearers of redemption, the Churches, in face of their responsibility, to give a lead in acknowledging their weakness and need for redemption. A common acknowledgment of that by Irish Church leaders and their followers seems the first requirement in preparing for the creative and redemptive activity of Christ and the Spirit. It could be that the visit of Pope John Paul II whose papal programme has been fashioned in terms of Christ as redeemer of humankind would be the occasion for opening Irish hearts and minds to their real condition and urgent need.

Such acknowledgment and openness at Church level will have to proceed patiently and persistently. The effective Christian leaders of any era are those who are sensitive to the historical conditions, and open to the workings of the Spirit as he seeks to renew the face of the earth and, in this context, that tiny blob of it, the island of Ireland.

163

The acknowledgment of failure and indeed of helplessness is not in Christian terms a collapse into despair but a beginning of hope. The initial steps devised by Alcoholics Anonymous in acknowledging one's problems, one's inability to handle them alone and need for help from some higher power, have deeply Christian roots and much wider application to individuals and groups, including the individuals and groups who constitute the Irish Churches. Until the Irish Churches attain the humility displayed by members of AA they will continue to be barriers to, rather than mediators of, the creative work of the Spirit. He will be forced to brood unfruitfully over the chaos of Irish waters.

In the shared spirit of humility they may dare to hope for the slow process of re-creation and redemption to begin. For it is a social redemption that is required to realise, in the fresh and apt phrase of the encyclical, that 'social love' which will liberate us from our present futility (§5). But the hope of social redemption and social love must be carefully nurtured. Creation even in biblical terms was accomplished by God through stages and over time (Gen. 1:2). In the scientific view of evolution, the time scale and the successive changes are even more clearly emphasised.

The Paradoxes of New Creation

In seeking to understand, be open to and promote new creation out of Irish chaos, the paradoxes of the process quickly appear. The relation of time and creation, just mentioned, is but one. Our traditional view of the divine activity saw it as timeless and in that sense instantaneous, although it had to be worked out in time, as we said, due to creaturely limitations. A more thoughtful consideration of creator and creature relationships as experienced in the faith of Israel and then in Christian faith, would have recognised how the creator, God himself, enters into the historical condition and humankind in his gradual wooing of human hearts, his sensitive, time-conscious transformation of human attitudes and structures. The writings of the Old Testament continually recount the loving gradualness of Yahweh's approach to his people in teaching and forming them as his people. The patient caring of Jesus in the formation of his disciples in face of their thoughtless ambition and eventual cowardice, reveals more clearly still the divine strategy in search

164

of new creation of Israel or creation of new Israel, reflecting the Genesis accounts of primary creation.

New creation takes time. It is a historical process, precisely out of divine respect for the human historical condition. And in that time dimension lies both its challenge and its excitement. The once-for-all historical events of Jesus Christ provide the model and the source for the continuous and universal events in every era, among every people, and in every human heart. The process has been initiated by the gift of the Spirit. It has been initiated in Ireland and Britain in each new generation. Yet it remains frustrated, subject to futility in critical and destructive ways. The challenge is to liberate it, to let it take its course, to let the Spirit loose. By savage irony the Churches, claiming the power to bind and loose on earth as in heaven, are helping to bind the Spirit or at best not letting him loose effectively. The excitement is in the loosing of the Spirit, in the historical development of his creative initiative. Such a new creation is never complete, always open to further development, always beckoning into the future. The temptation of instant solutions to which Jesus was also subject, if kneeling down he would adore the demon, is always very strong for the menaced humanity to which the encyclical is so sensitive (§16). Instant solutions lack roots in time. Instant achievement leading to instant satisfaction tends to be followed in the next instant by new dissatisfaction, calling for another instant solution. It reflects the childish need for immediate gratification turned into a way of life in the consumer society. Filling the void or overcoming the chaos by instant solutions usually leads to new void and new chaos, but above all it fails to grapple with the time-laden condition of humankind and the genuine and exciting possibilities of that condition. To take time seriously is to take it creatively, to see it as the basis for profound human growth, transformation and achievement.

The 'not an inch' and 'no surrender' of some unionists and the 'United Ireland now' and 'British withdrawal now' of some republicans, ignore the realities and possibilities of time. 1979 is not 1912 or 1916. Past solutions belong to another time and, like instant solutions, attempt to escape the threat and gift of time. Only in time can a new creation, a really transforming human solution be found. But there is no time to be wasted on recalling and defending formalised and now out-of-time past solutions.

Those who really wish Irish people to live in real peace and unity, the new creation on offer, have to accept the challenge and possibilities of time, in the manner of Jesus and his Father.

The manner of Jesus and his Father, which went to the extremes of taking on the human condition in its fullness in redemptive incarnation, illustrates further paradoxes of the divine-human creative relationships. By entering fully into human history as a human being, God carried his sensitive loving of the human other to the point of self-emptying and surrender (Phil. 2:6 ff.). It is the summons of the other and our response in self-surrender, loving them as Jesus loves us (John 13:34), which reveals the depths of our call and response in the realisation of new creation.

As republican and unionist, Protestant and Catholic, we are impeding the new creative activity of God, failing to follow the divine example, in so far as we are unwilling to be open to, receptive of, indeed to surrender to the others. 'No surrender' on either side is the very antithesis of Christian discipleship and it leads into the heart, the demonic heart of our situation, the idolatrous deification of power, political and economic, civil and even religious.

The idolatry of power, of control of the others by civil or religious leaders, was another aspect of Jesus' temptations and one against which he specifically warned his disciples. They were not to lord it over the others as the Gentiles do. The kingly service, to borrow the encyclical's phrase (§21), to which Christians and their leaders are called, offers a creative alternative to the powers and principalities of this world. In the post-Constantinian Church we are slowly (historically) learning that lesson and being liberated from the enslavement of power through self-surrender and service.

Such liberation and new creation take, as always, time. But a start must be made and a lead given in a situation as destructive as ours. In Christian perspective that lead should come from the Churches, the communities of professed Christians and their leaders. The openness to the others leading to self-emptying and loving service in imitation of the Master, requires thought and care, but most of all conviction and commitment. Protestant-Catholic relations have, as far as human judgment can discern, hitherto lacked conviction and commitment. They had more the appearance of political manoeuvre and power play, analogous to Salt II or Middle East negotiations, even if they were not simply a public relations exercise. Power and pretence are basic enemies of the conviction and commitment needed to realise mutual acceptance, surrender and service. We Irish Christians do not seem to have learned that lesson yet. Conviction and commitment have to be expressed carefully and thoughtfully. Instant ecumenical solutions are no more possible than instant political solutions. They all belong within the time-conditioned achievement of new creation. The care and thoughtfulness will, however, focus first on the other, not on the self. Catholics must be first of all sensitive to the realities and needs of Protestants, Protestants to the realities and needs of Catholics. Each side will look in turn to the resources it has, to meet in faith and hope and love the needs of the others. This will be a slow, painstaking, time-laden process. But again there is no time to be lost in recriminations about the past or haggling about the future. Christianity is not about a *quid pro quo*. It is about self-giving in love which undoubtedly carries the hope, but only the hope, that the other will be moved and transformed in turn by love. Christians cannot wait upon guarantees of return. That is how they help humankind to break out of the self-protective and so self-destructive barriers with which individuals and groups surround themselves. There is no salvation, no redemption, no new creation behind the barriers, be they political or religious. Unless the professed Christians give a lead in their inter-Church relations, to whom will men turn? (Jn 6:68).

The care and thoughtfulness of Jesus and the Father were expressed in continuing courtesy to individuals and groups, particularly the socially rejected, like harlots and publicans. The caring courtesy manifest in dealing with the Samaritan woman or the woman taken in adultery illustrate the continuing divine courtesy of him who stands at the gate and knocks, seeking admission to our hearts and worlds. The courtesy of God is grace. His graciousness in seeking us out, in coming to where we are, offers some guidelines to the Churches. They will seek out the others in the same thoughtful, gracious way, endeavouring over time to understand more fully, accept more deeply, in a creative process that leads to genuine surrender to the presence of God in these others. The long-term yet urgent task of redeeming and re-creating the Churches in their relations with one another requires concrete demonstration now. Would it be too much for them to acknowledge together this need for redemption and new creation in the light of the Pope's visit? Would the Catholic Church lose anything of its Christian character in entering into the pain and resentments its attitude and practice in inter-Church or mixed marriages cause many Protestants? If these Churches are, as Vatican II proclaims, really Churches, communities of Christian believers and vehicles of salvation for their members, does the Catholic Church have to insist that it is bound by divine law in regard to the Catholic upbringing of their children, when exceptions are already made elsewhere and undoubtedly on the basis that divine redeeming grace is also present in the Churches of the Reformation? Despite the difficulties involved in this and other inter-Church enterprises, have we, in the terms used by the Pope in precisely this ecumenical context, 'the right not to' (§6)? Should the Protestant Churches not finally break their connection with the Orange Order and clearly condemn the debasing political religion of Ian Paisley and his followers? Would not a joint prayer and peace centre, sponsored officially by the four major Churches and financed by them, be a fitting monument to the new relationships demanded of them?

There are so many other exciting possibilities open to the Churches to join together in releasing the Spirit in promotion of the new creation of which all Irish people are in such urgent need. The urgency of letting the process begin is so great that immediate announcement of some concrete agreements is imperative. And it would be an appropriate response to the gracious visit of Pope John Paul.

Politics and New Creation

Although new creation might appear the best and even the only possible description for a solution to the British-Irish, unionist-republican political difficulties, it may also appear unreal at least as far as the means of achieving it are concerned. A re-creation of inter-Church relationships would almost certainly have a liberating effect on the overall political stalemate. Yet how far do love and patience, self-giving and surrender provide any guidelines for political activity? And is it not precisely the power which Jesus condemned, its possession, distribution and use which must lie at the heart of the political difficulties and must be at the heart of their political solution? How far is the encyclical or similar Christian discussion relevant to the politics of Northern Ireland?

There can be no entirely satisfactory answer to these questions because we live in the era of hope of, not completion of, the new creation. For those who do not really accept Christianity no intelligible answer along these lines is possible at all.

The very hope of new creation raises our eyes to the prospect of new horizons so that we may no longer be confined by the past and now largely irrelevant visions of a stagnant republicanism or unionism. The possibility and hope of such a new vision will become effective as the dim outlines of it appear. The worth and dignity of every human person as expressed in creation and confirmed in the incarnation and redemption, a constant theme of the encyclical and the Church's gospel, must figure prominently in that outline. The social, historical identity which each person enjoys and cherishes must be understood and respected. The limitations of that identity, the shadow side of it as inherited or fostered, will only fade in the light of justice and love which reflect and realise the gracious courtesy of the Father. The further protection or promotion of that limited and warped identity by holding or seeking power through the violence of revolution or of repression will only yield to the respecting and enduring love of the others in their actuality and potential. It is that respecting and enduring love which promotes the true identity and fulfilment of threatening and threatened. And we are all both. In his letter from a Birmingham jail Martin Luther King tells of an old black woman who during a bus-boycott continued daily her tired and foot-sore walks amid the jeers of white observers. She explained: 'My feets is tired but my soul is at rest.' And patient walking emancipated not only the oppressed blacks in the South but also many of the oppressing whites.

The patient, respectful, non-violent way is the only way for Christians committed to love and justice to promote the new creation. But they must be committed. Such advice without actual engagement is likely to be no more than a plea for the protection of one's own comfortable ways. The way of new creation is long and difficult. The instant and violent solutions do not share in its radical and enduring character. The history of Ireland's violent failures on both sides provides some insight into

169

that. Time must be respected by human beings, as it is respected by God.

For all the patient endurance involved, the way of new creation can also be exciting and rewarding. Delicate openings, acceptances, transformations and emancipations are open to discovery which the trampling rush of violence destroys and frustrates. Exciting and enriching aspects of the others become accessible for the first time. The interaction of these ways provides the creative spark which leads to fuller and more refined transformation. The prospect of the Irish people really discovering one another over the next twenty years offers new life in a near hopeless situation. Such discovery with its gradual removal of fears and establishment of trust would begin to release each side from the tyranny of power, the demonic, idolised power to which they resort in their fear and self-interest. New ways of self-government would be devised and the power-struggle eventually resolved.

Further elaboration is possible and necessary. But it is best done by those who recognise their Christian vocation to engage in preparing and promoting the new creation of Irish society in the graciously divine manner revealed in Jesus Christ. It is an urgent vocation for Christians in Ireland today. Some of them must consciously and explicitly devote themselves to it. All Irish Christians must participate in it in various ways. Perhaps a new inter-Church clerical and lay ministry, a quasi-religious order is called for which will lead the way for the Churches and politicians. Unless some people make it their particular business now, it will never start or start much too late.

Human Fulfilment and Church

The new creation which the encyclical highlights as realisations of the redemptive activity of Jesus Christ, constitutes a primary responsibility for the Churches. Their mission in the Irish situation must be to grapple with the futility and frustration and menace as I have indicated. Their manner of mission is to be that of Jesus Christ, and of the Father who sent Jesus Christ, and of the Spirit sent by him. That manner, as I already noted, was to seek out, accept and even surrender to humankind. The direction of the divine mission is to humanity, each and every man and the whole man. The direction of the Church's mission must also be to each and every man and to the whole man

170

(§13ff.). Its purpose is the fullness of unity of each human being with Christ, the growing realisation of adoptive sonship and daughterhood of the Father, whether in the explicit Christian faith of the believing community or in the implicit faith employed by all authentically religious people and indeed by all even of good will (§13, §14). The further criterion of that Church mission and unity with Christ and divine daughterhood and sonship, is the fuller realisation of authentic humanity (§14, §15). Pope John Paul endorses very strongly the contemporary understanding of incarnation and redemption, with its historical and biblical roots, as the realisation, restoration and new creation of the human person, first of all in history and society and then eschatologically in the fullness of the kingdom (§13ff.). The kingly service to which the Church is called, which is another description of its mission, is the promotion of the more fully human in person, relationship and structure. Such a clear exposition of the Church's union and service should remove any doubts about the Pope's attitude to the Church's engagement in the promotion of social justice, human rights and political freedom. His expanded treatment of these topics confirms and develops the Council's document on 'The Church in the Modern World' and the 1971 Synod of Bishops' 'Justice in the World'. One of his striking images for the redemption achieved in Jesus Christ is that the Father found the fullness of justice in a human heart (§9). He speaks of the divine love, source of human love, as that which does whatever justice sees as necessary and, to repeat another of his striking phrases, he speaks of the 'social love' which clearly goes beyond personal loving or any restrictive idea of social justice (§5). There is much in this for the Irish Church and Irish society to meditate on, assimilate and apply. There are still too many Irish people deprived of the opportunities of human fulfilment which should be the concrete expression of their redemption. Too many Irish Catholics and other Christians are indifferent to the fate of others, particularly those physically, mentally and socially deprived. This very indifference precludes for the indifferent the human fulfilment available in Jesus Christ. Indifference and lack of human fulfilment may not be entirely overcome in time. But the task of the Church is to seek to overcome them in time or at least to give a lead in this respect. The Irish Church will examine carefully privation and indifference in Irish society, the degrading

171

poverty and offensive affluence now so evident in such close proximity, seek their origins and attempt to eradicate them. That calls for an even stronger social awareness than Church leaders have in various ways been recently manifesting. It calls still more for an acting out of that awareness in solidarity with the poor and deprived, and in prophetic awakening of the affluent and indifferent. Consciousness of the much wider world needs which has been increasing recently in Ireland must be further developed and given greater realisation in action. Ireland is by world standards a wealthy country materially and educationally. It must endeavour to share that material and educational wealth more broadly and more effectively. Such activity and sharing will express a new phase of the world mission of Irish Church and people.

Irish Mission and Irish Theology

The gospel as redemptive truth has to be understood and explored anew in different eras and cultures. Developing human experience (§13, §19), as the Pope puts it, challenges us to develop in understanding the gospel. Such is the task of theology. Where that task is neglected and theology stagnates, the gospel loses its redemptive power and the mission of the Church stagnates. It would be too much to say that Irish theology and theologians have been effectively engaged in this task over a long period. There are historical and social excuses to be offered. They may be offered with good conscience in regard to earlier generations, but are scarcely convincing today. The poverty of Irish theology is undoubtedly to the shame of the Irish Churches. The signs of that poverty are striking. The limited opportunities available for Irish theological work, which has been totally excluded for seventy years from the dominant National University system, may be the most striking. The meagre number of people engaged in theological work, their limited training and resources, and the limitations of time and encouragement under which they work, combined with the (necessary) emigration of some of the few excellent people, has stunted the growth of a vital theological community. The heavy but necessary dependence on foreign scholars and ideas for new thinking encourages a suspicion of theology which further restricts the development of a native tradition. And so the Church suffers in its mission sometimes in comfortable

172

unconsciousness of its own privations. Some of the need for redemption and new creation of Irish Churches and society derives from the lack of a vital and creative theology. Theology and theologians are no less in need of redemption than the rest of the Church and society. Church mission must include the revitalisation of a theology which can in turn contribute to new creation in Ireland.

A concrete expression of that Church mission in the Irish situation would be inter-Church collaboration in the development of theology. The Protestant Churches are no less theologically impoverished than the Catholic Church. Such inter-Church efforts would make better use of limited resources. More importantly they would embody ecumenical conviction, commitment and contact in the search for the liberating truth of the gospel in Irish conditions. If and when new university departments of theology are established, attention must be paid to this need. Meantime, Maynooth, Trinity College and Assembly College, Belfast, should provide continuous and effective participation by scholars and students of other Churches in their theological programmes. The Church character of theology does not exclude such collaboration. Vatican II's recognition of these Churches as Churches sharing the Christian faith has not really been fully understood or accepted yet. Certainly Church unity is not yet with us. It remains our duty to seek that unity and to acknowledge how much of it already exists. The reversal by Vatican II of the Counter-Reformation attitude to other Churches and the admission that the Catholic Church is always in need of reform, provide the stimulus and justification for collaborative reflection on and exploration of the faith we share with other Churches—the task of theology.

The Catholic theological tradition carried on in Catholic universities and faculties of theology has already been enriched by the work within the faculties themselves of scholars from other traditions. They help the Catholic tradition to recover some of what it lost in the historical divisions and the, historically understandable if very defensive, reactions to them. They help to prevent the Catholic tradition from making some of the mistakes made by their own, for example, by the liberal Protestant theology of the nineteenth century. And they provide a broader base in confronting the challenges of a future society as it grows tired of or indifferent to religion or to particular

173

Church expressions and organisations of it. These positive features are evident in the work of the Catholic Department of Theology at the Catholic University of Notre Dame in the US. They may be more applicable and are certainly more urgently needed at Maynooth and Assembly College, Belfast.

From Advent to Pentecost

The liturgical and theological period which dominates *Redemptor Hominis* is that of Advent. The Pope applies this in particular to the advent of the year 2000, the second millenium. But it has deeper roots in the document as a whole. The Pope's clear and enthusiastic approval of Vatican II would no doubt share the vision of it by Pope John XXIII and the Church as a whole as a new Pentecost. And Pentecost is both a completion and a beginning—of the redemption in Jesus Christ and the beginning of the Church and its redemptive task, the ending of the first phase of realising the kingdom and the waiting upon the second and final phase. For the Christians of the first Pentecost, the advent, the coming again of Jesus in glory was decisive. It was for that they waited and hoped. It was for that they laboured and preached. The mission activity into which Pentecost ushered them was also the prayerful waiting upon the final coming. The paradoxes of Pentecost and Advent are always with us. Sometimes the paradox is more clearly signalled by the Spirit. This encyclical provides such a signal. The spirit poured out at Vatican II demands active expression and patient prayer as we face the historical climax of the year 2000. It might indeed be seen as another Pentecost, to issue in the transforming activity and prayerful patience that are key to the new creation which is our only hope.

11
Church and State in Ireland

Historical Background

The topic of Church and State in Ireland has been written about from so many different angles and by so many interested and disinterested parties that it might appear entirely worn out. Historical works like those of John Whyte, David Miller and Emmet Larkin have created a remarkable background for discussing the tangled relations that developed over the past hundred years and more. Yet for all the scholarly historical background, there remains a lack of analysis of the kind one might expect from a theologian or a political scientist. This chapter then is directed towards a theological analysis of the relationships.

A theological analysis has to take account of the historical situation and of the changes in that situation. These include the movement from dependence on Britain to independence in the south, the continuance of the union between Northern Ireland and Britain, the consequent interactions between the Republic, Northern Ireland and Britain. All have a bearing on church/state relationships. Indeed, the present crisis centred in Northern Ireland has definite church/state dimensions. For all the assertions by religious leaders that this is basically a political conflict, the religious dimension complicates political division and reflects a history of church/state relationships over decades and centuries.

The changes I am concerned with here are theological changes, changes in the self-understanding of the Churches, particularly the Roman Catholic Church. As a Catholic I can speak more adequately for that community. As it is the dominant religious community in the Republic and by far the largest in Ireland as a whole, church/state relations as

175

historically discussed have tended to focus on the Catholic Church. To some extent this is misleading. It is misleading historically because the officially recognised church up to 1869 was the Church of Ireland as by law established. Perhaps since then, or at any rate since 1920, the Presbyterian Church of Ireland has enjoyed some of the recognition in the north which the Catholic Church has enjoyed in the south. There are however, theological reasons for not separating the Churches in this discussion. The deeper theological reasons are connected with how the Churches have defined themselves since the Reformation and the Council of Trent. They have defined themselves partly in relation to, or more correctly in opposition to, one another. With the division of the Reformation, particular groups of Christians began to emphasise whatever distinguished them from opposing groups and to suppress certain things held in common with the opposing groups. An obvious example of this in the Catholic tradition was the increased emphasis on ordained ministry of the faithful acquired through baptism. It is only in our time, the last thirty to fifty years that the role of the laity began to emerge in those ministerial terms. Similarly in the Protestant tradition the sacraments were obscured, particularly the Eucharist, in response to what was seen as Catholic emphasis and abuse. In our time, liturgical renewal has brought considerable convergence between the reform tradition and the Catholic tradition. It is not possible then to speak adequately of the Catholic Church as if it were not defined somehow in relation to the Reformation Churches and vice versa. This, of course, has been greatly compounded in Ireland by the political problem whereby the Reformation Churches were associated with the power of Britain and the Catholic Church with the resistance to that power. So for us to talk realistically about church and state in Ireland, one must always keep in mind how far the Catholic Church understood itself in opposition to the Protestant Churches, the Protestant Churches understood themselves in opposition to the Catholic Church and both traditions identified with a particular political stance.

Theological Development

I am supposing then that the changes which occurred in the Catholic Church's self-understanding since 1962 and the

176

contemporary changes in the self-understanding of the other Churches have somehow changed the usual theological presentation of church/state relations in the historical works already noted. John Whyte, for example, offers a concluding analysis in which he rejects the extreme positions of seeing the Republic of Ireland as a theocratic state, basically run by the Roman Catholic Church, or seeing on the other hand the Roman Catholic Church as just another pressure group like the trade unions or the farmer associations.

But he does not offer any more precise analysis than some in-between position (in his first edition). In his second edition he draws on Liam Ryan's interesting article in *The Furrow* (January 1979), where he speaks of the Church as the conscience of society. Suggestive as this article of Ryan's is, it does not seem to me to confront the theological/political problems which the suggestion involves. Is the Church the only conscience of society? Who as Church shall speak for the conscience of society? Is this a task for the bishops only, or bishops and priests, or the laity? Is it an ecumenical task for the Churches working together, or one for the Roman Catholic Church only? On what issues shall this conscience be voiced, on the traditional issues of sexual morality, respect for life in terms of abortion or political violence, on education, or is there a whole wider range of issues? How are these issues discerned? How are conscience judgments formed about them? Who shall listen to this conscience? How shall its judgment be offered or imposed? Yet this idea of the Church as the conscience of society has the merit of focusing on the kind of leadership or service which the Christian community might offer in any society. It, at least on the surface, undermines any particular claim that churchmen are the final arbiters of what counts as acceptable legislation and removes the discussion from the simple context of a power struggle. To do this adequately, however, there must be much further analysis of the Church, its role in society and the expression of that role in various ways. So what I am proposing here is a move from the developed understanding of the Church which we have acquired over the past twenty years, to an assessment of its place in society and its relationship with the political powers.

Church and Kingdom
Two significant moves were made at Vatican II Council

which influenced very considerably the Church's self-understanding. The first of these occurs in the first chapter of the document on the Church. In this first chapter, the emphasis is placed where it primarily and properly belongs, on the mystery of God's presence in the world. This coming of God in the world at his initiative and out of his love has a long history. It took particular shape in the history of Israel. It reached its climax in Jesus Christ. Now it finds expression in the community of Christ's disciples or followers. The importance of beginning the Church here reflects both an upgrading of the Church and a relativising of it. The upgrading attends to the divine initiative. The Church is the sign or sacrament of God's presence in the world. It is the people called by God and empowered by him to respond. It also reflects a certain relativisation. The dependence of the Church on God is underlined. What is also underlined is that this is not the complete presence of God in the world. It is not the kingdom that Jesus came to preach, the kingdom of God's presence and power finally and fully realised. It is a sign of that kingdom, of that presence and power. It is a servant of that kingdom. It is a herald or preacher of that kingdom. It is a partial and ambiguous realisation of that kingdom. The Church is relativised by being sharply distinguished from the kingdom in contemporary teaching. This was not always so. It is not always clearly so even now for people within and without the Church, for people who think the Church must claim to be identical with the final, or at least the historically full presence of God in the world.

The second chapter in the constitution on the Church speaks of the Church as the people of God. It is only in chapter three and subsequent chapters that particular divisions between the people, based on structure and function, emerge. This is a notable overturning of the presentation of the Church so common prior to Vatican II. In these presentations the Church was primarily an institution, a hierarchical institution. Yves Congar used the phrase 'hierarchology' to discuss the study of the Church in these presentations because the Church appeared to be primarily a hierarchy composed of popes and bishops, with a people attached. In an ecclesiology dealing with the ecclesia, or the called people, the people come first. The significance of this for the Church's engagement in society and with the world is not yet completely worked out. We still have many traces of the hierarchology of pre-Vatican II in the way ordinary Church members think of the Church as the bishops or the clergy, in the way bishops and clergy seem to think of themselves as the Church. This is betrayed in phrases such as 'the Church has said' when some bishop or group of bishops has spoken, or 'the Church acts' when we mean the activity of clergy. Yet if the Church is to speak and act effectively out of its resources, its God-given resources, then it must speak and act effectively as a people. We have not yet found the ways and means for the people to speak and act as effectively as they might. Developments of collegiality, as it is called, that is seeing the Church as a group of colleagues collaborating, have become more effective at the level of bishops together or of priests together in priest senates in the diocese, of people and priests in parish councils and of religious in the reorganisation of religious orders. Yet we are very far from having the structure and the motivation which would enable the Church to speak effectively as a people. The implications of this for how the Church speaks and acts in historical society are clear. We do not yet have a totally satisfactory way of enabling the Church in its fullness to speak and act in society.

Church in Society

This people, which is called by God and responds in faith, enjoys a mission in society, that mission we have spoken of already in terms of announcing and serving God's presence and power, God's kingdom. We may attempt to define that presence and power of God as it is operative in history and to give it certain content. That content could be expressed in terms of traditional values and virtues like justice, peace, freedom, love. It could be translated into more precise legal formulations in the language of human rights. It demands, at any rate, attitudes and activities, structures and relationships which reflect the image of God in every human being and the redemptive and transforming work for humanity achieved by God in Jesus Christ. This is not at all to say that somehow society must be incorporated into the Church. That would be to repeat the mistake of medieval times with its union of Church and emperor and its ideal of Christendom. These ideals and partial achievements may have been understandable in their time, but they did involve a basic confusion about establishing the kingdom of God on earth.

In that basic confusion the people, their freedoms and dignity suffered. The most horrendous example of that confusing cooperation was, of course, the institution of the Inquisition. The deeper failure was the failure to remember that the developments of the Church in the empire in the aftermath of the death and resurrection of Jesus Christ created for the empire a very troublesome gap between the people in their total lives and the people simply as members of the empire. The people in their total lives could never be defined again by membership of the empire because that dimension of them which responded to the God of Jesus Christ could not be captured and expressed in imperial terms. This cost Christians much suffering and death. The real thrust of the Church's call to respond to God was to create a duality between Church and the political order which should never be overlooked and could eventually never be overcome. That quality introduced a duality into social life itself. The social life of the members of the empire, or of the citizens of any modern state, is not coterminous with their political life. There is an irreducible gap between person and citizen, between society and state. We have seen this gap, of course, ignored and the citizens suffer in totalitarian regimes around the world in this century from Nazi Germany to Eastern Europe, to South Africa, to Latin America. Yet the gap must be maintained for the sake of the human beings who are citizens but more than that. The obvious symbol of the gap in the Roman Empire was the Church. It has not always lived up to that symbolic vocation.

Church, Kingdom, Society and State:
   In speaking of the relationship between Church and state, we are dealing with four distinct realities. We are dealing with the body of believers we call the Church. We are dealing with the kingdom which that Church must announce and promote in the world at large. We are dealing with the historical society at a particular time within which the world Church exists and which is in its simplest expression the whole range of relationships of a particular people, or in the modern shrinking world, of all people. We are dealing with the political organisation of people in a state. This is no longer a totally independent state, but an inter-dependent state in one way or another, yet a state with certain powers of self-government which it implements through

180

the law. That state and the citizenry that goes with it are not exhaustive of the society of which it is the political expression. The people and their relationships in society are richer, deeper and more extensive than their particular political structures, organisations, aspirations. As a footnote, one might say that in the nation state as it developed in the nineteenth and twentieth centuries when the nation, as a description of the people, wished to identify itself narrowly with the state, there was a danger of oppressing minorities who did not belong to the majority nation. Where the nation becomes fully politicised there is always a diminution of the citizenry. This diminution may occur only in emergency because of the many safeguards in a modern democratic state, but it can occur. The person who will not follow the flag or support country or nation, right or wrong, is readily seen as anti-Irish or anti-American. It is also part of the believing community's role to refuse to let the gap between society and state be closed by an idolatrous nationalism.

Historically and theologically the emergence of the Church has underlined the gap between society at large and its political organisation in the state, between the person and the citizen. It is on this basis that we have developed in Western politics a range of civil and political rights which, we say, the state does not grant, cannot take away, but should guarantee and protect. Another way of putting it would be to say that the first of these rights in historical and theological terms is the right to freedom of religion. In saying this, I am not maintaining that in countries where the Christian Church does not exist or is not effective such rights disappear. Neither am I saying that the Church and its existence has always ensured the maintenance of that space between society and the political within which such personal rights might survive and flourish. However, whether we look at contemporary Poland or medieval Christendom, the maintenance or disappearance of the gap between state and society has always been related to how church and state have interacted. In much of medieval Christendom that gap disappeared because the Church, the religious organisation, was elided into or absorbed the political organisation. The Holy Roman Empire may have had two swords and two heads, but the collaboration and coordination that existed, or at least was expected to exist, between them effectively excluded the gap within which the distinction between person and citizen might survive. So the

181

heretic very easily became treasonable. In contemporary Poland as distinct from so much of the eastern Socialist bloc, the vigorous presence of the Church has helped the people in some measure to define themselves as larger than the party, larger than citizens or subjects of an all-embracing government. That definition is given very practical expression in recent events. The Church's basic role in society is to continue the preaching and work of Jesus Christ in announcing, promoting and, to some extent embodying, the kingdom of God. By kingdom of God, we mean the presence and power of God as it enters into the shape of our human world, enters into it as judgment upon it, as challenge to it, as empowerment of it, to achieve the kind of human fulfilment for which God has destined his creatures. The reign of God we are talking about, therefore, takes shape in human beings, in human relationships, in social and historical structures, even as it took place, its inaugurating place, in the person of Jesus Christ, his relationships, attitudes and inter-actions with the structures.

The Church exists, therefore, for the kingdom in society. It must announce that gracious coming and presence and power of God. It must announce this in terms that have social and historical meaning. It must announce the attitudes and the values, the relationships and the structures, which correspond to the love of God embodied in Jesus Christ, a love that relates us to our ultimate origin and destiny and relates us to that origin and destiny by relating us to one another.

The Irish Experience

In the Irish situation, as in so many other situations, the distinctions between church, kingdom, society and state are frequently obscured, with serious loss to all four realities and to the Irish people as a whole, North and South. The demand so frequently heard in the past in Northern Ireland for a Protestant state for a Protestant people, and scarcely modified in some contemporary slogans, clearly collapses the basic distinction between church and state. En route it associates to the point of near-identity the people or society and the state, so that a particular cultural, ethnic and religious group dominates society and constitutes the state to the exclusion of another cultural, religious and ethnic group. That dominant association of Protestant people with Unionist party and Northern Ireland

182

state inevitably entailed discrimination for the Catholic minority. The complex problems of how far that minority withdrew or was excluded and where the original blame for either should be laid do not concern this article. What does concern it is that the Protestant Churches were unable to keep alive the critical distinction between society and state so that neither should be readily identified with their particular Churches. In that situation the distinctions of church and kingdom largely disappeared and with it the judgment and challenge which the kingdom as the emerging presence and power of God offers the Church.

The Catholic Church was drawn by these historical forces into closer alignment with the nationalist cause and also exposed to the risk of ignoring the basic distinctions. At hierarchical level in the nineteenth and twentieth centuries the Catholic Church did not consistently or even predominantly support nationalist movements for independence, certainly not those advocating or using violence. Reaction to the Fenians, IRB and the modern IRA confirms that. With the establishment of the Free State/Republic in twenty-six counties the church leaders, by a process of osmosis well described in John Whyte's book, became more closely, if informally, associated with government leaders. Such contacts, mainly informal, did not consciously and overtly influence much of the legislative and administrative activity of the new state. The occasional crisis as in the 1951 Health Act incident, did not, for all the misjudgments of the hierarchy, weakness of the government and self-interest of the medical profession, establish any clear-cut evidence of simple power-seeking by the bishops in the legislative process. What it did reveal was something which many much less dramatic events had frequently suggested, that what the Catholic Church leaders seemed to want was not a Catholic state for a Catholic people but a Catholic society, that is, a society whose ethos was informed by Catholic values. The references to 'this Catholic country' or to 'Catholic Ireland' were never simply reducible to the demand for a Catholic state with the Catholic Church established as the one true Church, although there were movements such as Maria Duce and various clerical and lay commentators who sought these goals. The aim of Catholic leaders was more a certain kind of society with definite attitudes, customs and structures, including legal structures.

183

Towards a Catholic Society

In promotion of this society or in the preservation of it, as some bishops and priests with a selective view of the past would put it, family and school were key structures and attracted the bulk of church attention and energy. The gaps in this attention as evident, for example, in the reluctance to support the first Adoption Bill (1952) or in the slow response to the need for sexual and premarital education did not take from the overall intent and the range of services provided. Indeed, without the church schools and hospitals much greater gaps would have occurred in the services available to the people.

This goal of a certain kind of society, spoken or unspoken, among church leaders, was shared in varying degrees by many people and many political leaders. With the legislators it occasionally translated into protective and preventive legislation as with the Censorship Act of 1929, the Criminal Law Amendment Act of 1935 (outlawing the importation and sale of contraceptives) and the prohibition against introducing divorce legislation in the 1937 Constitution. Yet church attention was never primarily focused on legislation over the decades, and state legislation was never primarily focused on the promotion or preservation of the Catholic ethos. The positive interaction between church goals, the social understanding and wishes of so many people and the particular policies and legal provisions of the government were much more complex, subtle and largely unspoken.

Any theological evaluation of attempts by the Catholic Church in Ireland to promote or maintain a Catholic society or social ethos must take into account the mission of the Church in society, the means by which that mission is pursued and the historical context in which all this occurs. A further qualification is appropriate in this particular discussion. I am concerned almost exclusively here with the Catholic Church as the dominant influence in the Republic and the Church of my own allegiance.

In current theology, as outlined here, the mission of the Church in society is to promote the coming of the kingdom in terms of the attitudes, values, relationships and structures adumbrated in the teaching of Jesus and the prophets, expressing, as these do, the historical role and power of God and the personal and social fulfilment of humankind. Freedom,

184

justice, peace and development for all persons in society constitute key features of the kingdom or rule of God already initiated in Jesus Christ but constantly inhibited and distorted by failure and sinfulness both personal and structural. Insofar as the Catholic Church is conscious of its mission in this fashion, it has had no alternative but to pursue it, however misunderstood and rejected it may be.

The misunderstandings may be, and historically certainly were, sometimes of its own making. A selective, and in our own context, conservative view of kingdom attitudes and values and of their appropriate embodiment in relationships and structures is always a temptation for church leaders and political leaders sharing their views. To this temptation the Catholic members in Ireland too readily yielded in their attitudes to book censorship where the kingdom values of freedom and truth were unfairly restricted and the kingdom resource of human creativity as expressed in literature demeaned. In the debates about legalising divorce and contraception the kingdom values of fidelity and self-disciplined sexual love as critical to a healthy society are undoubtedly at stake and in need of defence. However, their interpretation has sometimes taken on a narrowly conceived denominational significance and the values of respecting differences of interpretation and the freedom to pursue them may have been too easily obscured. In some of the education controversies the Catholic Church's historical service and theological mission deserves fair and open recognition, but the Church must not surrender to the anti-kingdom temptation to elevate power and control above the quality and range of service. The temptation to obscure social justice in the name of opposing communism and in an ethos of petty self-centred capitalism is being gradually overcome in church documents, as witness the recent pastoral *The Work of Justice* (1977). Much remains to be done.

In all this I have been endorsing the Church's basic mission to serve the kingdom in society while drawing attention to the inevitable and actual distortions of that mission in Ireland as well as to its undoubted achievements.

To some extent the manner of pursuing that mission has already been indicated, at least by the narrow and often authoritarian interpretations of that mission in issues concerning family life, education and censorship. Two further comments are in order. In its attempt to articulate its social mission, the Church, in line with the prevailing theological fashion, based its positions on natural law morality. This is still a very reputable tradition although it is undergoing serious philosophical and theological overhaul right now. Its traditional claim in the traditional form to break across religious divisions and to provide a basis for morality and law acceptable to believers and non-believers alike is no longer verified in much of the modern world, if it ever was. This applies more and more to Ireland. And, of course, the Reformed traditions never adopted natural law as an adequate basis for morality. When it became increasingly the case that even some reasoning Catholics did not arrive at or understand or even accept certain conclusions allegedly based on natural law, such as the universal prohibition on contraceptive intercourse, and that the dominant Catholic argument for these positions was not reasonable examination of human nature (now in disagreement) but what the Church teaches, the force of natural law argument in public debate on social issues was clearly weakened. Yet much of the natural law type of analysis and reasoning could still be applicable if developed in the new historical context and integrated for church purposes into a moral theology which was focused on the values of the kingdom as they are to be discerned and promoted in society. In this way the genuinely Christian concern for and commitment to the transformation of society for the fulfilment of humankind, could combine its religious roots with its social and secular concerns. The alternative to natural law thinking in social morality is not either superficial liberalism or inhumane collectivism.

With the combination of a natural law requiring continuous church interpretations and a Church conceived hierarchically clerically, the promotion of the kingdom translated as Catholic society, became a rather overtly clerical and religious enterprise. This obscured the real worth and weakness of the enterprise in the eyes of its proponents and of its critics. While the 'priest-ridden' society was always an unfair jibe, the mind and method of the Catholic society had unnecessary clerical tones and overtones.

The Irish context in which the Church sought to fulfil its mission in society has changed even more rapidly than the Church itself. Cultural influences through the media and travel,

186

rapid economic and demographic changes and the persistent problem of Northern Ireland present a very different social challenge to the Church in 1981 than it experienced in 1951. In this situation the distraction of a Catholic society must be replaced by a more thorough understanding of the kind of society in which we actually live and of the deeper and more discriminating call to promote genuine kingdom values in that society. The justice which would embody the righteousness of God's reign must be discerned and pursued by all members of the Church, all God's people, in ways that are only fitfully apparent at present. That justice will range over distribution of goods, facilities and power within Irish society and beyond Irish society to the needier parts of the world. In this promotion of kingdom justice, the witness and service of the Catholic Church and of any other Irish Church will be diminished and indeed contradicted by its failure to join honestly and fully with its sister Churches. The present polite and, at best, lukewarm church exchanges must give way to a common commitment and intimate collaboration in the service of a torn and distorted Irish society. Otherwise, the wounds of society will not be healed. The values of the kingdom will be further obscured and distorted. The Churches will have demonstrated their common failure and grow increasingly irrelevant.

The problems of church and state in Ireland do not reduce to any simple formulas of power struggles between bishops and politicians, of difficulties between law and morality, or seeking a Catholic society or a Protestant state. The Churches must once again humbly examine their mission in society and join together in a common understanding and promotion of that mission. In this they will be both judged and empowered by the incoming presence of the God they wish to serve. Just now they need to experience and appropriate that judgment as basis for their new empowerment in service of society and God's emerging kingdom. That service will not be primarily related to the state but can hardly avoid endorsing or rejecting some of the state's efforts to serve society in its turn.

In this view the Christian conscience of society will be articulated and witnessed to in service by the Church as people and the Church as ecumenical. The issues will be derived from the needs of all the people in society, with priority for the deprived and the victims. The responses will be shaped by the

187

values of the kingdom which express the divine attention to the fulfilment of everybody. The achievements will be judged and empowered by that presence of God which is discernible in history through faith in Jesus Christ and which we finally call the kingdom or reign of God.

12

Agenda for Irish and British Moral Theologians

Teaching and learning

In the course of conversation some years ago an Irish bishop remarked: 'Of course I wasn't a moral theologian; I was a moral theology teacher'. The accompanying wry smile emphasised the not entirely serious self-deprecation and the not entirely jocose thrust at the self-importance and pretentiousness to which theologians are often prone. Of more significance were the implicit historical facts and attitudes about the conditions of theology, including moral theology; conditions which still prevail in Britain and Ireland. Most people with a professional commitment to theology work in seminaries and other institutions with teaching loads so heavy and resources so limited that they operate and see themselves almost exclusively as teachers. And this is how their employers and superiors, including bishops, also view them. The small if increasing number of Catholic theologians working at secular universities and not directly subject to religious superiors enjoy rather different conditions, challenges and resources, although teaching necessarily plays a significant role for them too. And they do not include any Catholic moral theologians, as far as I know.

The stress placed here on teaching could easily be misunderstood. Most people engaged in tertiary-level education, including universities, see teaching as a primary duty. Only at university level is it significantly qualified to the point where research (and publication) is given equal status. And that equality is often more formal and theoretical than substantive and practical. (The major organisations of university academics in Britain and Ireland have adopted 'teacher' as their self-designation in the Association of University Teachers, AUT, and the Irish Federation of University Teachers, IFUT). If the university or any parallel institution is to operate at all as a community of scholars, the initiation of new scholars through effective teaching must be vigorously undertaken. The suggestions of limitation which (moral) theology teacher and (moral) theology teaching carried in the opening paragraph should not, then, obscure the necessity, value and, indeed, intellectual excitement which the activities of teacher and teaching involve in general and in theological institutions of various kinds. The worrisome source of limitation relates more to certain dominant models of teaching theology and theology teacher.

The model of teacher rather than theologian preferred by the bishop was dominant in seminaries where Catholic priests and hence (most) theology teachers received their initial training. The teacher's task was to instruct the seminarian in the accepted moral teaching of the Church so that he, on ordination, could instruct and apply it to the faithful in pulpit and confessional. Difficulties such as answers to new questions (I recall that of the use of tampons from my student days!) were resolved by more exact applications of the received rules, by appeal to the approved authors and by authoritative decisions, almost exclusively from Rome. There were excellent teachers, of whom I knew several, who transcended the limitations of the subject-matter and of the process to convey a genuine sense of morality as richer than rule, and of teaching as richer than instruction. But the basic movement was receiving the stuff from above (Rome, text-books, articles by approved authors) and handing it on below. My theology teacher was the middle-man between the authorities and the students, the primary teachers and the learners.

The element of caricature in this picture does not destroy its overall validity. And while it may be less true of seminaries today, one is frequently reminded that its passing is to be regretted and that its retention or restoration is desirable where possible.

The revolution in approach and method in moral theology already begun in the 1930s and greatly accelerated after Vatican II, which undermined the simple receiving-from and handing-on process of moral theology, is already very well known. It might be briefly summarised as the admission of large sections of Christian and human reality, biblical, doctrinal, psychological and social, into the moral-theology classroom so that the neat structures and divisions of the manuals simply collapsed. Another kind of reality principle was at work in locating the moral theology teacher in the Church's overall teaching activity. The isolation and professionalisation which he enjoyed (and it was always *he*) gave him a responsibility and authority which, for all its intermediate status, obscured where the action was really going on. Long before Vatican II's insistence on the Church as primarily *God's people* with its implications of the radical equality of faith and baptism, Christian teaching, including moral teaching, was occurring formally and informally far beyond the reach of moral theologians or their episcopal masters. Parents and lay-teachers were the primary formal educators while the informal ranged from friends and school peers to work-contacts, local political and trades-union leaders, to newspaper columnists, and the ever more informal messages of the communications media and the cultural ethos. There is abundant evidence throughout Britain and Ireland to show how the informal prevailed over the formal and the non-specialised/non-authorised over the specialised and authorised. Which bishops or theologians consciously promoted in their teaching racism or sexism, political violence, now enjoying not only practical support but moral justification among Christians and Catholics? On the other hand many admirable moral movements and activities, for peace, for the care of itinerants, prisoners, and the social, mentally and physically deprived did not originate in the class-room or bishop's study. All this helps to locate and relativise the moral theologian as teacher in a way that was obscured when he was in his old role as intermediary between hierarchy and ordinands (to simplify crudely), or in the more authoritative professional position which today is claimed by some theologians and resented by some bishops. The theologian is a teacher and with, one hopes, a mediating as well as professional and authoritative role but within a community in which teacher and taught are frequently interchangeable. The moral theologian as teacher has to collaborate with a whole range of formal and informal teachers from whom he may learn at least as much as he teaches about the basic direction and particular tasks of Christian discipleship, the stuff of Christian morality. However, his ability, training, skills, opportunities and position of leadership give him responsibility to ensure that the various formal and informal teachers in the Church are communicating effectively with one another and with the historic wisdom of the Christian Church in response to the changing problems of the day. With such an explosion of teachers, information and challenges, the moral theology teacher can no longer look only to his manuals, approved authors and Roman or episcopal documents. He can no longer be content to receive from above and hand down to below. And indeed, he is no longer simply 'he'—'she' is also beginning to assume her rightful responsibility and duty as moral theologian in confronting the meaning of discipleship for today's Christians. The further impact of this development on the future of moral theology will be enormous.

Recognition of the plurality of teachers in the Church reveals simultaneously the plurality of learners and learning processes. As mediator between the tradition and the students the moral theologian was always conscious of his learning tasks. But the new situation calls for a broadening and deepening of that consciousness as he engages in a collaborative enterprise as broad as humanity itself and as deep as the mystery of God itself. This is the Church's enterprise as it seeks to understand and live the mystery of God's presence through the full expression of humanity in history.

The complexity of contemporary life and the range of moral views, practices and possibilities through which Christians must chart the course of their discipleship emphasise the learning-role of the moral theologian and his or her responsibility to provide leadership in learning to chart that course. For theological as well as pedagogical reasons, an effective moral teacher today must be seen to be a continuing learner.

The kind of leadership in learning and discerning which the moral theologian offers in face of complexity and conflict of moral views and practices is first of all conservative. He is, after all, trying to understand and present discipleship of Jesus Christ to a contemporary audience. The first records of that discipleship in the New Testament provide the starting-point for his investigations and standard of judgment for his conclusions. The subsequent history of Christian life and reflection provides further illustration of and insight into how discipleship should and should not be realised. Familiarity with this continuing Christian story furnishes the moral theologian with a rich storehouse of heroes and villains from Pope John XXIII to Pope

John XII, of the ways of sanctity and of sin, of successful experiments (monasticism) and inglorious failures (the Inquisition), of the brilliant moral insights, analyses and syntheses of Augustine and Aquinas and the misleading, if persuasive, moralising of Montanists and Jansenists, of fidelity in understanding and living against great odds as with so many martyrs and of obstinacy in misunderstanding for reasons of convenience, as with the teaching on slavery.

The richness as well as the ambiguity of the past forces the genuinely conservative theologian to be also critical. He must evaluate the past, discern its truly Christian elements, to maintain continuity in discipleship. For responsible critique and discernment he needs information, skill, dedication and freedom—the time, energy, recognition and resources which encourage and enable him to act as a discriminating leader in calling to mind and so to life those truly Christian elements. With more dedication and freedom, the acceptance of slavery or the denial of religious liberty might not have afflicted Catholic moral teaching for so long. In face of current problems a greater awareness of past teaching and example in peace and violence, in wealth and poverty, or in power and service, might help to break the world-wide bonds of militarism, consumerism and exploitation, which Christians also support to their immediate profit. As an overall enterprise, in its various systematic sections and more particular challenges, moral theology is still seriously lacking in historical depth, leaving itself open to the temptations of either a rigid defence of one unexamined version of past experience and teaching or an equally uncritical rejection of all that is past. The conserving responsibility of the moral theologian must join fully with his critical responsibility in more detailed archaeology of his discipline's past.

Retreat into the past rather than active and critical recall of it in the present may also prove a temptation as one surveys the variety of problems and solutions which threaten to submerge all clear thinking and right doing today. The theologian's critical faculty is no less in demand as he attempts to order, analyse and illuminate today's problems and solutions for modern disciples. Although all Christians are called to be both teachers and learners, in charting the way of discipleship the moral theologian has a responsibility of leadership. The exercise of this leadership in learning occurs within the community of the Church but also within the community of his theological colleagues. The theological community in the strong sense of people actively and intellectually and continuously engaged in seeking to understand the faith may include people who do not teach at theological institutes or have not even studied at such. Britain has long had outstanding contributors to theology of this kind. Rosemary Haughton and Jack Dominian come to mind as present-day examples. In the dialogue with the world at issue here, in confronting new moral problems, views and practices, the theological community is greatly enriched by people whose background and life-engagement are far removed from the seminary or even the university.

The concentrated exposure to the contemporary scene which the moral theologian may not avoid, calls for discriminating fidelity to the tradition and critical openness to the present. The search for new ways will involve risk and mistake. And it calls for that third characteristic of the good moralist and theologian, creativity. Creativity should and frequently does characterise all human communication, including teaching. A good conversation, paradigms of much adult communication and moral activity, takes for granted the rules of vocabulary, grammar and syntax, as it moves over uncharted terrain, follows the spirit of the exchange and creates a dialogue that is itself creative of or transformative of the participants. The security and trust involved in such a successful venture, the community of language and tradition on which the participants draw and the genuinely personal creative activity involved, illustrate how moral behaviour is also human, creative interchange between people with a tradition and a community. In the critical understanding and creative promotion of that moral interchange, the moral theologian speaks on the frontier between the diverse communities to which he belongs, Christian and secular, historical and contemporary. His response to frontier dilemmas or conflicts may sometimes have to transcend his conserving and critical roles in genuinely creative work. Such creative response will inevitably involve the new. The moral theologian has the obligation to show how this novelty is not for its own sake but is demanded by his conserving and critical roles. Sometimes this will be readily recognised by the wider church community. More often, precisely because the moral theologian has had the opportunity and experienced the need to find a way forward for disciples, it will involve time, debate, perhaps initial rejection. And sometimes the moral theologian will be wrong. To enable the moral theologian and other theologians and Christians to engage in this creative as well as conserving and critical work while at the same time minimising the impact of mistakes, calls for continuing effort by all church members. Where the theologian pays effective attention to the work of his colleagues, to the broader insights and needs of the Church and to its overall co-ordination and guides, the pope and the bishops, the risks of mistake are reduced. In the difficulties that may arise, perhaps the Vatican reaction to the Molinists and Banezians of telling them to stop attacking each other may be more appropriate than the silencing of John Courtney Murray in the 1950s. At any rate, in the rather deprived theological world of Britain and Ireland, theologians need a lot more encouragement if their conserving, critical and creative work is to have any hope of enabling the Church to discern and meet its needs. The mistakes of creativity, in particular, are likely to be much less damaging than the simple repetition of answers drawn from 'authorities' in other times and other lands, which were almost certainly devised for rather different questions. A moral theology teacher may never be a simple 'repetitore' if his conserving function is to involve genuinely Christian and not merely verbal and mechanical fidelity to the past. Teaching is always the other side of learning with all the risks that implies.

Learning and living

Moral theology as a theology of discipleship for disciples today relates closely to Christian living. It has sometimes appeared as if moral theology should provide a theory of Christian living which might then be translated into practice. In the Christian tradition, however, theory never enjoyed such a simple priority. Theology was understood to be in important senses secondary to and based on Christian practice. Reflection with its accompanying insight came after the fact. This was obviously true of those earliest 'theological' documents, the books of the New Testament. Following Jesus Christ and living out discipleship anticipated writing about it. And this has been a recurring pattern in Christian life and theology. Many of the classical developments in moral theology from just-war theory

195

to approval of interest-taking occurred after certain critical facts: the establishment of the Church as the Church of the Empire with a belief in the responsibility of defending it, and a change in the economic system which found the old prohibition of usury increasingly ignored and eventually unreasonable.

The theory developed in turn affected events and facts. Practice was also influenced by theory or previous reflection and systematisation. The New Testament writings which embody reflection on as well as recording of the primitive discipleship play a normative role in all Christian theology and practice. Subsequent theological writing and community decisions based on reflection contribute to the self-understanding of the Church as it teaches and lives the way of discipleship. Moral theologians may ignore individual documents or passages but their primary attention has been directed to written sources with a heavy emphasis on the reflective in the theological and philosophical mould to the neglect of historical accounts of life or the re-creations of life in imaginative literature.

There has been a recent welcome recovery of history and story by theologians, including moral theologians, though it has not made much impact in Britain or Ireland as yet. This will enrich moral understanding and teaching although it cannot simply replace the tradition of conceptual analysis in which moralists, philosophical and theological, must still engage. More challenging in many ways for moralists is the tendency to give priority to practice, or 'praxis'—as the jargon tends to put it. This learning through *doing* and reflecting after the fact could pose serious problems for the study-bound moral theologian and indeed for other Christian teachers.

It is fairly obvious that the moral theologian cannot do research and reflection if he is entirely engaged in activity. Apart from the very difficult question of time and energy, different skills are developed in the one and the other. Yet the moralist above all must be in close and constant contact with the life on which he is to reflect. To some extent this happens automatically if sometimes unconsciously. The moral theologian is also a member of a family, of the Church, of a particular State. His active engagement with these and other communities may vary considerably but it is seldom negligible and can, with advertence, provide some active basis for his theological inquiry. A more self-conscious engagement in particular pastoral or social activity will usually make him more alert and aware in his theology. Theologians who have worked with special groups, the handicapped or alcoholics or prisoners or divorced or homosexuals, frequently display particular insight into these problems and can enlarge theological understanding in general.

The limits of this kind of engagement derive from time, energy, opportunity and ability. No moral theologian can cover a wide range of activity. He will therefore be dependent on dialogue with people engaged in particular activities, personally or professionally. A much more profound and continuing dialogue is demanded of the moral theologian in a whole range of areas today. In the areas of medical and bio-ethics, of business ethics and of law and morality, useful collaborative work has already begun. However it is only in the medical area and in the United States for the most part that real collaboration has been sustained over an effective period by a relatively large number of collaborators to yield substantial results. In Britain and Ireland especially, a much more systematic effort will be needed by theologians, other specialists and lay-people affected, if Christian discipleship is to be understood and taught and lived in response to challenges as diverse as the environment and its protection, political freedom and economic development, to take a few obvious instances.

Team-work of this kind with the moral theologian learning with and from the expertise and experience of so many others will be necessary to future moral theology. However, the professional moral theologian may not be the critical figure in some of these developments. It is important to recognise the responsibility of other professionals to provide leadership in discerning the way of discipleship in their own fields, in offering leadership in moral learning and teaching for the Christian community in their particular area. The moral theologian will be a partner to the enterprise of developing Christian morality for architects and accountants, politicians and lawyers. He will not necessarily be the dominant partner. However, he will remain a necessary link to the tradition and to the other areas in which Christian morality has to be exposed and lived. In this vision of a Church collaborating through its different members with their responsibilities and experience, the moral theologian will require commitment, knowledge, skill and opportunity far exceeding those suggested by phrases such as 'merely a moral theology teacher and not a moral theologian'. The demands on the moral theologian to be linked directly or indirectly with the great moral movements and issues of the day call for much greater support from the Church in its community resources and pastoral direction. Blame for the present apathy about or occasional hostility to moral theology may be variously apportioned. Its failures to meet the needs of the gospel community today will be harshly judged later.

British and Irish issues

What I have been saying applies to a large extent to the tasks of moral theology throughout the Church, although its particular limitations of personnel and other resources in Britain and Ireland have been briefly noticed. Britain and Ireland share many of the same tasks and issues, although sometimes with a particular quality or qualification of their own. Marriage breakdown has its own characteristics in England, somewhat different in Scotland perhaps, and more different still in Ireland. The abortion problem is, if one would excuse the crudity, developing as an export problem in Ireland while it has become an import as well as a native problem in Britain. Racism is predominantly a British issue although many Catholics of Irish origin or extraction are involved in it and had or have to suffer similar indignity. Sexism affects both islands in somewhat different degrees and fashions. Economic issues such as unemployment and the community's response to it, or the responsibilities and powers of management and unions move back and over the Irish Sea. So do the positive moral movements which have emerged to fight in some of these issues. A survey of the major current moral issues could take enormous space and time so I choose to concentrate on a few that have a peculiarly British-Irish character.

(a) Britain and Ireland. The first of these is undoubtedly the relationship between Britain and Ireland and the parallel but not identical relationship between British and Irish people. Despite their long and sometimes tragic history, their relationships have received very little attention from theologians, moral or other. Given the continuing tension between the countries and the peoples, expressed most destructively in the violence in

198

Northern Ireland but also at work as between Irish and English in Britain (the earliest of Britain's contemporary race problems!), and then in an insidiously destructive way within the Catholic Church in Britain, some more attention to this question by the Catholic Church and its theologians as well as its ordinary members is clearly called for.

I suggest three separate tasks for urgent attention:

(i) A historical-theological examination and appropriation of the history of British-Irish relationships. This needs some further explanation. The history is so long and tangled that it could take volumes to complete. Much of this work has already been published by reputable British and Irish historians. What I have in mind is a joint effort by theologians and historians on the basis of this material, to produce an accurate historical survey which would offer opportunity for theological or Christian understanding, forgiveness and reconciliation. Some of the work of Haddon Wilmer of Leeds on 'The Politics of Forgiveness', despite its slightly unhappy title, would be relevant here. At any rate it should be possible for theologians and historians with the support of the Churches to supply a basic and accurate account of the history with such theological reflection on its implications that it would lead to eventual repentance and reconciliation. Such a work should be required reading in all religious and moral courses.

(ii) The second task would involve a much more serious concentration on the role of religion in the Northern Irish and British-Irish conflict. History might again combine with theological analyses to help us understand and appropriate past and present. The object would be to enable the Churches to play a more positive role in the future rather than to convict them of failure in the past, although some recognition of and repentance for past failure are clearly demanded. In this as in other areas, the theologian will be collaborating with other academics such as historians and social scientists, and with more directly-involved people like politicians, community leaders including clergymen and the suffering masses. The life-experience will be critical to the learning-process.

(iii) The tensions between English and Irish Catholics, the evasion of these tensions and their historical and political background, have plagued the Church at least since the Veto controversy at the beginning of the nineteenth century. (It will

199

be remembered that this arose when the British sought a right to veto the appointment of Catholic bishops in Ireland in exchange for granting Emancipation.) The great improvements in relationships in past decades display an unhealthy middle-class blandness while the working-class Irish feel they may be excluded and excluding. The 'Paddy' references and the Irish jokes can be taken too seriously but they sometimes reveal a nasty edge and frequently express or feed a hidden hostility. In many ways the Catholic Church in Britain has not attempted to celebrate its ethnic pluralism. Perhaps it felt threatened or overwhelmed at an earlier stage by the Irish element. Some more thoughtful examination and reflection on these tensions are now required for the health of the Church in both countries, and indeed for the health of society generally, if traditional resentment is not to be replaced by a more destructive rootlessness.

(b) Protestant-Catholic relations. It is impossible to discuss British-Irish relations, past or present, without facing up to Protestant-Catholic relations. The progress made in the last two decades is enormous, as compared with the starting point, but looks very limited when compared with what is still to be achieved. The progress gives promise for the future but it could as easily lead to complacency in the present as the more serious and difficult problems arise. The impact of the agreed statements between Anglicans and Catholics has been limited through fear and disguised through complacency. The continuing scandal of Northern Ireland (and its genuine and universal Christian scandal may not be ignored) demands an honest and effective response from the Churches which they have so far failed to give, busy as they are with their own people, their own institutions and their own power. Only an ecumenism that involves inter-church surrender in love and forgiveness can help the Churches out of this impasse.

Meanwhile this scandal combines with a host of other religious, cultural and economic factors to undermine the traditional bonds uniting family, locality, school, common social activity and church-going. To survive as a believing Christian in the future will call for much more self-conscious allegiance by the believer and a new set of structures or communities of support. In that situation, and it is already here for many young Christians, the divisions between Churches with their restrictive regulations for joint celebrations of Eucharist, marriage or death, will look increasingly fussy and irrelevant. How to avoid simple anarchy in inter-church relations and yet prevent the current regulations from alienating a growing number of young people will be a major task for pastors, theologians and believers in the next decade. It has special urgency in our islands.

(c) Economics and discipleship. To ascribe all our woes to economic conditions would hardly satisfy even the Marxists among us. Yet there is an increasing recognition that economic conditions play a significant role in the development of a humane society and in its break-down. Church and theologians have hitherto lacked the interest and the skill to confront in any significant way the problems posed for discipleship at what the jargon calls the macro- and micro-economic levels. The present economic difficulties in Britain and Ireland, the uneasy state of the European Economic Community and the north/south or first world/third world tensions in which we are all involved, economically and politically, suggest a much more serious approach to studying the economic responsibility of discipleship. Such an approach would need the knowledge and experience of a range of Christians. In the British and Irish situation it would provide an excellent focus for international and inter-church collaboration. In that very collaboration itself, new aspects of discipleship would almost certainly emerge.

The Cost of Morality and of Moral Theology

As learner as well as teacher, as learning from life as well as from books, the moral theologian is confronted with the meaning of discipleship for himself as he attempts to chart it for others. In the transparent world in which Christians now live it is very difficult to get away with simply instructing the others. My own jocose remark to a student twenty years ago, 'I teach this stuff, you don't expect me to live it as well', I would not dare risk today. The teacher and learner of moral theology must also be a disciple, and discipleship is costly. So moral theologians, by giving a lead in learning and in learning for living, have to face the further tasks of Christian living for themselves. The standard lecture on famine in the Third World after a sumptuous

201

banquet is so crass as to be easily dismissed. The more modest but still very comfortable life-style of the moralist who is struggling to relate the pervasiveness of poverty to the meaning of justice for today's disciples is much more subtle and much less easy to cope with. But it must be coped with if Christian discipleship is to offer a way out of the present consumerist enslavement of the first world and the impoverished enslavement of so much of the third.

The insulation of university and seminary, of education and class, of prestige and worthwhile, enjoyable work, all conspire to blind theologians to the real moral conditions of our world. What is the moral theologian prepared to sacrifice in order to come to grips with that real world, and in order to offer some vision of true discipleship to the Church he is called to serve?

Conflict with Church Authority

Recent difficulties between church authorities (pope and bishops) and theologians may have been inevitable and even healthy in the rapid transitions which the Church had to make in the 1960s and 1970s. They are regrettable, however, in so far as they reflect fear and arrogance, instead of trust and humility. They may even be more easily avoidable if the collaborative learning to which the Church is called by word and world becomes the dominant concern of all church members, with of course special responsibilities for theologians and final practical authority for the pastors. In the service of the Church by his deciphering of discipleship, the moral theologian has to take risks and be willing to pay the price. These are critical tests of his own discipleship and of his authority to investigate and explain it for others.

13

Peace and War:
A Task for American Moral
Theologians

The emergence of the peace and war issue as dominant for
European and American Christians, has intensified the obligation
of people engaged in moral theology and Christian ethics to
analyse anew the complex problems involved. This task affects
American theologians in a particular way because of the United
States' nuclear power status and because of the freedom,
resources and prestige which American theology now enjoys.
The example of so many Catholic bishops and other Church
leaders, together with a range of other Christians, in questioning
or protesting about current American policy, should provide
any further stimulus needed to American theologians.

In this chapter a European who has much reason to be
grateful to the United States and its theologians, Catholic,
Protestant and Jewish, attempts to illuminate the basic issues
facing Christians in this great debate of our time. He does this in
full awareness of European limitations and American responsibilities.

Christian understanding and witness must combine various
dimensions of particularity and universality. As disciples of
Jesus Christ, baptised and nurtured in Christian tradition and
community, Christians have a particular moral vocation. They
must understand and witness to the particular truth, salvific
power and way of life revealed in that most particular of people,
Jesus Christ. Yet the vocation of Jesus Christ himself, which his
disciples share, points beyond himself to the Father, to the
inbreaking presence and power of God in his reign or kingship.
This particular vocation points to, promises and realises the
universal care and power of the God of universal creation and
redemption. In elaborating the Christian understanding and
witness to affairs of peace and war, the particularity of the

Christian tradition has to meet the universality of the concerns of the Christian God. The Catholic concern with natural law provided one model of attempting to integrate the universality of divine concern with the particularity of Christianity. It is not the only model or necessarily the best one. Other Christian Churches have approached the problem differently. All Churches must attempt to speak out of the Christian tradition to humankind at large, above all on the universal topic of peace and war. This speaking out of, and to, also involves listening to. It demands real communication in both directions, real dialogue. One very important illustration of dialogue for this chapter lies in the attempt to listen to and integrate the achievements of Gandhi in his understanding and use of non-violence.

A further dimension of the relationship between the particular and universal follows from the peculiar power of the United States and its consequent planet-wide role in matters of peace and war.

The tension between moral analysis, evaluation and advocacy can never be theoretically resolved for moral theologians. On different issues at different times the emphasis will necessarily be put on analysis, on exposing the component parts of a particular moral issue. This will involve evaluation—moral analysis is always about values—although the evaluation may emerge only indirectly in the choice and presentation of the component parts and of the arguments about them. Whether evaluation is direct or indirect the analysis will also carry a persuasive intent and effect. It will bear its own witness, contain its own advocacy, at least in terms of relevant factors and acceptable argument. Moral theologians of 'liberal' mind usually prefer this implicit advocacy although they do not always recognise it. In a moral theology of discipleship it may seem inadequate. Yet the strengths of such implicit advocacy may not be denied, and the dangers of the more explicit may not be ignored. The contemporary issue of peace and war is a particularly difficult source of tension for Christian moral analysts and their diverse attitudes to advocacy. This chapter consciously attempts to combine both advocacy and analysis but must also consciously concede the strains and distortions which such attempts at combination may involve.

The Current Crisis
Pervasiveness and Totality of War. The twentieth century has experienced radically new developments in the pervasiveness and totality of war. Two world wars and the links connecting local wars—in the Middle-East, South-east Asia, Southern Africa and Latin America—with the super-powers effectively demonstrate the pervasiveness of contemporary warfare. Wherever it occurs it is likely to have worldwide repercussions. The totality characteristic of modern warfare is even more frightening. This is partly the technological fulfilment of von Clausewitz's nineteenth-century analysis that military at war will use every means available to succeed. And the means now available to the superpowers, and bound to be progressively available to lesser powers, are total in the full planetary range of that predicate. The refusal by the Americans to use nuclear weapons in Vietnam and that by the Russians to use them in Afghanistan are not encouraging exceptions to the new technical range of von Clausewitz's dictum. The technical range of means used in Vietnam equivalently demolished that restraint on the conduct of war which the distinction between combatants and non-combatants maintained in the light of the 'just war' theory. That distinction and restraint had disappeared during World War II with its blitzkrieg and saturation bombing of cities such as Dresden and Hamburg even before its final obscenities of Hiroshima and Nagasaki. The irrelevance of 'just war' theory was finally and cruelly exposed.

The 'Cold War' which is still with us turns on the 'balance of terror' in a world in which the arms race between the superpowers gives them the possibility and, in many people's minds, the emergent probability of total planetary destruction. Meanwhile the 'arms trade' increases the destructive capacity of even small and poverty-stricken nations. At the level of locally containable violence as well as at the level of possibly universal and total violence the human weakness for mutual destruction threatens every single person today.

The enormity of the threat may so far exceed our moral imaginations that we decide to ignore it. The hope of dealing with it in any effective way may seem so remote that we turn apathetically to more manageable problems or more cheerful distractions. The contemporary preoccupation with superficial consumer satisfactions across the whole range of our lives may be an attempt to shield ourselves from confronting the threatening question-mark that hangs over our planet. What we cannot influence, we must ignore.

Emergent Responses. The totality and pervasiveness of modern warfare, which render 'just war' theory as a form of restraint totally inadequate, have however been matched at other levels by the emergence of three distinct responses. The first of these, the United Nations Organisation, has not fulfilled its early hopes of providing some basic international order backed by effective international peace-keeping and enforceable sanctions. Yet as a forum it can provide for useful debate of particular conflicts and for the analysis and condemnation of the 'arms race' and 'arms trade'. Its peace-keeping function is still very limited in range and effect. But it does exist and has proved useful. The development of the United Nations as a more effective promoter and maintainer of the peace is clearly important and gives some limited ground for hope in an otherwise chaotic and frequently violent international scene.

A rather different sign of hope may be discerned in the recent popular movements in Europe and to some extent in the United States, calling for nuclear disarmament. These seem to me quite different from earlier 'Ban the Bomb' movements in the breadth of their appeal, the quality of their commitment and the reasonableness of their arguments and demands. The concern, for example, of a growing number of US Catholic bishops about the manufacture and possession of nuclear weapons is a sign from a body normally conservative on this issue, that a serious change is under way. The recent mass-meetings in Bonn and London and other European cities confirmed the conviction that a genuine and general people's movement has begun.

Of course such movements have come and gone in the past. The most notorious of these in terms of quick growth and equally quick collapse was the Peace Movement in Northern Ireland inspired by the leadership of Nobel Prize winners Máiréad Corrigan and Betty Williams. This example may be instructive in a number of ways. Developed out of a particular incident (the death of Máiréad Corrigan's sister and her sister's children) it obviously matched a mood of the moment. Its subsequent growth created a climate in which people with power in the community, politicians, British and Irish, and

206

Church leaders, Catholic and Protestant, could have taken some imaginative, radical steps to break through the old barriers and establish new structures of communication and community. When this did not happen and the magic mood passed, people retreated behind the old barriers. The work of the 'Peace People' has left its mark, for some in hope, for others in disillusionment. The lesson remains. Unless mass-movements can affect practical policies and practising politicians, they eventually lose momentum.

It is at this point that the third significant peace achievement of the twentieth century becomes particularly relevant. The non-violent philosophy and policies of the Mahatma Gandhi represent the most important twentieth-century achievement in the search for peace with justice and freedom. The Gandhian way involved certain principles of reverence for all living things (*ahimsa*), the force of truth (and so of God) in the pursuit of political change (*satyagraha*) and a discipline of community life (*ashram*). By his adoption of these principles in his political campaign to emancipate the Indian peoples, Gandhi showed remarkable insight into the enslavement of the British as well as the Indians in the colonial system and their need for mutual emancipation as distinct from the elimination of one or both through violence. His further grasp of the relation of ends and means, how the means must anticipate and be fulfilled in the ends sought, strengthened his conviction on non-violent means. The means themselves were both varied and sophisticated, and they demand as much education, discipline and training as one would expect from a highly trained army. Although few resources have been devoted to developing these means further, either for the promotion of political change in conditions of internal oppression or—still less—for defence against external aggression, enough progress has been made to justify people opposed to violence and war in hoping for alternatives. The obvious influence of Jesus and the New Testament on Gandhi's thought and life, and the inner connecting points between his philosophy and policies and the Christian tradition, make him a critical figure in discussing the Christian contribution to peace today.

The Christian Meaning of Peace
In Christian terms peace is a divine gift and an eschatological

reality. The peace attained in Jesus Christ and accessible to us through him, the peace which he embodies and offers, is God's gift, establishing loving and binding relationships among men and women, overcoming their hostilities and divisions. Its fullness lies beyond history in the completion of God's presence to us and our presence to him. For all its divine and eschatological origin and completion, peace is also a human and historic task. We have to realise, in history and by our human efforts, the peace which has been given to us in anticipation of the final Kingdom. The discernment, promotion and embodiment of the Kingdom with its Kingdom values and relationships constitutes the mission of Christians in the world. Central to the Kingdom, its values and relationships, is the gift and task of peace. We are committed to being peace-makers by our faith in Jesus Christ and our share in his inauguration of the Kingdom.

The early Christians recognised how opposed war and its waging was to the example and teaching of Jesus Christ. The long history of subsequent Christians' involvement in war, as they moved from the catacombs to the basilicas, is too well known to need rehearsal here. The two main strands in that historical tradition, the acceptance of the 'just war', the dominant strand, and the rejection of all war, a much weaker strand, still confront Christians today as they contemplate a world with its actual limited wars and its threat of unlimited war. The inaugural gift of the Kingdom we call the peace of Christ can with difficulty be discerned through inter-state rivalries and hostilities, the continuing violence within states between establishment forces and the forces of insurrection, and bellicose threats of the superpowers. The absence of major i.e. total war between the great powers is something to be thankful for. It can hardly be described in 'peace of Christ' terms. And it is in continuing danger of ending war and peace in the extinction of the human world on earth in a nuclear holocaust. The fine balance of deterrence is exposed to all too many possible upsets, particularly with the nuclear arms race so obviously renewed and no longer confinable to the two great powers of the United States and Soviet Russia.

So far from confining ourselves to an understanding of peace as the absence of war, of armed hostilities between organised groups for political ends, whether inter-state or within states, we need to analyse the peace of God's Kingdom in terms of the covenant by which it is established and the covenant relationships and values which apply to the communual living of human beings.

The Qualities of 'Kingdom Peace'. Righteousness or justice as coming from God and transforming human beings and their relationships is central to the New Covenant as to the Old. It forms a distinctive and basic characteristic of the Kingdom in its pre-Jesus and post-Jesus phases. As a quality of relationships it embraces the recognition of, respect for and response to others, divine and human, which in the narrower tradition of commutative justice is described as their due. In the broader biblical sense, which is analogous to the general virtue of justice as analysed by Aristotle and adopted by Thomas Aquinas and which for them is the overall characteristic of the good person, what is due in justice moves from elementary respect for life through a whole range of diverse virtues, values and rights. Whatever is due to a human being in the light of God's communication of the fullness of his saving righteousness in Jesus Christ comes under the virtue and value of human righteousness or justice. The Kingdom is to be a kingdom of righteousness. Without righteousness true peace is not possible. Wherever injustice in the broader or narrower sense prevails the Kingdom is obscured if not entirely excluded and the absence of armed hostilities carries only the appearance of peace. The Christian as peace-maker is always the Christian as justice-seeker. The truly Christian justice-seeker is also peace-maker. The overcoming of hostility by reconciliation is an overcoming in justice, whereby the hostile parties can now relate in trust and love because the injustice which separated them has been overcome. Reconciliation, trust and love enter into the making of Christian peace but they are truly Christian only where they promote or express justice.

The Kingdom of God is a universe of freedom. Christians are set free for freedom in Paul's words. And freedom involves the capacity and the space to be ourselves, to make our own decisions, to achieve our own fulfilment and destiny. The conditions of our freedom as biological, psychological, social and spiritual beings may become obstacles to our freedom in physical illness, mental distress, social oppression and sin. Peace-making Christians seek to overcome these obstacles for themselves and for others. Liberation at these different levels has become a catchword of contemporary theology. Yet it captures an essential aspect of the inbreaking Kingdom of God and its gift of peace.

Christian freedom is not the individualist freedom of an effete liberalism. It is freedom in communion of the fellowship which is the Kingdom. It involves a free commitment to others in community, a solidarity with them in their attempts to achieve freedom and justice. The solidarity of the Body of Christ is the Christian goal and measure of all human community. The quest for such solidarity among all peoples, in which people are primarily enriching for one another and not primarily destructive, provides the scope of the Christian search for peace.

Peace as a quality of the reign or Kingdom of God derives from God's empowering presence. Any social expression of the Kingdom involves the exercise of human power. The words of Jesus to the disciples about not lording it over people as the Gentiles did has implications for all human power-holders.

Power is the capacity to achieve one's intention or will. In this social context the power is the capacity to achieve certain intentions, certain willed ends for a society or state. Such achievement may be simply for the benefit of the power-holder and divorced from the good of the society for which the power is enjoyed. The power may and frequently does oppress the people it is meant to serve, diminishing and disabling them in various ways. Social or political power can be properly exercised by combining the political theory of representation with the Christian idea of service. The representatives of people, however appointed, enjoy power for the sake of the people, to enable the people to achieve righteousness in freedom. Power, properly conceived and exercised, is an enabling reality, enabling people to be themselves, to achieve their fulfilment and destiny in freedom. Abuse of power is a disabling of people, preventing them from being themselves and achieving their destiny. It effectively removes people's freedom and usually other requirements of justice also. The oppression of disabling power is not compatible with the peace of the Kingdom.

Peace is a dynamic or developing characteristic of social relationships within states and between states, involving justice, freedom and solidarity with the further implications of these virtues and values. It is always incomplete, as a historical reality

210

awaiting its eschatological fulfilment. It is always ambiguous, containing and often concealing various abuses of power which disable people in their search for fulfilment. It is a divine gift constituting a human challenge. It is the business of Christians to be primary discerners of the gift and primary respondents to the challenge.

The Christian Ethical Imperative
The search for true peace within and between states as constituent element of the Kingdom of God preached by Jesus, forms a primary ethical imperative for Christians. It is indeed an ethical imperative for all human beings if they are to attain human fulfilment in history and avoid now the nuclear holocaust, terminating the individual, the community and history.

It may be best to begin analysing this peace imperative and its implied demands by examining more localised violations and requirements and leaving the universal threat and demand until later. At the local level of individual states the threat or violation of peace may occur within a particular nation or state. Institutionalised oppression and disabling power exist in varying degrees throughout the world. In many states they have apparently gone beyond the reach of constitutional correction and provoked extra-constitutional opposition, non-violent or, in many cases, violent. We need not list all the countries in which institutionalised oppression or institutional violence is provoking violent opposition. The phenomenon is widespread and clearly frustrates the gift and call of peace in Christ.

In many of these situations violent revolution is seen as the only alternative to total submission to oppression. For Church believers this alternative is justified along the lines of the 'just war' theory. In discussing such situations from the outside it is important to remember one's 'outsider' limitations lest they lead one into offering superficial advice about the immorality of violent response to violent oppression. Yet the 'outsider' may not be entirely excluded from dialogue partly because of his sympathy with the particular oppressed, partly perhaps because of his direct experience of similar situations elsewhere and partly because the legitimation invoked in 'just war' theory is a universal possession of the Christian churches. In that dialogue Christian 'outsider' and 'insider' have a number of significant issues to discuss which involve in their resolution important practical steps.

The actual oppression may appear to affect the 'insider' only and be of such a character as to qualify as a just cause under just war (revolution) theory. Yet the 'outsider' may well be involved because his country or the alliance to which his country belongs, may be involved in supporting oppressor or oppressed. In the Western world we are becoming increasingly, if all too slowly, conscious that we are tied into a number of oppressive regimes throughout the world either directly through military and economic aid or indirectly through endorsing the overall political, military and particularly economic structures which in particular cases endorse oppression. In that perspective we may all be oppressors, at least indirectly. The range of indirect oppression in our world is measured to a large extent by the range of our economic, military and political privilege. The practical implications of this for the 'outsider' include his political influence in his own government's policies, his attitude to and action on the economic structures involved and his stand on his country's supply and others' use of arms in achieving or preventing political change.

The supply and use of arms by different sides create some of the most difficult ethical questions today. Again, without presuming to deny the 'insider's' right and duty to decide for himself in such a situation the 'outsider' can and should question the current international arms trade and his own country's or bloc's involvement in it. That the United States with Britain, France and the Soviet Union are the main merchants of violence in the world through their arms dealings, is in shocking contradiction of our pious aspirations for peace and our decrying of the growth of armaments in the Third World, armaments which replace the very necessities of life in some of the poorer countries. That section of the military-industrial complex in advanced countries should be given close scrutiny and effective opposition.

Alternatives to Violence. The deeper question remains of how far violent means are any longer appropriate in our world. Leaving aside for the moment the risk of total destruction which even a local war may pose by involving the superpowers, and these may never be left aside for long, let us concentrate on alternative means to removing oppression and establishing a just peace within countries and between them. The absence of an effective international arbiter on border disputes and other interstate difficulties leads neighbouring states to solve their problems by warfare in particular circumstances. The development of such international arbiter(s) seems both necessary and appropriate in the interlocking world in which we live. The failure of the UN or other similar agencies to provide effective arbitration should not discourage us from seeking to promote more effective means of arbitration. This is a topic to which we will have to return later.

Apart from mutually acceptable arbitration between states and particularly in the more common problem today of response to oppression within a country, the development of alternatives to violent response should be pursued and promoted much more vigorously. The Gandhian breakthrough has yet to be assimilated by countries influenced by the West with its cult of war as the ultimate way to achieve political ends. This places Western leaders, civil and religious, in a weak position in recommending non-violent means to countries struggling with oppression in the rest of the world. The position would be enormously strengthened if the developed countries were to switch some of their resources from arms research and development to the research and development of non-violent means for their own defence and for the protection and achievement of human rights throughout the world. Without the example of their own serious interest and with the counter example of their own arms trade, developed countries simply endorse the ways of violence for developing countries with problems of oppression. The full price of this foolish, indeed wicked, strategy may be paid in violent response by the southern hemisphere against the northern, which is so manifestly oppressive in its trade arrangements and its supply of arms to local southern oppressors. How far such a war by even a few southern countries could lead to nuclear exchange, and so to the holocaust, is difficult to assess. President Carter's remarks in 1980 that the US would defend 'its vital interests' in the Persian Gulf with all the necessary means incluing military means, should be interpreted in the context that the USA could not hope to match Russian conventional means in that area and so would seem to be relying on its nuclear capacity. There are perhaps a dozen such flash-points around the world where a local struggle can readily involve the

213

superpowers and so place the world at risk. This should emphasise all the more the need for non-violent means of effectively overcoming oppression.

Apart from the multiplier effect local wars may have, their own destructive capacity leaves the societies involved weakened and disrupted. This may include the seeds of further civil war as many Western examples including the United States and Ireland confirm.

The transforming effect on the actual participants of the non-violent philosophy and strategy inspired by Gandhi is already liberating people by restoring to them their self-esteem and their dignity. This was a notable result under Gandhi in India and also among black Americans in the nineteen sixties. That transformation of the participants prepares the way for the transformation of the society by establishing a whole new set of relationships and power-structures which are genuinely enabling for all the people. In that social transformation the oppressors, also enslaved in privilege by the disabling structures, may be transformed or converted. At worst they will be prevented from exercising their old disabling power, without being violently eliminated. This approach provides at every stage of achievement the basis for further transformation and liberation but does not, unlike violent revolution, encourage counter-coups as the only means of further development. In the historic perspective of continuing transformation in pursuit of justice, freedom and solidarity, non-violent means offers a dynamic vision of Kingdom peace being progressively realised in society. The mutual emancipation at which it aims and the mutual reconciliation with its implied forgiveness which it makes possible, are typically social and historic expressions of the Kingdom achievement of salvation and redemption.

The value of the non-violent programme, which includes an enormous range of flexible methods, is not confined to national or international difficulties. It can be adapted to quite confined and local issues. Some of these methods such as strikes, sit-ins, boycotts are already operative at the local level in many countries and on many issues. They are, however, usually divorced from any philosophy of the transformation of the participants, still less of their opponents. They are for the most part straight power-struggles. This is a pity because all these difficulties are opportunities for genuine human growth and

214

development for both sides. It is only when we realise this in action that we will begin to appreciate the full depth of Gandhi's insight and programme. It is only then that we will become convinced and convincing exponents of the non-violent alternatives.

With our new-found conviction we may be able to extend the philosophy and its practice throughout our own society. More importantly we may, through an awakening public consciousness, be able to harness some of society's resources to the research and development which is at least as necessary here as in the arms industry. Some of our countries, particularly the smaller and militarily non-aligned, could give a lead by establishing research centres and training academies for non-violent national defence as well as for non-violent radical change. This could lead to non-violent or unarmed peace-keeping groups that would be available to monitor critical confrontations and maintain truces long enough to allow negotiations to find a solution. Research centres, training academies and unarmed peace-keeping forces should be sought in our own countries either through government sponsorship or independently.

The Threat of Nuclear War. The non-violent dimension of peace-seeking and peace-keeping could obviously be a very significant contribution to the prevention of local wars, of defence or revolution. What bearing has it on the threat which looms over all of us, the threat of nuclear war? In so far as local wars might escalate, as we saw, their prevention has also a multiplier effect in promoting peace in the world. The demonstrated effectiveness of non-violent means can undoubtedly play a role in preparing the way for alternative strategies for the nuclear powers. Yet there are urgent needs now at the global level which must be met if the nuclear holocaust is not to engulf us through accident or design.

I have no desire to repeat all the arguments pro and con the policy of nuclear deterrence. Yet there are a number of points which will bear repetition, I think.

1. It is highly improbable that any kind of limited nuclear war can take place. Talk of tactical weapons in some theatre of war, e.g. Europe, is illusory as some of the American leaders like Casper Weinberger and Alexander Haig have recently admitted.

215

At the very least the northern hemisphere will be annihilated and the damage to the total ecosystem of the earth would be such that life will be seriously affected if not destroyed everywhere.

2. Deterrence rests on the principle of Mutually Assured Destruction (MAD). This involves a balance of forces between West and East. The capacity for mutual destruction many times over is already in the possession of the superpowers. Further research, development, manufacture and deployment of nuclear weapons is unnecessary to any policy of deterrence and leads to a leapfrogging on both sides which is strategically unneccessary, hideously wasteful and increasingly dangerous.

3. Deterrence rests on the principle that each side has sufficient weaponry to survive a first strike by the enemy and to launch an equally crushing second strike. The logic of this position is vulnerable to the objection that if your society is destroyed in the first strike, there will be no point in destroying the other side, except for the morally disreputable, if humanly understandable, desire of revenge.

4. The moral weakness of deterrence derives from the position that to be effective deterrence it must be credible in the sense that each side is committed to annihilate the other should it strike first, or indeed may engage in a pre-emptive first strike if it knows/believes/suspects that the other is about to launch a first strike. Either way—as pre-emptive first strike or equally annihilating second strike—the theory of just war becomes irrelevant. What just cause could justify the double annihilation? What just cause can you defend by destroying yourself as well as the enemy? At the limit what just cause could justify the destruction of the whole world?

5. There are further moral weaknesses in nuclear strategy. The inability of the superpowers to control the spread of nuclear weapons extends the possibility of their coming into the possession of somebody entirely irresponsible or insane.

6. The growing complexity of nuclear weaponry increases the hazards of computer or human error. Errors of that kind have already been experienced in the US warning system and the series of errors uncovered at the Three Mile Island Nuclear Power Station are unlikely to be totally unique or confined to civilian installations. To place so much of humanity at risk in this fashion seems obviously immoral.

216

7. The immorality of devoting so much of the world's resources in material and personnel to developing further unnecessary means of destruction is highlighted by the consequent neglect of attention to the world's genuinely needy.

A host of other objections might be added to these seven points. They suffice for the moment to underline the obligation to rid the world of the nuclear menace. So far the politicians responsible in the various countries have been unable to break out of the double-bind of maintaining the threat of destroying the world in order to preserve it to their liking. They will only move when their base is eroded, when they find themselves increasingly isolated by the people's movement that wants to preserve the world for themselves and their posterity and effectively rejects the nuclear deterrence strategy. This is an enormous but not a hopeless task. As the world was finally rid of slavery, so it may be finally rid of war. As a popular movement in the United States compelled the leaders of the world's greatest power to withdraw from the Vietnam War, so popular movements throughout the world may restore the sanity which is clearly lacking in the arms race and is scarcely more evident in the deterrence policy. The recent European movements for nuclear disarmament and the first real stirrings of such a movement in the United States are offering people fresh hope.

A great deal of hard thinking, organisation and discipline will be demanded for the success of these movements. In the US, for example, the movement to freeze all armaments at their present level seems an important first step. In Europe the goal of a nuclear-free zone, which might be approached in segments, has obvious attractions. In this connection the unilateral renunciation by Britain and France of their nuclear weapons would be helpful examples without taking from the overall deterrence programme of the West based on fear of Russia. Reciprocal movements on the other side of Europe could generate the beginnings of a trust that might eventually overcome fear. There are many possibilities in need of exploration to be followed by action by which the people of the world may lead their leaders back from the brink of nuclear disaster to a sane concern for our common world and its future.

As nuclear disarmament becomes a possibility, radical changes in methods of defence, in arbitration of disputes and in economic structures will be needed.

217

It is unlikely that disarmament can stop at nuclear weapons. With the continuation of conventional weapons and the possibility of conventional war, the fresh development of nuclear weapons may become too much of a temptation. The knowledge of how they are produced can never now be unlearned. So the temptation will remain to look to the more destructive means to victory if the less destructive prove inadequate. That is how they were developed and used in the first place. The progress towards total disarmament will take considerable time but it will undoubtedly be hastened by progress in the development of non-violent methods.

The need for inter-state arbitration will likewise become more urgent. Here the question arises whether we can in the future endure as sovereign independent states and still avoid war with its possible escalation. Some kind of world authority with effective peace-keeping and acceptable arbitration must sooner or later emerge if we are to survive. The United Nations Organisation is far from providing such an authority at present. If there is sufficient consciousness of the threat of total destruction and of the need to provide a different structure for our world to save it, obstacles might be removed and progress made. Such progress will start with the people, their movements, their activities, their emerging world-wide relationships. A world-wide public and public conscience will finally move the leaders in the direction of world-wide structures. The restructuring of the economic world which disarmament will demand will only yield to similar popular and political pressure.

The Christian imperative of peace, the eschatological gift which is to be sought and realised in history, must take shape at local, national, international and planet-wide levels. The difficulties of that imperative and the strategies available to overcome them extend beyond the confines of the Christian Churches. Yet if the imperative is finally Christian, deriving its meaning, urgency and ultimate fulfilment from God's activity in Jesus Christ, Christians in community, as Churches, have their own particular communal role and responsibility. To that role and responsibility we now turn. I will speak of the Church rather than the Churches as better adapted to their common vocation in this area.

The relationship between Kingdom and Church has undergone different interpretations and diverse attempts at realisation in the course of history. At present we distinguish but do not separate the two. The Church is the partial, ambiguous, historical expression of the Kingdom, which it must discern in the world, to which it must bear witness and which it must provoke. The partial nature of the Church's realisation of the Kingdom refers not merely to its historical limitations vis-à-vis eschatological fulfilment, it refers also to the fact that the Kingdom may and does emerge beyond the confines of the Church. The Church's ambiguity in realising, discerning and promoting the Kingdom derives from its continuing sinfulness in person and structure.

Despite all these limitations, the Church remains the primary conscious locus of the Kingdom. Its role and responsibility in discerning and promoting the Kingdom and its values are without parallel. Among these values or qualities of the Kingdom peace is central, as we have seen. The Church's responsibility to true peace as realisation of the Kingdom goes to the root of its God-given role and remains permanent and urgent in history. In seeking to clarify this role and responsibility we define the Church as a community created and structured by the power of God exercised in word and sacrament.

Word and sacrament embrace the creative as well as the salvific work of God. The Word of salvation, the same Word of God through whom creation took place, is directed to the restoration, transformation and fulfilment of human beings and their earthly home to be finally achieved in the fullness of the Kingdom. The current nuclear threat is directly opposed to that creative and salvific Word and its sacramental expression. By annihilating the earth and cutting off all future as well as present generations, nuclear war assumes a dimension that is traditionally thought of as demonic in its total opposition to the creative and saving work and Word of God. Christians and their Churches must understand this depth of the nuclear threat and seek urgently to remove it.

The creative and saving Word of God, which is addressed to the world and emerges in history in the community of faith, the Church, provides a means of binding all the nations of the earth together. The community of faith constitutes a global network of communication in which the judging and saving Word of God illuminates, summons and empowers the Church and, through it, the human community, in discerning and opposing the counter-kingdom as well as in discerning and promoting the true Kingdom. As peace constitutes an essential element in and sign of the true Kingdom, so wars and above all the prospect of total war characterise the counter-kingdom. So much the enlightening Word of God reveals. So much the network of communications which is the universal Church repeats.

In this network of communication we are addressed by one another as mediators of God's Word to promote justice, freedom and solidarity, constituents of Kingdom peace. The presence of this Word in any one place with its promise and power, may be and should be taken up elsewhere as we Christians seek a co-ordinated response to the counter-kingdom forces of injustice, slavery and fragmentation, the seeds of war.

As we seek to develop a people's movement to abolish nuclear weapons and outlaw war we have our local communities of the Word to enlighten and empower us. That Word with its global and transcendent character moves outward to other local communities or Churches and so we get a movement of Christian people that should be the leaven of the whole human community in confronting these basically human problems. Through the network of local Churches the ripple effect of the most limited and local protest, resistance and political activity may reach and enrich the whole world.

The sacramental dimension of the Church may be no less significant in inspiring and sustaining peace movements. Sacramentality stresses cosmic and human dignity in mediating the presence and power of God. The extinction of humanity and its planet which nuclear war promises is total denial and rejection of that dignity and of its divine originator.

Particular sacraments reinforce the same Christian understanding and demand the same Christian commitment. The Eucharist in its celebration of Kingdom fellowship emphasises the unity and fulfilment of the human race on this earth and through its fruits, the bread and wine. Its positive celebratory attitude to human and cosmic reality is in total opposition to the negation of nuclear war. Its graceful remembering of God's triumph over sin and death in the death and resurrection of Jesus Christ gives us hope that the total death now possible through human sinfulness and nuclear destruction may be avoided, that God will save his people if only they repent and abandon their destructive ways.

The sacramental expression of repentance and reconciliation in the sacrament of Penance is a further reminder of human failure and division and of the saving and forgiving power of God. In human terms the sacrament of reconciliation moves outward from reconciliation with one's immediate brother before bringing one's gift to the altar, to match the gift and call of brotherhood at the furthest reaches of our communications and potential community. Increasingly the liturgy of penance is taking account not just of individual sin and reconciliation but of the structural sins which divide sexes, nations, races and classes and their need for communal reconciliation. The further development of this tendency could unsettle many of the accepted lines of division as Christian groups begin to transcend their national and other limits in seeking Christian reconciliation. What has been called the 'politics of forgiveness' might enable the Church to break down the barriers of enmity and distrust which fuel the arms race and spark off wars. The relation of peace to forgiveness, and of reconciliation to new creation, underlines the role of Christian communities and their sacramental life in overcoming wars and rumours of wars.

As a community of Word and Sacrament the universal Church enjoys the promise and the power of promoting the peace of the Kingdom in a badly wounded and fragmented world. Its response in grace to this ethical imperative rests with every individual Christian, particular communities of Christians, American and non-American, and the world-wide community of Christians.